T0254106

Lecture Notes in Computer Science 12041

More information about this series at http://www.springer.com/series/7407

Ivona Brandic · Thiago A. L. Genez ·
Ilia Pietri · Rizos Sakellariou (Eds.)

Algorithmic Aspects of Cloud Computing

5th International Symposium, ALGOCLOUD 2019
Munich, Germany, September 10, 2019
Revised Selected Papers

Springer

Editors
Ivona Brandic
Vienna University of Technology
Vienna, Austria

Ilia Pietri
Intracom Telecom
Paiania, Greece

Thiago A. L. Genez
Department of Engineering
University of Cambridge
Cambridge, UK

Rizos Sakellariou
University of Manchester
Manchester, UK

ISSN 0302-9743 ISSN 1611-3349 (electronic)
Lecture Notes in Computer Science
ISBN 978-3-030-58627-0 ISBN 978-3-030-58628-7 (eBook)
https://doi.org/10.1007/978-3-030-58628-7

LNCS Sublibrary: SL1 – Theoretical Computer Science and General Issues

This Springer imprint is published by the registered company Springer Nature Switzerland AG
The registered company address is: Gewerbestrasse 11, 6330 Cham, Switzerland

Preface

The International Symposium on Algorithmic Aspects of Cloud Computing (ALGOCLOUD) is an annual event that aims to tackle the diverse new topics in the emerging area of algorithmic aspects of computing and data management in the cloud.

The aim of the symposium is to bring together international researchers, students, and practitioners to present research activities and results on topics related to algorithmic, design, and development aspects of modern cloud-based systems.

As in previous years, paper submissions were solicited through an open call for papers. ALGOCLOUD welcomes submissions on all theoretical, design, and implementation aspects of modern cloud-based systems. We are particularly interested in novel algorithms in the context of cloud computing, cloud architectures, as well as experimental work that evaluates contemporary cloud approaches and pertinent applications. We also welcome demonstration manuscripts, which discuss successful elastic system developments, as well as experience/use-case articles and reviews. Contributions may span a wide range of algorithms for modeling, practices for constructing, and techniques for evaluating operations and services in a variety of systems, including but not limited to, virtualized infrastructures, cloud platforms, data centers, cloud-storage options, cloud data management, non-traditional key-value stores on the cloud, HPC architectures, etc.

Topics of interest addressed by this workshop include, but are not limited to:

- Analysis of algorithms and data structures
- Resource management and scheduling
- Data center and infrastructure management
- Privacy, security, and anonymization
- Cloud-based applications
- Virtualization and containers
- Performance models
- Cloud deployment tools and their analysis
- Novel programming models
- Storage management
- Fog and edge computing
- Economic models and pricing
- Energy and power management
- Big data and the cloud
- Network management and techniques
- Caching and load balancing

ALGOCLOUD 2019 took place on September 10, 2019, in Munich, Germany. It collocated and was part of ALGO 2019 (September 9–13, 2019), the major annual congress that combines the premier algorithmic conference European Symposium on Algorithms (ESA), and a number of other specialized symposiums and workshops, all related to algorithms and their applications, making ALGO the major European event for researchers, students, and practitioners in algorithms.

There was a positive response to the ALGOCLOUD 2019 call for papers. The diverse nature of papers submitted demonstrated the vitality of the algorithmic aspects of cloud computing. All submissions went through a rigorous peer-review process and were reviewed by at least three Program Committee (PC) members. Following their recommendations, the PC chairs accepted seven original research papers in a wide variety of topics that were presented at the workshop. We would like to thank all PC members for their significant contribution in the review process.

The program of ALGOCLOUD 2019 was complemented with a highly interesting keynote, entitled "New Horizons in IoT Workflows Provisioning in Edge and Cloud Datacentres for Fast Data Analytics," which was delivered by Rajiv Ranjan (Newcastle University, UK), and an informative and well-thought-out tutorial entitled "Algorithms for a Smart Construction Environment," which was delivered by Vlado Stankovski (University of Ljubljana, Slovenia). We wish to express our sincere gratitude to both our esteemed invitees for their contributions.

Finally, we would like to thank all authors who submitted their research work to ALGOCLOUD and the Steering Committee for volunteering their time.

We hope that these proceedings will help researchers, students, and practitioners understand and be aware of state-of-the-art algorithmic aspects of cloud computing, and that they will stimulate further research in the domain of algorithmic approaches in cloud computing in general.

September 2019

Ivona Brandic
Thiago A. L. Genez
Ilia Pietri
Rizos Sakellariou

Organization

Steering Committee

Spyros Sioutas	University of Patras, Greece
Peter Triantafillou	University of Warwick, UK
Christos D. Zaroliagis	University of Patras, Greece

Symposium Chairs

Ivona Brandic	Vienna University of Technology, Austria
Thiago A. L. Genez	University of Cambridge, UK
Ilia Pietri	Intracom SA, Greece
Rizos Sakellariou	The University of Manchester, UK

Program Committee

Olivier Beaumont	Inria Bordeaux, France
Luiz Fernando Bittencourt	University of Campinas, Brazil
Valeria Cardellini	University of Rome Tor Vergata, Italy
Alex Delis	University of Athens, Greece
Elisabetta Di Nitto	Politecnico di Milano, Italy
Katerina Doka	National Technical University of Athens, Greece
Fanny Dufossé	Inria Grenoble, France
Thomas Fahringer	University of Innsbruck, Austria
Sarunas Girdzijauskas	KTH Royal Institute of Technology, Sweden
Anastasios Gounaris	Aristotle University of Thessaloniki, Greece
Raffaele Montella	Parthenope University of Naples, Italy
George Pallis	University of Cyprus, Cyprus
Alessandro Papadopoulos	Mälardalen University, Sweden
Guido Proietti	University of L'Aquila, Italy
Krzysztof Rzadca	University of Warsaw, Poland
Rafael Brundo Uriarte	IMT Lucca, Italy

Additional Reviewer

Thanh-Phuong Pham	University of Innsbruck, Austria

New Horizons in IoT Workflows Provisioning in Edge and Cloud Datacentres for Fast Data Analytics (Keynote Talk)

Rajiv Ranjan

Newcastle University, UK
raj.ranjan@ncl.ac.uk

Abstract. Supporting Internet of Things (IoT) workflow enactment/execution on a combination of computational resources at the network edge and at a datacentre remains a challenge. Increasing volumes of data being generated through smart phones and IoT devices (which can vary significantly in scope and capability), need to be processed in a timely manner [2]. Current practice involves using edge nodes (e.g. sensors or other low-capacity devices) as a means to acquire/collect data (i.e. as an "observation" mechanism). Subsequently, this data is transmitted to a datacentre/cloud for analysis/insight. Increasingly, the limitation with the use of a large-scale, centralised datacentre is being realised (such as speed of response for latency-sensitive applications), with the emergence of a number of paradigms to address this concern – such as fog computing, edge computing, Cloud-of-Things, etc. [1]. All of these propose the use of dedicated servers (with varying capacity and capability) within micro/nano datacentres at the network edge, to overcome latency constraints associated with moving data to a central facility and (lack of use of) increasing computational capability within edge devices. These paradigms also closely align with work in content distribution networks (e.g. from Akamai CDNs), which attempt to place data servers within one (or a small number of) hop-of-end users (currently 85% of users are supported in this way, with >175K Akamai servers).

A key objective of this keynote talk is to understand how such emerging paradigms can be used to enable cloud systems (supported through large scale computational facilities) to be "stretched" to the network edge, to enable data-driven IoT workflows to be enacted efficiently over such combined infrastructure. We propose the combined use of (varying) capability at the network edge (referred to as an Edge DataCentre (EDC)) with capability within a Cloud DataCentre (CDC). Collectively, IoT devices and edge resources, like gateways (Raspberry Pi 3), software-defined network systems (Huawei CloudEngine 6800), and smart phones equipped with sensors, constitute a new set of computing resources – and are potential components of an EDC [1, 3].
This keynote talk will have the following outline:

1. Overview of the research challenges involved with composing and orchestrating complex IoT workflows in cloud-edge continuum infrastructure.
2. Discuss two case studies in healthcare and smart cities domain to understand how data-driven workflows can be applied to create/compose next-generation IoT applications.

3. Discuss our experience with running the UK's largest IoT infrastructure, namely, the Urban Observatory (http://www.urbanobservatory.ac.uk/).

References

1. Nardelli, M., Nastic, S., Dustdar, S., Villari, M., Ranjan, R.: Osmotic flow: osmotic computing + IoT workflow. IEEE Cloud Comput. **4**(2), 68–75 (2017). https://doi.org/10.1109/MCC.2017.22
2. Ranjan, R., et al.: The next grand challenges: integrating the internet of things and data science. IEEE Cloud Comput. **5**(3), 12–26 (2018). https://doi.org/10.1109/MCC.2018.032591612
3. Villari, M., Fazio, M., Dustdar, S., Rana, O., Ranjan, R.: Osmotic computing: a new paradigm for edge/cloud integration. IEEE Cloud Comput. **3**(6), 76–83 (2016). https://doi.org/10.1109/MCC.2016.124

Contents

Algorithms for a Smart Construction Environment

Petar Kochovski and Vlado Stankovski(✉)

University of Ljubljana, Ljubljana, Slovenia
vlado.stankovski@fri.uni-lj.si

Abstract. Every building project is one of a kind. Unique are its design, location, collaborating people and organizations, time-frame, cost and many other aspects. Setting up smart services and applications that would support the building process is on the wish list of every construction company. Such applications, however, have time-critical requirements that must be addressed in the application designing process. There are four broad types of converging technologies that are currently used to build smart applications. These include the Internet of Things (IoT), Artificial Intelligence (AI), Cloud Computing and Blockchain. The EU-Korean research and innovation project DECENTER intends to play a pivotal role in the integration of such technologies in a new Fog Computing Platform. The DECENTER Fog Computing Platform would help address the resource requirements of smart applications and provide high Quality of Service (QoS) to various AI-based applications. Due to the various uncertainties of the Fog Computing environment, the project aims at also providing Service Level Agreements for the offered services, which include assurances, ranking and verification of Edge-to-Cloud deployment options. Our present work focuses on the use of stochastic methods, particularly, the Markov Decision Process to deliver a QoS model of the smart application in relation to the available Cloud computing resources. This work presents the algorithm, which is used to achieve high QoS of smart applications and its implementation considerations. Our findings support the understanding that dynamic Edge-to-Cloud computing environments require a stochastic approach to establish assurances for high QoS operation of the applications. It is shown that the required assurances can be expressed as a probability value for confidence, which is calculated by the stochastic method.

Keywords: Internet of Things · Artificial Intelligence · Cloud · Fog · Edge · Blockchain · Markov Decision Process · Decision-making

1 Introduction

Smart applications may be required to operate at actual building sites in order to address problems of resources and assets management, building process monitoring, construction site automation, robots assisted construction, infrastructures

I. Brandic et al. (Eds.): ALGOCLOUD 2019, LNCS 12041, pp. 1–14, 2020.
https://doi.org/10.1007/978-3-030-58628-7_1

monitoring, safety monitoring and similar. In order to develop smart construction applications, their development and deployment stages may require to address a variety of requirements including those for high performance or response time, i.e. high Quality of Service (QoS). In order to achieve this goal, some applications require high network performance (e.g. Web real-time communication), whilst other require more processing power (e.g. video-stream analysis) or storage capacity (e.g. data management system). Often, Internet of Things (IoT) and Edge devices run on batteries and are lacking processing power, which leads to the necessity of placing the computations at nearby micro-servers and data centers, where higher frequency processors can be obtained. Generally, the network performance metrics (e.g. latency, network throughput, packet loss) are relevant for smart applications in order to achieve high levels of dependability. Hence, to reach their business value, smart applications in construction must satisfy very specific technical, performance-related requirements. In summary, requirements analysis must take into consideration network and performance-wise QoS attributes, particularly non-functional requirements, such as reliability, availability, security, safety and similar, which are commonly known in systems engineering as dependability attributes.

In order to facilitate efficient and effective development of smart IoT-based applications, they come hands-in-hands with component-based software engineering approaches and tools, which introduce radical improvements of the software lifecycle. An important improvement is the ability to use container images within workbenches i.e. Interactive Development Environments(IDEs), such as SWITCH IDE [17] or Fabric8[1]. Existing open-source technologies for interoperability, such as Docker Swarm[2] and Kubernetes[3] allow to orchestrate containerized applications across the Edge-to-Cloud computing continuum. The process of placing i.e. deploying a containerized smart application in the computing continuum is a complex problem, because during this stage of the application, it is necessary to choose optimal or close-to-optimal Cloud deployment option among large quantity of options by considering multiple quality constraints. As a result, various trade-offs between the constraints must be considered and uncertainties which can only be addressed at the time of deployment. For instance, one trade-off can be the service cost versus the infrastructure processing power. The decision-making process during the deployment stage can be expressed as a complex multi-objective decision-making problem, which is too challenging to be addressed manually by the software engineer.

The ongoing Horizon 2020 European Union-Korea project DECENTER[4] is inspired by four main use cases, which fit in the context of Smart Homes, Smart Cities, Smart Construction and Robot Logistics. The smart applications that are designed for these domains, require data integration and processing that is constantly streamed from large amounts of sensors and data sources. Once the

[1] https://fabric8.io/.
[2] https://docs.docker.com/engine/swarm/.
[3] https://kubernetes.io/.
[4] https://www.decenter-project.eu/.

data is gathered, it is necessary to extract some useful information by using various Artificial Intelligence (AI) methods. Due to the different application scenarios and requirements, the data is processed, filtered, integrated and visualized at different stages of the Big Data pipeline, starting from the Edge computing nodes to the high performance Cloud data centers.

The DECENTER project currently integrates four technology types: the IoT, AI, Cloud computing and Blockchain, in order to build a new Fog Computing Platform, which offers new opportunities for the development of smart applications in a wide range of domains. It also provides a workbench that helps software engineers to use Edge-to-Cloud resources to carry out a substantial amount of computation, storage, communication from the Edge to the Cloud, and thus addresses the requirements of Big Data pipelines, which start at the Edge of the computing network and may run across multiple computing tiers up to various public or private Cloud providers. While providing mechanisms for seamless integration of resources necessary for smart application deployment, the project aims to achieve high QoS guarantees for its services provided as Service-Level Agreements (SLAs). This whole effort is necessary in order to provide dependability to the operation of smart applications.

Hence, DECENTER has potential to improve the development of dependable smart environments, notification systems, Ambient Intelligence solutions and even Cyber-Physical Systems. DECENTER can be used to dynamically integrate both static (e.g. sensors, cameras, actuators) or moving (e.g. sensors, vehicles, drones, robots) Things. Application domains include smart cities and communities, smart buildings and homes, smart trading chains, the circular economy, sustainable food production, sustainable tourism, factories of the future, e-health, smart mobility and beyond, and are well exemplified by projects of the Slovenia's Smart Specialization programme of research and innovation.

This paper focuses on the decision-making process when deploying smart applications in the cloud. The key objective is to design specific algorithms that may help maintain high Quality of Service during the operation in conditions where the execution context may dynamically change (e.g. varying network bandwidth) and thus influence the resulting QoS. This work also intends to provide an overview of various decision-making mechanisms that can be utilized in such circumstances.

The rest of the paper is structured as follows. Section 2 describes various smart application scenarios for smart construction environments. Section 3 presents the different computing paradigms, requirements that can be used when developing applications for different scenarios for the purposes of Smart Construction environments. Section 4 describes the necessity of utilizing multi-objective decision-making mechanisms in order to achieve optimal QoS and an evaluation results of the implemented Markov Decision Process (MDP). Section 5 discusses the importance of trust in smart environments and the role of Blockchain in achieving trust. Section 6 concludes the paper and discusses future challenges in the field.

2 Smart Application Scenarios

In order to illustrate the benefits of implementing multi-layered architectures for smart construction environments, this section describes three of the analyzed smart applications. Each application is built from reusable components, which can be deployed in three-tier architecture (Edge-Fog-Cloud).

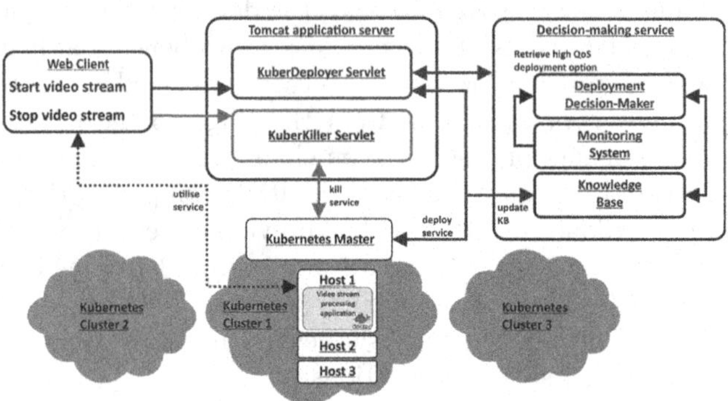

(a) Video stream application workflow

(b) Video stream Graphical User Interface

Fig. 1. Video stream application scenario

Web real time communication represents an important communication method potentially to be used at a smart construction site. It can be complemented with various other features, such as Deep Learning Neural Networks for AI video analysis, and other real-time communication functions in order to address safety and security risks, improve teamwork and prevent delays in the construction process.

In this scenario, the video conferencing application is developed by using the open-source videoconferencing service Jitsi Meet[5], which is virtualized as

[5] https://jitsi.org/.

a Docker container. The containerized application can be run on any physical device or Virtual Machine where the Docker Engine is running. The videoconferencing session is initiated via a Web link, which forwards the users to a containerized Jitsi Meet software running on an Edge computing node.

In this scenario, the Jitsi Meet application does not run constantly on a dedicated service. In fact, upon user's request the KuberDeployer Servlet calls a Decision-Making service, which retrieves a Cloud deployment option satisfying high QoS. Once an optimal deployment option is retrieved, the application's container image is deployed and run on the computing node by the Kubernetes Orchestrator. This approach allows to save resources on the Edge computing node, when the service is not required, and thus save on operational costs. In addition to that high QoS is achieved due to the use of Edge computing. More details of this scenario are depicted on Fig. 1 and are explained elsewhere [10], [12].

Video surveillance and safety violations detection is a scenario in which a containerized application is designed and deployed in order to increase the safety at construction sites by analyzing video surveillance data. The application is composed of three containers, which cover the complete Big Data pipeline. Each container runs on different layer in the Edge-to-Cloud continuum.

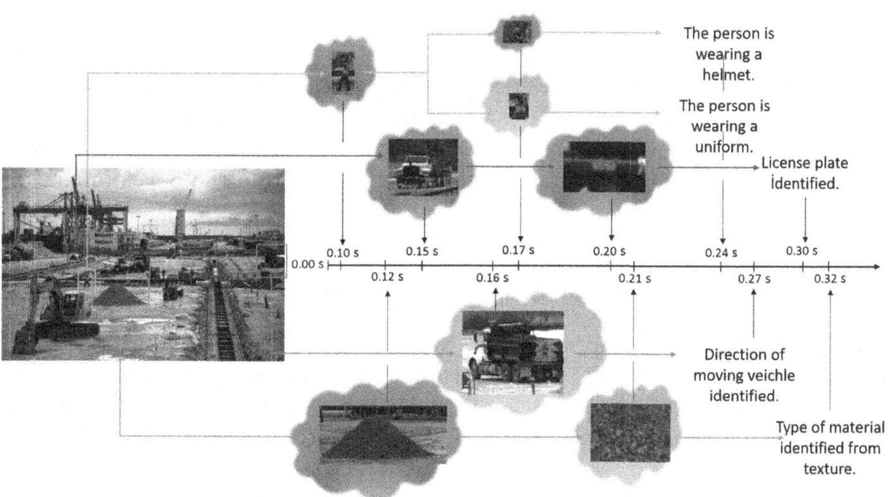

Fig. 2. AI processing workflow for video surveillance data

The video streaming data is firstly processed on the network Edge in order to detect presence of meaningful data for further analysis. Once a subject or object is detected, the data is forwarded to the Fog computing layer, where AI empowered Microservices use the surveillance footage as input data to detect safety violations. Figure 2 shows how surveillance data is fragmented into small fragments that are separately analyzed in order to retrieve safety violations. Finally the results of the analysis are stored on the top layer, which is the Cloud computing layer, where Cloud data is present, and additional data analyses and visualizations are performed on high power computing cloud infrastructures.

Data management and documentation are very important processes during construction. In larger projects, delays and data-loss are probable, thus documenting and backing up data from the overall construction process is essential. In order to achieve high QoS in such scenarios, when large files are constantly exchanged, it is necessary to store the files in close proximity to the users.

In this scenario, the smart application takes advantage of decentralized storage services that are part of the Fog computing layer. In particular, the application is deployed on the optimal infrastructure as a Docker container, which allows file transfer through HTTP RESTfull APIs. The container is created, served and destroyed for each individual file upload request. The application components are described in the following study [10], whilst [9] describes a multi-tier architecture for achieving high QoS when computing data in multi-tier distributed computing systems.

3 Edge-to-Cloud Computing for Smart Environments

The implementation of Big Data pipelines from the Edge of the computing network up to the Cloud data centres poses some important requirements that have been addressed by new architectures, standards and technologies for Edge computing. In the following we present some outstanding initiatives in this context, and the summary of important requirements that underpin the development of the DECENTER's Fog Computing Platform.

3.1 Computing Layers for Smart Environments

Following the latest standards, defined by the Cloud Native Computing Foundation (CNCF)[6], the OpenFog Consortium [7] and the Edge Computing Consortium Europe (ECCE)[8], smart application and data produced by them can be computed across the whole Edge-to-Cloud computing continuum as depicted on Fig. 3.

The Edge-to-Cloud computing paradigm, that is, the plethora of various computing resources and connections can be differentiated among properties such as: computing performance, network performance and geographic distribution. Cloud computing is a centralised computing approach that offers high computing power in large data centres, often being too remote from the data sources. In

[6] https://www.cncf.io/.
[7] http://www.openfogconsortium.org/.
[8] https://ecconsortium.eu/.

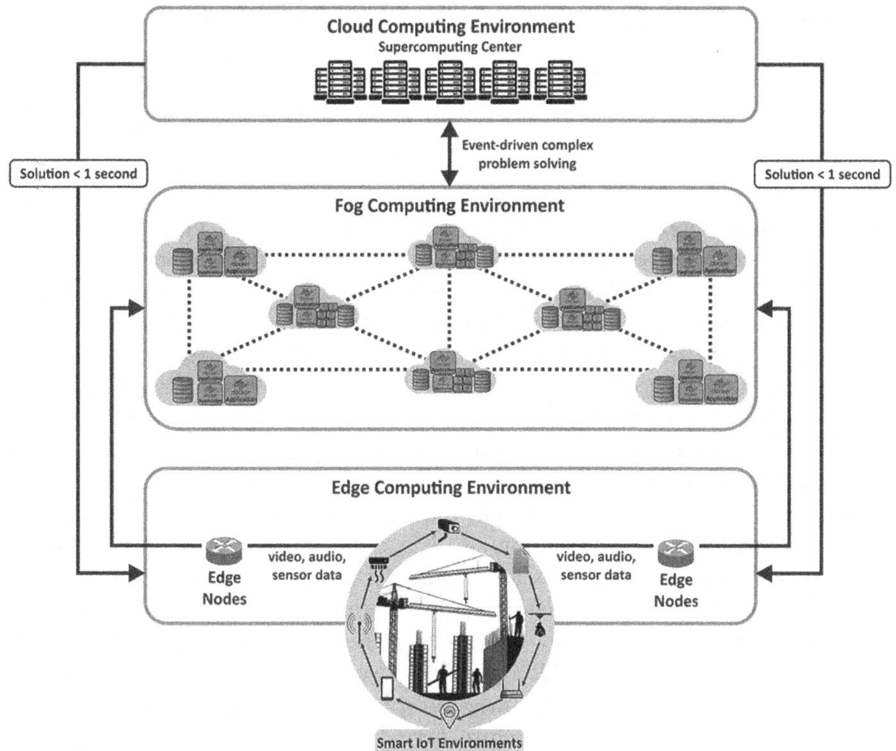

Fig. 3. Smart construction environment and IoT applications

order to address the network quality issues, Cloud computing is being complemented by emerging computing paradigms that extend the computing capacity closer to the sources of data, such as Edge computing.

According to the OpenFog Consortium, Fog computing is a computing paradigm that distributes computing, storage, control and networking functions closer to the users along the Cloud-to-Things continuum. Moreover, it can be considered as Cloud resources that exist between the Edge devices and the traditional Cloud computing data centres that offer high computing performance with improved network performance.

Edge computing is the lowest layer of computing, which is designed to guarantee high network performance. It is highly distributed and allows processing data on various multiprocessor devices that operate in close proximity to sensors (e.g. Raspberry Pi, BeagleBoard or PCDuino). Although, edge computing offers high network performance, it is not recommended for intensive computing operations.

3.2 Summary of Requirements for Smart Applications

Smart applications have a range of functional and non-functional requirements that have to be addressed at their design phase. Here follows a brief summary of such requirements.

- Non-Functional Requirements are system requirements that specify how a system should operate. Areas in need of smart applications in civil engineering include construction monitoring, construction site management, safety at work, early disaster warning, and resources and assets management. So far, smart applications in these areas have not taken off due to significant Quality of Service (QoS) requirements. For such applications, geographic proximity, low latency and high bandwidth may be the only feasible options. Moreover, using sensors in construction sites may pose privacy or security challenges. Whatever is identified from sensor or video streams may need to stay locally and under strict access control.
- Functional Requirements are system requirements that specify the behavior of the system. Every construction site is a dynamic place: various Artificial Intelligence and other Big Data analytics software should dynamically adapt. It is therefore necessary to provide an orchestration technology that is event-driven as various services may be needed in real time, to be deployed, used and destroyed. Benefits for QoS metrics have already been observed when such microservices are deployed in geographic proximity of an actual smart construction site [10]. It is therefore necessary to provide a system design for smart applications, which may benefit from an event-driven orchestration technology for containers that are deployed in close proximity to the locations of the sensors. Based on this rationale we proceeded by designing an application that is container-based and suitable for Fog computing.

4 Multi-objective Decision-Making for the Selection of Cloud Deployment Options

4.1 Decision-Making Mechanisms Summary

Managing non-functional requirements of smart applications that need to be deployed in the Edge-to-Cloud continuum requires detailed understanding of their trade-offs. For instance, utilizing greater processing power, requires higher operational cost. Moreover, it is necessary to address the uncertainties present at application deployment time. Usually, the application deployment processes has to take into account multiple non-functional requirements, hence the process is complex and can be formulated as a multi-objective decision-making problem.

Several studies that address this problem from deterministic and stochastic point of view were investigated for this study. The studies [3,4,6] approach the application deployment problem by implementing deterministic decision-making solutions based on the Analytical Hierarchy Process (AHP). This method implements threshold values to various metrics selected by the developer and helps rank the considered Cloud deployment options. Furthermore, there are studies [5,13] that propose algorithms based on Pareto front decision-making. However, these studies are limited to the amount of non-functional requirements that are being considered in the decision-making process.

Stochastic decision-making approaches allow for suitable probabilistic evaluation and may help achieving the required application QoS in addition to assurances, ranking and verification of Cloud deployment options. For example, MDP is a suitable stochastic method to address the stochastic nature of the Cloud computing domain which has been exemplified in related studies [11,14,16].

4.2 Markov Decision Process

MDP is a powerful decision-making method for dynamic environments where the results are partly random and partly under the control of a decision maker. In other words, MDP is a method for planning in stochastic environments. Our hypothesis is that this method is suitable for container deployment, that is, Cloud deployment options decision-making because it is capable of: (1) autonomous evaluation of all possible outcomes, whilst analyzing all events that can take place in the stochastic environment; (2) utilize prior knowledge of the system behavior to determine the best set of actions in a stochastic environment; (3) calculate the utility i.e. usefulness of each deployment option in order to prepare a ranking list and determine an optimal deployment option. Moreover, the method can be used to provide assurances for the QoS expressed as probability values. This property makes it suitable for implementation of SLAs within the DECENTER Fog Computing Platform.

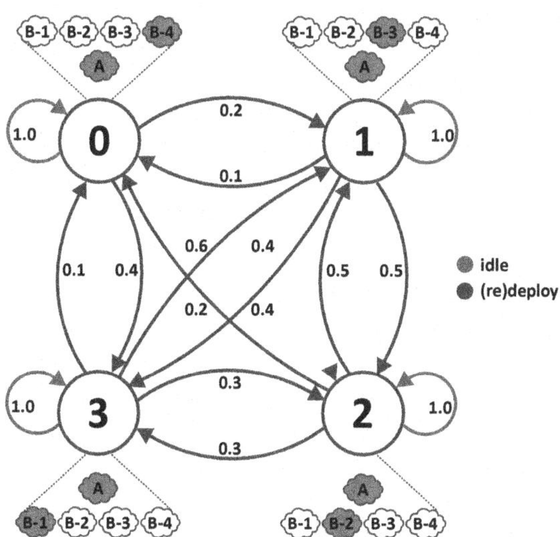

Fig. 4. Example of a MDP model where each state represents a federation of computing infrastructures

In order to illustrate our algorithmic approach to the decision-making for Cloud deployment options, we have prepared an illustrative example in Fig. 4. The MDP model is defined as a tuple of elements $M = (S, A, P, R, \gamma)$, where: S is a finite set of states (i.e. each state can represent one or a federation of deployment options in the Edge-to-Cloud computing continuum); A is a finite set of actions (i.e. re/deploy, idle); P is the transition probability from one state to another due to an specific action; R is the expected reward for transitioning from one state to another; and γ is a discount factor, which exists to reduce the number of iterations when evaluating the model.

As we can see from the figure, the MDP probabilistic model is a finite automaton, which is necessary for delivering a decision for deployment an application on an optimal Cloud deployment option. Each MDP model has to satisfy the Markov rule, which states that for any given time, the conditional distribution of future states of the process given present and past states depends only on the present state and not on the past states.

Mathematically, the Markov property is expressed as follows:

$$P[S_{t+1}|S_t] = P[S_{t+1}|S_1, ..., S_t] \tag{1}$$

In our case, the MDP model is generated for each software component (or set of software components) and can dynamically change due to the variability of available deployment options and their input non-functional requirements. Within the model, each transition from one state is a probabilistic choice over multiple next states, where the probability value is estimated from prior usage data.

Transitions between states represent different actions: (re)deployment, which is responsible for retrieving an optimal deployment option; and idle state, which is selected to terminate the process, once a deployment option is retrieved. Each state in the model is mapped to a different reward value, which are derived from the metrics thresholds that the state satisfies.

Finally the deployment options are ranked by their utility values, which are derived by performing value iteration over the Bellman equation:

$$u(S) = r(S) + \gamma \max_a \sum_{S'} P(S'|a, S)u(S') \tag{2}$$

Detailed information on the method and a previously developed model for single-tiered applications, are elaborated in our previous study [7]. In this work, however, we address the possibility to address the requirements of multi-tier applications that are comprised by several Microservice containers. This is represented by combinations of states $A - B_1$, $A - B_2$, $A - B_3$ and $A - B_4$, that is from Edge to Cloud in the above presented Fig. 4.

4.3 Probabilistic Decision-Making Evaluation

In order to prove the feasibility of implementation the above described decision-making mechanism, a two-tier application composed of two AI methods that had to be deployed on optimal or close-to-optimal pair of computing infrastructures. The infrastructure pairs are enlisted in Table 1, where infrastructure A is a powerful small computer NVIDIA Jetson Nano that runs at the network Edge i.e. in close proximity to data sources; and infrastructure(s) B-type can be computing instances hosted by Amazon AWS EC2[9] i.e. a1.medium, a1.large, a1.xlarge, a1.2xlarge or Google Cloud Platform[10] i.e. n1-standard-1,2,4 in Europe. For the needs of the evaluation, the following non-functional requirements were taken into account: latency between the paired infrastructures lower than 60 ms, throughput between the paired infrastructures higher than 10 Gb/s, packet loss lower than 2% and cost of infrastructure B lower than 90$.

The results, presented in Table 1 show the scores and the ranking of infrastructure pairs for the two-tier application. Due to the prior usage data that was used for generating the probabilistic model and the rewards that were estimated from the current monitoring data, the optimal deployment pair with highest score in this evaluation was the NVIDIA Jetson Nano + a1.large infrastructure pair.

Table 1. Deployment ranking results of the infrastructure pairs

Rank	Infrastructure pairs		Score
	A	B	
I	NVIDIA Jetson Nano	a1.large	115.8
II		n1-standard2-Frankfurt	115.44
III		a1.xlarge	115.17
IV		a1.medium	105.49
V		n1-standard1-Frankfurt	104.03
VI		n1-standard1-London	103.99
VII		n1-standard1-London	97.33
VIII		a1.2xlarge	96.98
IX		n1-standard4-London	95.68
X		n1-standard4-Frankfurt	95.48

*Edge computing infrastructures;
**Fog and Cloud computing infrastructures.

The presented results show the suitability of the MDP method to take into account information at both design and runtime in order to calculate the optimal Cloud deployment option for two-tiered applications. This fits the requirements of the use cases scenarios that we investigated. Moreover, in the following we discuss the possibility to use Blockchain-based services to provide high-level of trust in the operation of such applications.

[9] https://aws.amazon.com/ec2/.
[10] https://cloud.google.com/.

5 Trust as a High-Level Requirement

Besides addressing the QoS requirements of smart applications, MDP can be used to also address high-level requirements such as trust, dependability, availability and others. Smart applications usually face many threats in various domains, including smart constructions, particularly when it is necessary to deploy them in the Edge-to-Cloud computing continuum, that is, in a computing environment that spans across different administrative domains and employs heterogeneous and dynamic infrastructures. Achieving trust among the participating entities is of crucial importance in such environments. Usually trust is defined as subjective probability with which an entity assesses that another entity or group of entities will perform a particular action. In computer science the question of trust is still not investigated thoroughly. Few isolated studies have aimed to define a trust ontology [15]. The role of trust has also been investigated when maintaining reliable services, preventing incidental failures and handling misbehavior issues [1,2].

An overreaching goal of our work is therefore to incorporate trust management principles in the context of the DECENTER's Fog Computing Platform. DECENTER is designed to orchestrate AI microservice containers across the Edge-to-Cloud computing continuum. For this purpose several trust-related attributes, such as availability, credibility, privacy, response time, throughput, security, transparency and traceability have to be satisfied.

In order to assure that the complex interactions among humans and the smart applications are trusted, the DECENTER Fog Computing Platform implements a Blockchain layer. Blockchain is an immutable ledger with operations which are transparent. Its data is consistent among all the participants. Autonomous trust management in the DECENTER Platform is supported through the execution of Smart Contracts. Smart Contracts are computer protocols intended to facilitate and enforce digital contracts between different entities. All Smart Contracts are executed on the Blockchain, hence all transactions are irreversible, transparent and traceable. In complex and dynamic Edge-to-Cloud computing environments, such as those mentioned before, Smart Contracts may use timely monitoring data provided by less costly off-chain services. A Smart Oracle is a mechanism that can provide tamper-proof off-blockchain data to Smart Contracts, which can be used in the runtime.

In our ongoing work in this domain, we assure trust in the three smart application scenarios by using Smart Contracts [8]. Each Cloud application deployment scenario was complemented with three trust management scenarios: assuring trust between sensors or cameras and users, assuring trusted data flow in the Edge-to-Cloud continuum and assuring high QoS in the Edge-to-Cloud continuum. The architecture, system workflow and the Smart Contracts logic in achieving trust in smart construction environments.

6 Conclusions

The goal of our work is to address the QoS requirements of smart applications for highly dynamic and heterogeneous Edge-to-Cloud environments. In our study we focused on various Edge-to-Cloud deployment options and on providing assurances and ranking that can be used for SLA management. In our work we implemented a Markov Decision Process that can be used to address not only QoS, but also various other high-level requirements including trust. Moreover, we experimented with the development of Smart Contracts that would provide transparency and traceability to the overall smart application adaptation process in the Edge-to-Cloud environment. Our work indicates that MDP based decision-making can effectively be used to also address the needs for trust management, which is an essential requirement in Fog Computing.

Our plans for future work is to improve the decision-making mechanism and introduce new components to the whole architecture that will provide secure and safe data management in smart construction environments. We currently investigate cross-border data management facilitated through the use of Smart Contracts.

References

1. Alrawais, A., Alhothaily, A., Hu, C., Cheng, X.: Fog computing for the internet of things: security and privacy issues. IEEE Internet Comput. **21**(2), 34–42 (2017)
2. Corradini, F., De Angelis, F., Ippoliti, F., Marcantoni, F.: A survey of trust management models for cloud computing. In: CLOSER, pp. 155–162 (2015)
3. Garg, S.K., Versteeg, S., Buyya, R.: A framework for ranking of cloud computing services. Future Gener. Comput. Syst. **29**(4), 1012–1023 (2013)
4. Gonçalves Junior, R., Rolim, T., Sampaio, A., Mendonça, N.C.: A multi-criteria approach for assessing cloud deployment options based on non-functional requirements. In: Proceedings of the 30th Annual ACM Symposium on Applied Computing, pp. 1383–1389. ACM (2015)
5. Guerrero, C., Lera, I., Juiz, C.: Genetic algorithm for multi-objective optimization of container allocation in cloud architecture. J. Grid Comput. **16**(1), 113–135 (2017). https://doi.org/10.1007/s10723-017-9419-x
6. Karim, R., Ding, C., Miri, A.: An end-to-end qos mapping approach for cloud service selection. In: IEEE Ninth World Congress on Services (SERVICES), 2013, pp. 341–348. IEEE (2013)
7. Kochovski, P., Drobintsev, P.D., Stankovski, V.: Formal quality of service assurances, ranking and verification of cloud deployment options with a probabilistic model checking method. Inf. Softw. Technol. **109**, 14–25 (2019)
8. Kochovski, P., Gec, S., Stankovski, V., Bajec, M., Drobintsev, P.D.: Trust management in a blockchain based fog computing platform with trustless smart oracles. Future Gener. Comput. Syst. **101**, 747–759 (2019)
9. Kochovski, P., Sakellariou, R., Bajec, M., Drobintsev, P., Stankovski, V.: An architecture and stochastic method for database container placement in the edge-fog-cloud continuum. In: IEEE International Parallel and Distributed Processing Symposium (IPDPS), pp. 396–405. IEEE (2019)

10. Kochovski, P., Stankovski, V.: Supporting smart construction with dependable edge computing infrastructures and applications. Autom. Construct. **85**, 182–192 (2018)
11. Naskos, A., et al.: Dependable horizontal scaling based on probabilistic model checking. In: 15th IEEE/ACM International Symposium on Cluster, Cloud and Grid Computing (CCGrid), 2015, pp. 31–40. IEEE (2015)
12. Paščinski, U., Trnkoczy, J., Stankovski, V., Cigale, M., Gec, S.: QoS-Aware orchestration of network intensive software utilities within software defined data centres. J. Grid Comput. **16**(1), 85–112 (2017). https://doi.org/10.1007/s10723-017-9415-1
13. Štefanič, P., Kimovski, D., Suciu, G., Stankovski, V.: Non-functional requirements optimisation for multi-tier cloud applications: An early warning system case study. In: IEEE SmartWorld, Ubiquitous Intelligence & Computing, Advanced & Trusted Computed, Scalable Computing & Communications, Cloud & Big Data Computing, Internet of People and Smart City Innovation (SmartWorld/SCALCOM/UIC/ATC/CBDCom/IOP/SCI), pp. 1–8. IEEE (2017)
14. Tsoumakos, D., Konstantinou, I., Boumpouka, C., Sioutas, S., Koziris, N.: Automated, elastic resource provisioning for NoSQL clusters using TIRAMOLA. In: 13th IEEE/ACM International Symposium on Cluster, Cloud and Grid Computing (CCGrid), 2013, pp. 34–41. IEEE (2013)
15. Viljanen, L.: Towards an ontology of trust. In: Katsikas, S., López, J., Pernul, G. (eds.) TrustBus 2005. LNCS, vol. 3592, pp. 175–184. Springer, Heidelberg (2005). https://doi.org/10.1007/11537878_18
16. Yang, J., Lin, W., Dou, W.: An adaptive service selection method for cross-cloud service composition. Concurr. Comput. Pract. Exp. **25**(18), 2435–2454 (2013)
17. Zhao, Z., et al.: A software workbench for interactive, time critical and highly self-adaptive cloud applications (switch). In: 15th IEEE/ACM International Symposium on Cluster, Cloud and Grid Computing (CCGrid), 2015, pp. 1181–1184. IEEE (2015)

Developing a Cloud-Based Algorithm for Analyzing the Polarization of Social Media Users

Loris Belcastro[1], Fabrizio Marozzo[1,2], Domenico Talia[1,2(✉)], and Paolo Trunfio[1,2]

[1] DIMES, University of Calabria, Arcavacata, Italy
{lbelcastro,fmarozzo,talia,trunfio}@dimes.unical.it
[2] DtoK Lab Srl, Rende, Italy

Abstract. Social media analysis is a fast growing research area aimed at extracting useful information from social media. Several opinion mining techniques have been developed for capturing the mood of social media users related to a specific topic of interest. This paper shows how to use a cloud-based algorithm aimed at discovering the polarization of social media users in relation to political events characterized by the rivalry of different factions. The algorithm has been applied to a case study that analyzes the polarization of a large number of Twitter users during the 2016 Italian constitutional referendum. In particular, Twitter users have been classified and the results have been compared with the polls before voting and with the results obtained after the vote. The achieved results are very close to the real ones.

Keywords: Social data analysis · Cloud computing · Big Data · User polarization · Sentiment analysis

1 Introduction

With the growth of utilization of social media, every day millions of people produce huge amount of digital data containing information about human dynamics, collective sentiments, and the behavior of groups of people. Such data, commonly referred as Big Data, overwhelms our ability to make use of it and extract useful information in reasonable time. Cloud computing systems provide elastic services, high performance and scalable data storage, which can be used as large-scale computing infrastructures for complex high-performance data mining applications. Combining Big Data analytics and machine learning techniques with scalable computing systems allows the production of new insights in a shorter time [5]. The analysis of such information is clearly highly valuable in science and business, since it is suitable for a wide range of applications: tourism agencies and municipalities can know the most important regions-of-interest visited by users [6], transport operators can reveal mobility insights in cities such as

I. Brandic et al. (Eds.): ALGOCLOUD 2019, LNCS 12041, pp. 15–24, 2020.
https://doi.org/10.1007/978-3-030-58628-7_2

incident locations [12], business managers can understand the opinions of people on a topic, a product or an event of interest.

In this work we propose a new parallel and distributed algorithm for discovering the polarization of social media users in relation to a political event, which is characterized by the rivalry of different factions or parties. Examples of political events are:

- municipal elections, in which a faction supports a mayor candidate;
- political elections, in which a faction supports a party;
- presidential elections, in which a party (or a coalition of parties) supports a presidential candidate.

To deploy and run the designed algorithm on the Cloud, it has been written using ParSoDA (*Parallel Social Data Analytics*) [7], a Java library for building parallel social media analysis algorithms and simplifying the programming task necessary to implement these class of algorithms on parallel computing systems. To reach this goal, ParSoDA includes functions that are widely used for processing and analyzing data gathered from social media so as to find different types of information (e.g., user trajectories, user sentiments, topics trends).

The algorithm is designed to deal with Big Data. For this reason, it is based on the MapReduce model and can be executed in parallel on distributed systems, such as the HPC and Cloud platforms. The main benefit of using ParSoDA is that it was specifically designed to build Cloud-based data analysis applications. To this end, ParSoDA provides scalability mechanisms based on two of the most popular parallel processing frameworks (Hadoop[1] and Spark[2]), which are fundamental to provide satisfactory services as the amount of data to be managed grows.

To assess the accuracy of our algorithm, we present a case study application to extract the political polarization of Twitter users. In particular, the algorithm has been applied on a case study that analyzes the polarization of a large number of Twitter users during the 2016 Italian constitutional referendum. The obtained results are very close to the real ones and significantly more accurate than the average of the opinion polls, assessing the high accuracy and effectiveness of the proposed algorithm.

The paper is organized as follows: Sect. 2 discusses related work and compares other techniques with the one proposed here. Section 3 introduces the algorithm details and Sect. 4 discusses the case study on which the proposed algorithm has been used. Section 5 draws some conclusions.

2 Related Work

Several researches are working on the design and implementation algorithms for measuring public opinion and predicting the polarization of social users according to political events.

[1] https://hadoop.apache.org/.
[2] https://spark.apache.org/.

Graham et al. [10] performed an hand-coded content analysis for understanding how British and Dutch parliamentary candidates used Twitter during the 2010 general elections. Anstead and O'Loughlin [2] analyzed the 2010 United Kingdom election and suggested the use of social media as a new way to understand public opinion. Gruzd and Roy [11] investigated the political polarization of social network users during the 2011 Canadian Federal Election by analyzing a sample of tweets posted by social media users that self-declared political views and affiliations.

Marozzo and Bessi [13] presented a methodology aimed at discovering the behavior of social media users and how news sites are used during political campaigns characterized by the rivalry of different factions. The idea behind this technique is to use the keywords inside a tweet to classify it by calculating the degree of polarity. Ceron et al. [8] proposed a text analysis methodology for studying the voting intention of French Internet users during the 2012 Presidential ballot and the subsequent legislative election, comparing their results with the predictions made by survey companies. El Alaoui et al. [9] proposed an adaptive sentiment analysis approach for extracting user opinions about political events. Their approach classifies the posts by exploiting a series of word polarity dictionaries built from a selected set of hashtags related to a political event of interest. Oikonomou et al. [14] used a Naïve Bayes classifier for estimating the winning candidate of USA presidential elections in three US states (i.e., Florida, Ohio and North Carolina). Ahmed et al. [1] compared three different volumetric and sentiment analysis methods in order to predict the outcome of the elections from Twitter posts in three Asian countries: Malaysia, India, and Pakistan. Olorunnimbe et al. [15] presented an incremental learning method, based on a multiple independent Naïve Baye models for predicting the political orientation of users over time.

Our algorithm analyzes the tags used by social media users for supporting their voting intentions. As an important aspect of the analysis process, we evaluated the statistical significance of collected data, which gives strong indications about the users and if they are voters of the political event under analysis. The algorithm has been applied to a real case study: the 2016 Italian constitutional referendum. We studied the behavior of about 50,000 Twitter users by analyzing more than 300,000 tweets posted on the referendum by them in the five weeks preceding the vote. The achieved results are very close to the real ones and significantly more accurate than the average of the opinion polls, assessing the high accuracy and effectiveness of the proposed algorithm.

3 Algorithm Details

As mentioned in Sect. 1, this work proposes a new algorithm for estimating the polarization of social media users during political events. Given a political event $\mathcal{E}$, a set of the factions F, and a set the keywords K associated to $\mathcal{E}$, the proposed algorithm consists of the following steps (see Fig. 1):

- *Data collection*: during this step all tweets that contain one or more keywords in K are gathered from Twitter[3] through public API.
- *Data preprocessing*: at this step several operations are done for cleaning data, including removal of duplicates and tweets without tags, normalization of texts;
- *Tweet polarization*: during this step, each tweet is assigned to a specific faction f by considering the polarization of the tags it contains.
- *User polarization*: for each social media user u, a heuristic is used to calculate a score v_u, which represents the polarization of the user u towards each faction under analysis.
- *Result visualization*: at this step, the polarization scores are exploited for creating info-graphics that presents the results in a way that is easy to understand to the general public.

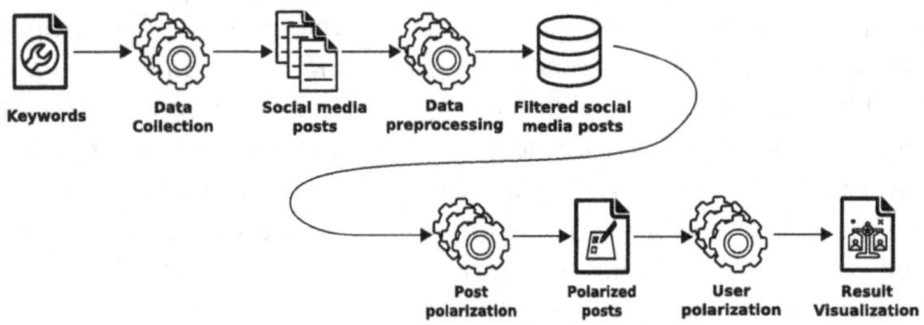

Fig. 1. Main steps of the proposed algorithm

3.1 Definition of Keywords K

A political event $\mathcal{E}$ is characterized by the rivalry of different factions $F = \{f_0, f_1, ..., f_n\}$. The algorithm requires a set of the main keywords K used by social media users to write tweets associated to $\mathcal{E}$. Following the same approach used in [3], such keywords can be divided in *neutral* or in *favor* of a specific faction, i.e., $K = K^{\bigcirc} \cup K_F^{\oplus}$. Specifically:

- $K^{\bigcirc}$ contains all the keywords that can be associated to $\mathcal{E}$, but not to any faction in F.
- $K_F^{\oplus} = K_{f_0}^{\oplus} \cup ... \cup K_{f_n}^{\oplus}$, where $K_{f_i}^{\oplus}$ contains the keywords used by social media users for supporting $f_i \in F$.

Usually, this preparation step requires a minimal knowledge of the domain, that means it could be easily automated. In fact, keywords used for supporting a specific faction usually match some fixed patterns, such as the form "#vote + (faction/candidate/yes/no)". In data gathered from Twitter, such patterns can be searched in hashtags or words.

[3] https://developer.twitter.com/.

3.2 Data Preprocessing

During this step, the tweets collected are pre-processed for making them suitable for the analysis. In particular, they are filtered and modified so as to:

- remove duplicates and stopwords;
- normalize all the keywords by transforming them in lowercase and replacing accented characters with regular ones (e.g., IOVOTOSI or iovotosí → iovotosi);
- improve data representativeness by filtering out all tweets having a language different from the one spoken in the nation hosting the considered political event.

The following operations are performed in parallel on multiple computing nodes exploiting the data parallelism provided by the MapReduce programming model. Since the algorithm has been developed using the ParSoDA library, it can run both on a Hadoop and a Spark cluster. In particular, some performance evaluation experiments we run show that the Spark version of ParSoDA is able to greatly reduce the execution compared to the Hadoop version of the library [4].

3.3 Tweet Polarization

At this step, each tweet is assigned to a specific faction by considering the polarization of the tags it contains. In particular, if a tweet t contains only keywords that are in favor of a specific faction f, then t is classified as in favor of f; otherwise, t is classified as *neutral*. Algorithm 1 shows the pseudo-code of the tweet polarization procedure.

ALGORITHM 1: Polarization of tweets.

Input : Set of tweets T, set of factions F, set of keywords K_F for the different factions
Output: Dictionary of $\langle$tweet, faction$\rangle$ D_T

```
for t ∈ T do
    v_f ← [];
    for i = 0; i < F.size; i++ do
        if contains(t, K_{f_i}) then
            v_f[i] = 1;
    if sum(v_f) = 1 then
        f ← argmax(v);
        D_T ← D_T ∪ ⟨t, f⟩;
return D_P
```

3.4 User Polarization

Using the classified tweets obtained at the previous step, the algorithm exploits a heuristic for estimating the polarization of each social user. Specifically, in a two-factions political event, characterized by the rivalry between the factions f_0 and f_1, the polarization of a user u is defined as:

$$v_u = 2 \times \frac{|f_0|}{|f_0| + |f_1|} - 1 \tag{1}$$

where $|f_0|$ and $|f_1|$ represent the number of tweets published by u that have been classified in favor of f_0 and f_1 respectively. A value of v_u close to 1 means that user u tends to be polarized towards the faction f_0, while when v_u is close to -1 the user is polarized towards f_1.

To obtain more robust results, the algorithm requires a threshold th, usually set to a high value (e.g., 0.9), to select users with strong polarization in favor of f_0 or f_1. Specifically, we consider users with $v_u > th$ as polarized towards $|f_1|$, users with $v_u < -th$ as polarized towards $|f_1|$, otherwise *neutral*. The pseudo-code of the user polarization procedure is shown in Algorithm 2.

ALGORITHM 2: Polarization of users.

```
Input  : Dictionary of ⟨tweet, faction ⟩ D_T, threshold th, two factions f_0 and f_1
Output: Dictionary of ⟨user, faction⟩ D_U
D_F ← ∅;
for t ∈ D_T do
    u ← t.user;
    f ← t.faction;
    D_F(u, f) + +;
D_U ← ∅;
for u ∈ D_F.users do
    v_u = 2 × |D_F(u,f_0)| / (|D_F(u,f_0)|+|D_F(u,f_1)|) − 1;
    if v_u > th then
        D_U ← D_U ∪ ⟨u, f_0⟩;
    else if v_u < −th then
        D_U ← D_U ∪ ⟨u, f_1⟩;
return D_U
```

3.5 Results Visualization

Results visualization is performed by the creation of info-graphics aimed at presenting the results in a way that is easy to understand to the general public, without providing complex statistical details that may be hard to understand to the intended audience. Displaying quantitative information by visual means instead of just using numeric symbols - or at least a combination of the two approaches - has been proven extremely useful in providing a kind of sensory evidence to the inherent abstraction of numbers, because this allows everybody to instantly grasp similarities and differences among values. In fact, basic visual metaphors (e.g., the largest is the greatest, the thickest is the highest) enable more natural ways of understanding and relating sets of quantities [16].

4 Case Study and Results

The algorithm has been applied to a case study that analyzes the polarization of a large number of Twitter users during the 2016 Italian constitutional referendum. The referendum, focused on changing the second part of the constitution, was characterized by the rivalry of two factions: *yes* and *no*. The results of the referendum saw the victory of the *no*, with about 60% of the votes. We collected the main keywords used as hashtags in tweets related to the political event. We collected the main keywords K used as hashtags in tweets related to the political event under analysis. Such keywords have been grouped as follows:

- $K^{\bigcirc}$ = {#referendumcostituzionale, #siono, #riformacostituzionale, #referendum, #4dicembre, #referendum-4dicembre}
- $K^{\oplus}_{yes}$ = {#bastaunsi, #iovotosi, #italiachedicesi, #iodicosi, #leragionidelsi}
- $K^{\oplus}_{no}$ = {#iovotono, #iodicono, #bastaunno, #famiglieperilno, #leragionidelno}

4.1 Statistical Significance of Analyzed Data

The goal of this section is to assess the statistical significance of the dataset used for the analysis. Specifically, we studied whether the Twitter users included in our analysis were actual voters of the referendum, i.e., whether they were Italian citizens aged at least 18 years old. We also extracted aggregate information on the language used to write a tweet (e.g., "it" for Italian or "und" if no language could be detected) and on the location of users who wrote it. In addition, from the user metadata we analyzed the location field, which indicates the user-defined location for the accounts profile (e.g., Rome, Italy). By analyzing the metadata described above, we can say that:

- All the tweets under analysis have been written in Italian. Such language is mainly used by Italians who reside in Italy (about 60 million) or abroad (about 4 million). Italian is used as first language only by a small part of Swiss (about 640,000 people), and a very small part of Croats and Slovenes (about 22.000 people).
- 98% of users who have defined the location in their profile live in Italy.

We calculated that there is a strong correlation (Pearson coefficient 0.9) between the number of Twitter users included in our analysis and the total number of citizens grouped by Italian regions. Similar results are obtained by comparing the number of users and the total number of citizen grouped by Italian cities (Pearson coefficient 0.96). These statistics give us strong indications about the users analyzed in our case study: it is highly likely that they are voters of the political event under analysis.

4.2 Analysis Results

In the last few weeks before the mandatory stop to the polls, the *no* clearly prevailed on the *yes* in the totality of the opinion polls, maintaining about 4% of advantage. Figure 2 shows the comparison among the results achieved by our algorithm, the real voting percentages, the average of opinion polls before voting, and the post-voting percentages estimated for users aged 18–49. Specifically, our analysis focuses on two opposing factions, those in favor of the constitutional reform (i.e., *yes*) and the opposites (i.e., *no*).

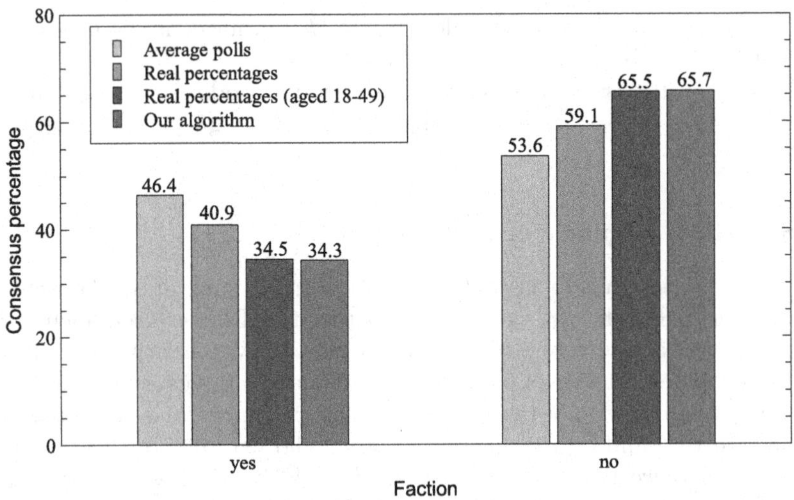

Fig. 2. Comparison between the obtained results, the real ones and the average of opinion polls.

The results achieved are very close to the real ones. This result assesses the high accuracy and effectiveness of the proposed approach. In particular, our algorithm estimated a consensus of 65.7% in favor of *no*, which is a slightly higher than the real one (59.1%), but really close to that estimated after the vote for users aged 18–49 (65.5%). Opinion polls underestimated the vote in favor of *no*, estimating only a percentage of about 53.6% for it. Differently from opinion polls, which tend to underestimate the results, our algorithm tends to overestimate them. This is most likely due to the Twitter data used for the analysis. As 75% of global Italian Twitter audiences were aged between 18 and 49 years, while only 14% of them are 50 or older[4]. An analysis carried out after the referendum[5] showed that the distribution of the vote by age was as follows:

[4] https://datareportal.com/reports/digital-2019-q2-global-digital-statshot (page 43).
[5] https://www.youtrend.it/2016/12/09/referendum-costituzionale-tutti-numeri/.

- age 18–34: 64% *no*, 36% *yes*;
- age 35–49: 67% *no*, 33% *yes*;
- age 50–64: 57% *no*, 43% *yes*;
- age 65+: 51% *no*, 49% *yes*;

Since the majority of Italian Twitter users are aged between 18–49 (75% of audiences), our results strongly respect the distribution of the vote for these age groups. On the contrary, the polls are more cautious and generate more conservative estimates that tend to offset this gap.

5 Conclusion

With the growth of social media, every day millions of people produce huge amount of digital data containing information about human dynamics, collective sentiments, and the behavior of group of people. In this work we presented a new parallel and distributed algorithm for discovering the polarization of social media users during political events, which are characterized by the rivalry of different factions or parties. The algorithm is based on the MapReduce model and can be executed in parallel on distributed systems, such as the Cloud, ensuring scalability as the amount of data to be analyzed grows. To validate the proposed algorithm, it has been applied to a real case study: the 2016 Italian constitutional referendum. The achieved results are very close to the real ones and are significantly more accurate than the average of the opinion polls, revealing the high accuracy and effectiveness of the proposed approach.

Acknowledgment. This work has been partially supported by the SMART Project, CUP J28C17000150006, funded by Regione Calabria (POR FESR-FSE 2014–2020) and by the ASPIDE Project funded by the European Union's Horizon 2020 Research and Innovation Programme under grant agreement No. 801091.

References

1. Ahmed, S., Jaidka, K., Skoric, M.M.: Tweets and votes: a four-country comparison of volumetric and sentiment analysis approaches. In: Tenth International AAAI Conference on Web and Social Media (2016)
2. Anstead, N., O'Loughlin, B.: Social media analysis and public opinion: the 2010 UK general election. J. Comput. Mediated Commun. **20**(2), 204–220 (2014)
3. Belcastro, L., Cantini, R., Marozzo, F., Talia, D., Trunfio, P.: Discovering political polarization on social media: a case study. In: The 15th International Conference on Semantics, Knowledge and Grids, Guangzhou, China (2019)
4. Belcastro, L., Marozzo, F., Talia, D., Trunfio, P.: Appraising SPARK on large-scale social media analysis. In: Heras, D.B., Bougé, L. (eds.) Euro-Par 2017. LNCS, vol. 10659, pp. 483–495. Springer, Cham (2018). https://doi.org/10.1007/978-3-319-75178-8_39
5. Belcastro, L., Marozzo, F., Talia, D., Trunfio, P.: Big data analysis on clouds. In: Zomaya, A.Y., Sakr, S. (eds.) Handbook of Big Data Technologies, pp. 101–142. Springer, Cham (2017). https://doi.org/10.1007/978-3-319-49340-4_4

6. Belcastro, L., Marozzo, F., Talia, D., Trunfio, P.: G-RoI: automatic region-of-interest detection driven by geotagged social media data. ACM Trans. Knowl. Discov. Data **12**(3), 1–22 (2018)
7. Belcastro, L., Marozzo, F., Talia, D., Trunfio, P.: ParSoDA: high-level parallel programming for social data mining. Soc. Netw. Anal. Min. **9**(1), 1–19 (2018). https://doi.org/10.1007/s13278-018-0547-5
8. Ceron, A., Curini, L., Iacus, S.M., Porro, G.: Every tweet counts? How sentiment analysis of social media can improve our knowledge of citizens' political preferences with an application to Italy and France. New Media Soc. **16**(2), 340–358 (2014)
9. El Alaoui, I., Gahi, Y., Messoussi, R., Chaabi, Y., Todoskoff, A., Kobi, A.: A novel adaptable approach for sentiment analysis on big social data. J. Big Data **5**(1), 1–18 (2018). https://doi.org/10.1186/s40537-018-0120-0
10. Graham, T., Jackson, D., Broersma, M.: New platform, old habits? Candidates' use of Twitter during the 2010 British and Dutch general election campaigns. New Media Soc. **18**(5), 765–783 (2016)
11. Gruzd, A., Roy, J.: Investigating political polarization on Twitter: a canadian perspective. Policy Internet **6**(1), 28–45 (2014)
12. Lee, R., Wakamiya, S., Sumiya, K.: Urban area characterization based on crowd behavioral lifelogs over twitter. Pers. Ubiquit. Comput. **17**(4), 605–620 (2013). https://doi.org/10.1007/s00779-012-0510-9
13. Marozzo, F., Bessi, A.: Analyzing polarization of social media users and news sites during political campaigns. Soc. Netw. Anal. Min. **8**(1), 1–13 (2017). https://doi.org/10.1007/s13278-017-0479-5
14. Oikonomou, L., Tjortjis, C.: A method for predicting the winner of the USA presidential elections using data extracted from Twitter. In: 2018 South-Eastern European Design Automation, Computer Engineering, Computer Networks and Society Media Conference (SEEDA_CECNSM), pp. 1–8. IEEE (2018)
15. Olorunnimbe, M.K., Viktor, H.L.: Tweets as a vote: exploring political sentiments on Twitter for opinion mining. In: Esposito, F., Pivert, O., Hacid, M.-S., Raś, Z.W., Ferilli, S. (eds.) ISMIS 2015. LNCS (LNAI), vol. 9384, pp. 180–185. Springer, Cham (2015). https://doi.org/10.1007/978-3-319-25252-0_19
16. Tufte, E.R.: The Visual Display of Quantitative Information. Graphics Press, Cheshire (1986)

Coordinated Data Flow Control in IoT Networks

Nipun Balan Thekkummal(✉), Devki Nandan Jha, Deepak Puthal, Philip James, and Rajiv Ranjan

School of Computing, Newcastle University, Newcastle upon Tyne, UK
{n.b.thekkummal1,d.n.jha2,deepak.puthal, philip.james,raj.ranjan}@newcastle.ac.uk

Abstract. An IoT cloud environment consists of connected physical devices communicating with the cloud, sending telemetry data and accepting actuation information. For sensors, the data flow is from the physical devices to the cloud. The IoT edge device is responsible for collecting this data and forwarding it to the cloud environment for processing. The time it takes for the data to be made available for processing in the cloud is critical, and the network connectivity, bandwidth and latency are the bottlenecks. In this work, we created a flow controller which adaptively controls the flow of the data from the edge device to the cloud. While rate limiting is a trivial technique to control data flow, it is crucial how the edge devices dynamically control the data rate by re-configuring the IoT devices to send data based on the current network condition and load on the Edge device. We tested this system with a simulated data flow from 10 sensors to a Raspberry Pi Device which performed the rate limiting.

Keywords: Internet of Things · Data flow control · Edge computing · Co-ordination algorithm

1 Introduction

IoT (Internet of Things) aims to connect physical devices to the Internet, and data comes from a variety of resources including industrial sensors and control systems, business applications, open web data, etc. [27]. It was reported that IoT would generate 508 zettabytes, termed as "Big Data", by the end of 2019 [24]. These big data is eventually sent from IoT devices to cloud for further analysis, which is a grand challenge.

There are two leading solutions for transferring the IoT data, i.e. (i) the sensor sends data directly to the cloud, or (ii) the edge node collects the data from IoT devices and then forwards the collected and processed data to the cloud. The former solution does not have sufficient flexibility to reprocess the IoT data on the ground due to the limited computing resources of the sensors. In some scenarios, this solution may cause high latency when the network is

I. Brandic et al. (Eds.): ALGOCLOUD 2019, LNCS 12041, pp. 25–41, 2020.
https://doi.org/10.1007/978-3-030-58628-7_3

unstable, wasting network bandwidth to forward entire data to the cloud where we only require some aggregated information.

The integration of edge and cloud solutions has been applied in many state-of-the-art systems [5,28]. However, these systems consider replacing the analytic jobs close to the data source, thereby reducing the latency. ApproxIoT system [33] was designed to utilise edge computing resources such as mobile phones, network gateways and edge data centres at ISPs where the approximate computing is performed by achieving low latency analytics. However, the uncertainty of the IoT network affects the stability of edge devices and its communication to the cloud. For example, the available bandwidth of a cellular network is extremely variable due to the changing number of devices connected to a base station. Also, the cellular network is dynamically changing among 2G, 3G and 4G in rural areas where there are not enough base stations. In many cases, high-frequency data is not required when there is no significant variance in the value, or there is no imminent real-world situation demanding a high data rate reading and analysis of sensor data. The sensor types, the location and real-world scenarios are the factors which determine the data sending rate or frequency. For example, a sensor installed for measuring the ambient temperature of a factory floor may send its values twice a second while a vibration sensor installed in a compression pump at a critical location sends data at a rate of 100 values per second as any significant change in vibration within a short period can cause severe damage if it is not acted upon quickly.

In this work, we build a data flow control system which can adapt the data forwarding from edge to cloud based on the uncertainly of the IoT network. To this end, we develop an *Edge Gatekeeper (EGK)* which monitors the status of each edge node while dynamically adapting the data ingestion rate from the IoT sensors to edge nodes, and edge nodes The design of the *EGK* allows the edge node to process and deliver only a subset of the data to reduce the latency.

Our proposed system needs to consider the following two research questions:

- *how to decide the size of the subset of the data on each edge node*
- *how to efficiently coordinate a large number of heterogeneous edge nodes sending data to a cloud simultaneously*

To address the research questions mentioned above this work makes the following contribution

- We propose a system and a reference architecture for IoT which coordinates the operations of edge devices to ensure stable and resilient operation using an adaptive data flow control mechanism. It is capable of coordinating a large number of heterogeneous edge nodes to utilise the computing resources in the cloud efficiently. We also provide a formal model of data flow in an IoT analytics system.
- We validated our proposed models and the system architecture through a set of experiments using real-world data and testbed. Our experimental results support the effectiveness of flow control for the stable operation on edge devices and resilience to the changes in the number of sensors and the data rate from the sensors.

Outline. The remaining paper is organised as follows. Section 2 sets the background and reviews some related work. Section 3 explains the proposed system architecture including Edge GateKeeper (3.1) and Adaptive Flow Controller (AFC) (3.2). The proposed model and algorithm is explained in Sect. 3.3 followed by the implementation details in Sect. 4, evaluation and future works in Sect. 6.

2 Background and Related Work

In this section, we first present the background of *edge+cloud IoT* architecture, and then discuss the desired properties of a stream processing application, in the context of IoT, following which we briefly introduce the two mainstream computational models. Finally, we illustrate the techniques that we used in our system.

2.1 *Edge+Cloud* IoT Architecture

The increasing number of sensors or IoT devices in smart manufacturing facilities and smart cities are continuously generating and emitting high volumes of data across distributed infrastructures. Further, more powerful devices such as Raspberry Pi, edge gateway, PC or edge cloud collect the emitted data and perform the data aggregation, sampling, filtering, projections or transformation into other formats over these collected data in the edge. This processed data is forwarded to the cloud for more complex analysis. This processing workflow is running over the *Edge+cloud* architecture as shown in Fig. 1. The *Edge+cloud* architecture helps in reducing latency, increasing privacy and saving network bandwidth [21] compared to the architecture where the sensors or IoT devices are connected directly to the cloud. [8] uses *Edge+cloud* architecture to extend the cloud computing paradigm to the edge layer by moving some of the processing workloads to the edge layer.

2.2 IoT Data Flow Challenges

The data flow management challenges in IoT network are well studied, and both industry and academia have proposed multiple solutions. Lukić, Mihajlović and Mezei (2018) [19] study various methods to establish a data path between sensor nodes and web-or cloud-based IoT applications. In this work, the authors studied the details of data flow challenges in the IoT network while using long-range, low power networks such as LoRAWAN and NB-IoT. Tomasz Szydlo et al. (2019) [29] used the concept of data flow transformation to run parts of the computation, closer to the origin of data, on edge devices with constrained resources.

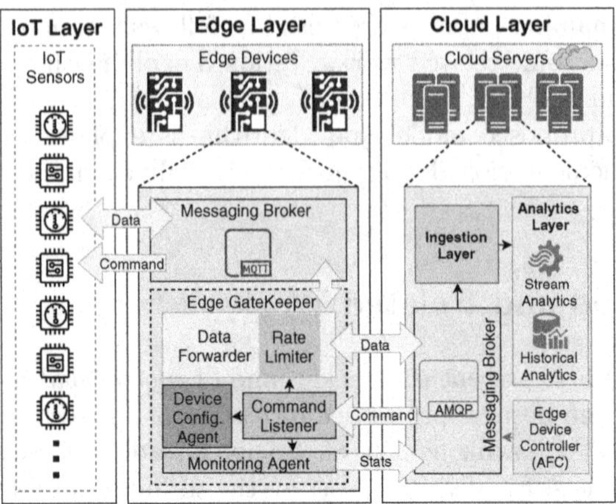

Fig. 1. Architecture

2.3 IoT Data Streams

Stream processing, which started from a single machine system such as Aurora [1] and TelegraphCQ [10], has been studied for decades. With the increasing amount of input data, stream processing has been moved to a distributed processing paradigm, for example Spark Streaming [34], Storm [30], Flink [9], Google Dataflow [4]. Furthermore, stream processing in the IoT environment requires systems that can utilise the computing resources from both edge nodes and cloud to achieve low latency and high throughput [33]. In this paper, we re-use the existing sampling technology and priority queue to ensure the QoS when the computing resources are limited. IoT data streams have some desirable properties for its applications:

High Throughput. In *edge+cloud* solutions, an edge node may connect with a large number of sensors; similarly, a large number of edge nodes are continuously sending data to the cloud. Therefore, high throughput processing is the key to keeping up with the incoming streams. For example, more than 15,000 sensors (attached to around 1,200 sensor nodes) were deployed in the Santander project for smart city research [11], and Boeing 787 creates half a terabyte of data per flight reported by Virgin Atlantic [7].

Low Latency (Data Freshness). The latency or data freshness is defined as the elapses between a sensor sensing the value from an IoT device and that data arriving at the cloud. Data latency is a crucial performance parameter in the sensor network as delayed or stale data could result in wrong analysis/decision making. Consider a real-time traffic monitoring application which collects the traffic data across the city. If the latency is too high because of limited network bandwidth or computing resources of edge nodes, this application may not be able to make a correct decision or may provide inaccurate information for users. Consequently, low latency is very important for this distributed IoT data stream processing system. The system designer should use techniques like sampling [33] and edge processing to ensure low latency in low bandwidth/high latency IoT networks.

Adaptability. Computation resources are geo-distributed in *edge+cloud* architecture and the underlying hardware are heterogeneous. As a result, the system needs to be adapted to the dynamic IoT environment. For example, cloud-based distributed stream process systems have frequently experienced crash-stop node failures [3,32], and IoT environments have much more uncertainty than cloud environments [25].

2.4 Computational Models for IoT Data Streams

For IoT data, several streaming computation models are preferred depending on the use cases. This section introduces a few computation models in use.

Bulk-Synchronous Parallel (BSP). This model has been used in many stream processing system such as Spark Streaming [34], Google Dataflow [4] with FlumeJava. In this model, the computation is a directed acyclic graph (DAG) of operators (e.g. sum, group by, join), the DAG is partitioned into the available computing resources. Moreover, the *mini-batch*, which reserves the streaming data for **T** seconds, is processed over the entire DAG.

Continuous Operator Streaming (COS). In this model, there is no blocking *barrier* like *mini-batch* to sync all operators in a defined time period. These operators are long-running operators, and the messages can be transferred directly among them. The representative systems are Naiad [23], Stream Scope [18] and Flink [9].

Approximate Computing. Sampling techniques have been applied in distributed big data analytics to obtain a reasonable output efficiently [2,13,16]. This approach is based on the observation that, for many applications, only an approximate value of the sensor reading is required for its desired functionality. Chippa et al. reported in [12] that by reducing 5% accuracy of the k-means clustering algorithm, 50 times energy can be saved. As a result, we leverage a similar strategy by using a sampling algorithm to overcome the trade-off between the limited computing resources and processing the large volumes of IoT data in real-time.

Next, these techniques are widely applied in stream processing [6,26], which demonstrated well that the proposed systems could balance the quality of output and computation efficiency. Unfortunately, these systems only work on cloud-based environments and cannot utilise the computing resources from edge nodes.

Wen et al. (2018) [33] share the same architecture in their work and use the simple technique to overcome the issue of how to sample IoT data in *truly* distributed environments while ensuring low latency and high throughput.

Simple Random Sampling (SRS). SRS is a naive approach for sampling, in which n samples are drawn from a population in such a way that the chance of sampling every set of n individuals is equal. Thus, SRS is an unbiased surveying technique which means the selected subset can represent the population as the whole.

3 Architecture

The purpose of the flow controller is to actively control the rate of data being processed and forwarded from the edge device to the cloud. To reduce the amount of data being sent by the sensors, the edge gateway can reconfigure IoT sensors to set the data rate. This acts as a stabilisation mechanism for the varying workload at the edge layer. While designing the reference architecture (Fig. 1), we considered the type, frequency and priority of the sensors. We considered the scenario of a single-hop star network where the sensor IoT devices are interacting directly with the edge device. It consists of 1) IoT layer which contains the IoT devices/sensors having the lowest processing capacity, 2) Edge layer which consists of devices which acts as the entry points to the larger cloud network and is also capable of doing some processing of the sensor data, 3) Cloud layer with the highest processing capacity of all the other layers. Data flows from the IoT to the cloud layer through the edge layer. The data flow control is done using Edge GateKeeper (EGK), which is deployed in the edge layer and Adaptive flow controller (AFC) deployed in the cloud layer. This work proposes the system architecture for dynamically reconfiguring the edge device based on the number of devices connected and the priority of each sensor in the network.

3.1 Edge GateKeeper (EGK)

An extensive IoT network contains 1000 s of sensors connected to 100 s of edge devices. The load on the edge device is proportional to the volume and velocity of data. Edge devices can either send the full data as-it-is to the cloud layer or perform sampling/pre-processing before sending to cloud. The proposed reference architecture uses a coordinated data flow control to allow the edge devices to balance the data flow by dynamically reconfiguring sensors to send data at different frequency allowing control of the volume and velocity of data. This acts as a stabilisation mechanism for a varying workload at the edge layer. The reference architecture consists of IoT sensor devices, which have a data channel and control channel for communication with the edge device. The edge device is a low powered computer with essential traffic management and processing capacity.

Edge GateKeeper (EGK) is a lightweight application running on the edge device which acts as the gateway for all communication to and from it. It consists of i) Lightweight local message broker, ii) Sensor data ingest and Forwarder, iii) Pre-processor, iv) Rate Limiter, v) Command listener, and vi) Device reconfiguration agent. The Sensor data reader reads the data from the message broker to which sensors send their readings in real-time. The pre-processor performs essential pre-processing and filtering operations. Figure 4 explains the functionality of EGK.

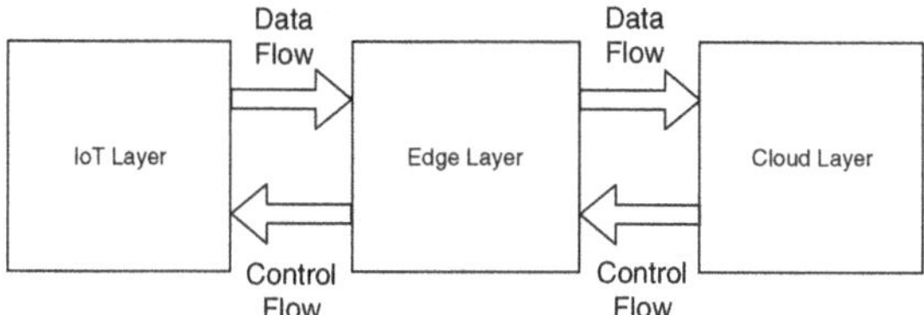

Fig. 2. Data flow and control flow between the layers: For IoT sensors, data flow happens from IoT layer to cloud while the control flow is from cloud layer to IoT layer

3.2 Adaptive Flow Controller (AFC)

The Adaptive Flow Controller (AFC), hosted in the cloud layer, controls the reconfiguration decisions. EGK and cloud layer are connected using a data channel and a control channel. The data channel carries data forwarded by the EGK from the IoT layer to the cloud ingestion layer. The control channel carries commands to control the edge layer and IoT layer. Sensors are registered to EGK, and EGK registers itself and its connected sensors to the ingestion layer in the cloud. The AFC stores the full map of the IoT network as a graph. The graph can be represented as a 2D sparse matrix M (Fig. 3). Edge devices are represented as rows, and IoT devices are represented as columns. The value at $M[i][j]$ represents the data rate of IoT device D_j to edge device E_i. Three scenarios can trigger a reconfiguration. i) More IoT devices are added to an edge device. ii) Edge devices' processing capacity becomes a bottleneck for the data flow. iii) There is a demand for higher data rate by some of the sensors. The maximum forward rate is set on the edge device based on the resource capacity of the edge device and network stability. We assume this value is set for each edge device during the initial setup. When additional IoT devices are added, the edge device informs the AFC. The AFC, in turn, recalculates the data rate allocation for each IoT device and sends back to the edge device. The data rate allocation problem is formally defined in Sect. 3.3. An algorithm (Algorithm 1) has been developed to dynamically set the data rates and runs periodically in the AFC. The edge device has a device reconfiguration agent which configures the IoT device with the new data rate.

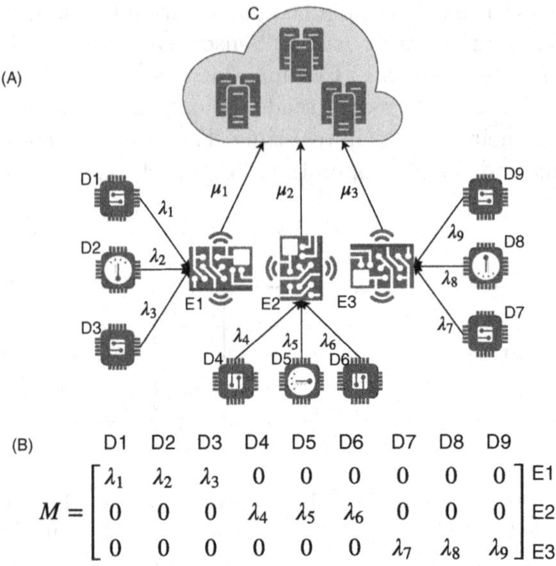

$$M = \begin{bmatrix} \lambda_1 & \lambda_2 & \lambda_3 & 0 & 0 & 0 & 0 & 0 & 0 \\ 0 & 0 & 0 & \lambda_4 & \lambda_5 & \lambda_6 & 0 & 0 & 0 \\ 0 & 0 & 0 & 0 & 0 & 0 & \lambda_7 & \lambda_8 & \lambda_9 \end{bmatrix}$$

Fig. 3. Shows data flow from sensor network to cloud through edge. D1–D9: IoT sensors, E1–E3: Edge Devices, C: Cloud Layer. λ_1–λ_9: Data from from D1–D9 to the connected Edge devices. In matrix M rows represent the edge devices (E1–E3) and columns represent IoT devices (D1–D9)

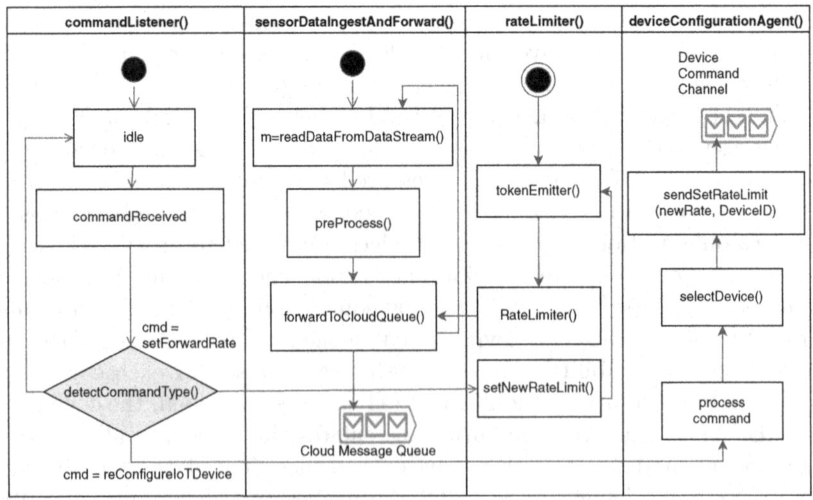

Fig. 4. Edge GateKeeper workflow

3.3 Model

Assume that we have a set of IoT devices D, and each one $D_i \in D$ has its priority $\mathcal{P}_i$ and sending rate λ_i. These devices are partitioned into K groups, and each group $G_k, k \in K$ interacts with only one edge node E_j. As a result, the total number of edge node $|E|$ equals the number of groups K, where E is a set of edge nodes. Finally, all edge nodes forward the received data streams to the cloud datacenter DC. We define the data flow as a tuple $\langle \mu_j, \lambda_i \rangle$, where μ_j is the forwarding rate of E_j while λ_i represents the data injection rate from D_i to E_j. We consider the situation that IoT devices are generating more data streams than the edge node can process and forward. This situation can occur because of two main reasons, i) Edge does not have enough resources to process and forward the amount of data it receives ii) Edge node has assigned a maximum data forwarding rate it could perform to the cloud when the total incoming data rate is higher than the forward rate. For example, the injection rate of a group of IoT devices G_j which are connecting with edge node E_j is larger than the forwarding rate of E_j, noting μ_j, i.e., $\sum_{i \in G_j} \lambda_i > \mu_j$.

To overcome this, we design a flow control method that prioritises the data streams which are coming from high priority IoT devices by dynamically reducing the injection rates of the less critical IoT devices. We set weights to each sensor according to the priority. Possible values of priority $\mathcal{P}$ are {HIGH, MEDIUM, LOW}. Weights W corresponding to these priorities are {3, 2, 1}. Weights associated with IoT device D_i is represented by W_i.

The data rate allocation for device D_i is given by

$$A_i = \frac{W_i}{\sum_{k \in G_j} W_k} \times \mu \tag{1}$$

Algorithm 1 finds the data rate of individual IoT devices. Data stream ds for each IoT device is again a tuple $ds = \langle \lambda_i, S_i \rangle$ where, λ_i and S_i are the data rate and size of data generated by the IoT device D_i. We therefore define the dataflow mapping as a tuple $\langle E_j, \mathcal{C}, \lambda_{\{D_i \to E_j\}}, \lambda_{\{E_j \to C\}} \rangle$, where the $\lambda_{\{D_i \to E_j\}}$ represents the data rate from device D_i to edge E_j and $\lambda_{\{E_j \to C\}}$ represents the data rate from edge E_j to cloud data center C. Consider there are X number of edge devices each represented by the tuple $\langle id, \mathcal{C}, \lambda_{\{D_i \to E_j\}}, \lambda_{\{E_j \to C\}} \rangle$ where id is the identifier of the edge device, $\mathcal{C}$ is the capacity of the edge device which is again a tuple $\mathcal{C} = \langle \mathcal{R}_S, \mathcal{R}_H \rangle$ where $\mathcal{R}_H$ and $\mathcal{R}_S$ are the hardware and software support provided by the edge device. Similarly, cloud datacentre C is represented as a set of components (VMs or containers) with an incoming data rate constraint of λ_C.

Based on the given priority of IoT devices D_i, the edge to cloud communication is sampled according to the function $\mathcal{F} : \lambda_{\{D_i \to E_j\}} \to \lambda_{\{E_j \to C\}}$. To perform this operation, the edge needs to compute the data rate for each IoT sensor device which enables the sampling of the data.

Problem Formulation: Given the IoT infrastructure, D, E, C,

$$\text{maximize}\{\lambda_{\{E_1 \to C\}}, \lambda_{\{E_2 \to C\}}, ..., \lambda_{\{E_K \to C\}}\}$$

with constraint to:

$$\sum\{\lambda_{\{E_1 \to C\}} + \lambda_{\{E_2 \to C\}} + ... + \lambda_{\{E_K \to C\}}\} \leq \lambda C \tag{2}$$

$$\exists_i \exists_j \{\sum_i \lambda_{D_i} \leq \lambda_{E_j}\} \tag{3}$$

where there is a mapping between D_i and E_j

Constraint 2 explains that the data rate of all the edge to cloud communication should be less than the available data rate of the cloud. Similarly, Constraint 3 explains the data rate limitation of each edge device E_j (Table 1).

Algorithm 1: Data Rate Controller Algorithm

Input : $A[n][m]$: A 2-D matrix where rows represent Edge devices and columns represent IoT Devices; Values represent the data rate from the IoT device to the Edge device; n edge device; m IoT devices

$\mathcal{P}[n][m]$: List of Priority for each Edge device; n=number of Edge Devices

λ: Total data rate of all IoT devices connected to an Edge device

μ_j: Data rate from edge to the cloud

Output: Data rate allocation matrix A[n][m]

```
Initiate weight matrix W[n][m]
Initiate total weight array tw[n] with 0
for i=0 to n-1 do
    for j=0 to m-1 do
        if P[i][j]='HIGH' then
            W[i][j]=3
            tw[i] = tw[i] + 3
        end
        else if P[i]='MEDIUM' then
            W[i][j]=2
            tw[i] = tw[i] + 2
        end
        else
            W[i][j]=1
            tw[i] = tw[i] + 1
        end
    end
end
Initiate data rate allocation matrix A[n][m]
for i=0 to n-1 do
    for j=0 to m-1 do
        A[i][j] = (W[i][j] / tw[i]) × μ
    end
end
```

Table 1. A summary of symbols and abbreviations used within the formal definition.

Symbol	Explanation
D_i	IoT Device
$\mathcal{P}_i$	Priority of IoT device D_i
K	Number of partitions of IoT devices
G_k	Group of IoT devices
E_j	Edge device
$\lvert E\rvert$	Total number of edge nodes
λ_i	Data emission rate of ith IoT device
S_i	Data size of each value of ith IoT device
N	Number of IoT devices
K	Number of Partitions of IoT devices
$\langle\mu_j, \lambda_i\rangle$	Data Flow
μ_j	Forwarding rate of Edge node E_j
λ_j	Data injection rate from D_i to E_j
W_i	Weight given to the IoT device D_i
$A[n][m]$	Data rate allocation matix. Rows represent edge devices and columns represent IoT devices

4 Implementation Details

We used Raspberry Pi 3B+ as edge nodes and for emulating sensors. Raspberry Pi is a credit-card-sized single-board computer (SBC) [31] mainly developed for simulation and teaching purposes. As it has a small form factor, is reliable and has low power requirement, this device is increasingly being used for industrial and IoT applications [22].

We set up a proof of concept system, consisting of the three layers, namely, IoT layer, Edge layer and Cloud layer. We used real sensor values from Newcastle Urban Observatory (UO) [15], which is an IoT based city environment monitoring system which consists of about 1000 sensors forwarding around 5000 data points a second. To test this system, we developed a sensor emulator which sends data points to edge devices at a configured frequency. The sensor emulator runs on three Raspberry Pi devices, each emulating a subset of sensors (Fig. 5).

The system is implemented based on the reference architecture (Fig. 1) proposed in this paper. We used Raspberry Pi 3B+ devices as the edge nodes. Devices are installed with Raspbian OS running in shell only mode. A lightweight MQTT broker, Mosquitto [17] is installed in each edge device to queue data from the sensors. As mentioned in the architecture section, sensors are partitioned, and each partition is connected to one Raspberry Pi device through LAN connectivity. An instance of Edge Gatekeeper (EGK) software is configured to run in each edge node. EGK is designed to run with minimal memory and CPU footprint and is developed in GoLang [20]. One topic is created for each sensor for command communication, while a single topic is used for data communica-

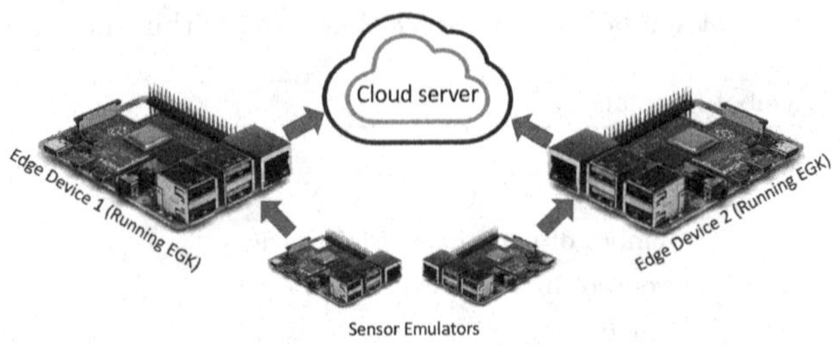

Fig. 5. Prototype implementation

tion from sensors to edge. Sensors receive commands from the device configuration agent in EGK by subscribing to the command topic to which it publishes reconfiguration commands. Sensors send the readings as streams of data points in JSON format to MQTT broker. As MQTT is a pub/sub based messaging protocol working over TCP/IP, both (emulated) sensors/IoT devices and edge devices communicate through network sockets. We selected a QoS Level 1 [14] which promises "AT LEAST ONCE" delivery assurance to ensure delivery of every message. Elevating to QoS Level 2 has a significant performance impact. All the sensors publish data points to the topic "sensor data". Upon startup, EGK initiates the data forwarder sub-service as a thread which subscribes to the topic "sensor data". EGK receives the messages from all the sensors publishing to its local broker at the configured publish rate. EGK receives data from all the sensors connected to it, and it forwards this to the cloud messaging queue. The data forwarding rate is preset at each edge device, which can be reconfigured by the Adaptive Flow Controller (AFC) in the cloud data centre.

EGK also runs a service which listens to the commands from the (AFC). We have defined reconfiguration commands (Table 2) to set data rate/frequency of both IoT devices and edge devices. A reconfiguration command could be addressed to an IoT device (using sensor_id) or edge device (using edge_id). AFC sends the reconfiguration command to the corresponding edge node. The device reconfiguration agent running as a service in edge gatekeeper is responsible for reconfiguring the edge and IoT nodes. If it is a command addressed to the edge node, it reconfigures itself with the new data rate. If it is addressed to a sensor, the device configuration agent sends the reconfiguration command to the sensor, which sets the new data rate and continues its normal operation.

AFC is a program running in the cloud environment which has the information of all the sensors and edge nodes. The data rate allocation algorithm (Algorithm 1) is triggered whenever a new sensor is added to the network.

5 Evaluation

For the validation of the proposed system, we designed four experiments to run on the prototype. The primary objective of the experiments is to understand the impact of a different rate of data flow for a fixed load on the edge device. The

Table 2. Device reconfiguration commands

Command	Description
SET E_FWD_RT ⟨*edge_id*⟩⟨*datarate*⟩	Set data forwarding rate of an edge node
SET S_RT ⟨*sensor_id*⟩⟨*datarate*⟩	Set data rate of a sensor node/IoT device
START E_FWD ⟨*edge_id*⟩	Instructs an edge node to start forwarding data
STOP E_FWD ⟨*edge_id*⟩	Instructs an edge node to stop forwarding data
START S_SND ⟨*sensor_id*⟩	Instructs a sensor node to start sending data points
STOP S_SND ⟨*sensor_id*⟩	Instructs a sensor node to stop sending data points

second objective is to understand the point at which the edge device is rendered into an unstable state, where data flow backpressure starts building on the edge device. The third objective is to understand how adaptive flow control deals with the backpressure and how it impacts the data freshness ingested into the cloud layer.

Experiment Setup: The experiment setup consists of two sensor emulators emulating 10 sensors each. These sensor emulators are connected to two edge devices with a balanced configuration where each edge device is receiving 10 sensor streams. Both sensor emulators and edge devices are implemented on Raspberry Pi devices. All these devices are connected to the network using wired LAN cables through a 1 Gigabit LAN switch. A router is connected to the switch providing edge layer access to the cloud layer.

5.1 Performance Baseline

Experiment 1: The processing load on the edge device is the prepossessing and forwarding overhead. This experiment establishes the baseline performance of the edge device for different data rates for the fixed load. Data rates are incrementally set on the IoT devices so that the total data rates are varied from 10 records per second to 450 records per second for each sensor. ie values are set for λ_{D_i} such that $\sum_{k \epsilon G_i} \lambda_{D_i}$ is varied from 100 to 4500 records per second. The effective forward rate is measured for each data rate for a fixed period (Fig. 6).

The results show that the forward rate is matching the receive rate until capped forward rates (1000, 2000 records/sec) after which backpressure started building and affecting the data forward performance making the forward rate dip.

5.2 Stability Analysis

Experiment 2: In this experiment, we try to identify the point at which the system reaches an unstable state while the backpressure in the edge device starts building. For this, each edge device is set with a forward rate of 5000 records per second. The data rates of sensors are elevated gradually to identify the point

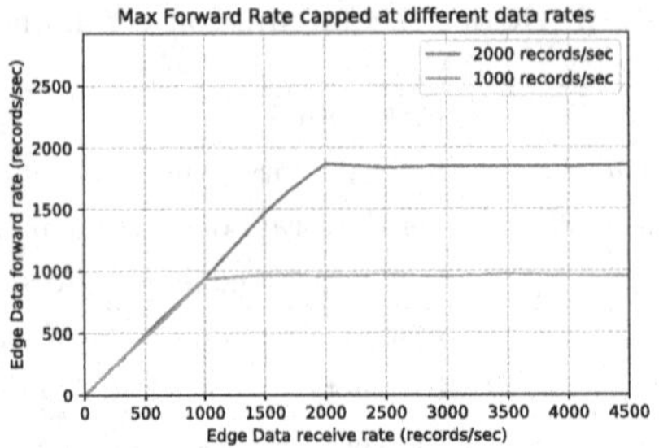

Fig. 6. Results of baseline performance in terms of forwarding rates for different data arrival rate

at which the edge is not capable of forwarding all the data received. CPU and memory stats of the edge device are monitored and plotted against the data receive rate. Results show the point at which the backpressure of the data spikes up the resource utilisation, especially the memory utilisation (Fig. 7).

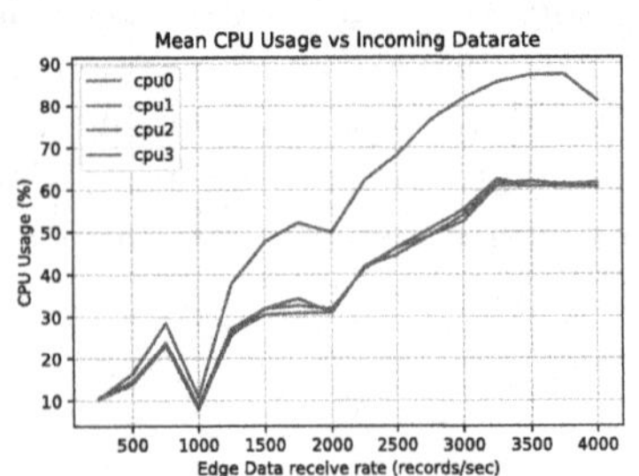

(a) CPU usage for different data rates

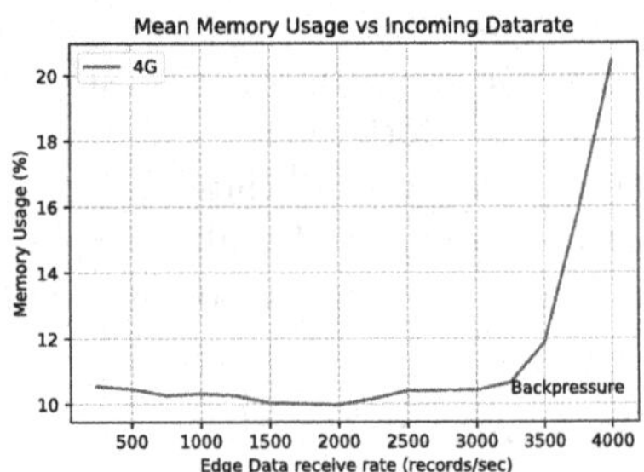

(b) Memory usage for different data rates

Fig. 7. CPU and memory usage of edge device for different data rates

5.3 Data Freshness and Backpressure Recovery Time with AFC

Experiment 3: The clocks of all the devices are synchronised using a standard Network Time Protocol (NTP) server. Each record produced in the sensor simulator is attached with an epoch time. These records are passed to the cloud environment through edge devices. The edge device attaches its current timestamp to the record before forwarding it to the cloud. This timestamp attached by the sensor is compared with the epoch time in the cloud environment to measure the latency/data freshness. The latency is tested with three different network scenarios 4G, 3G and GPRS. The results show that the latency is showing a sharp spike at the point of the forward rate limit (Fig. 8).

The following table (Table 3) shows the recovery time from the backpressure for each data rate when AFC is engaged.

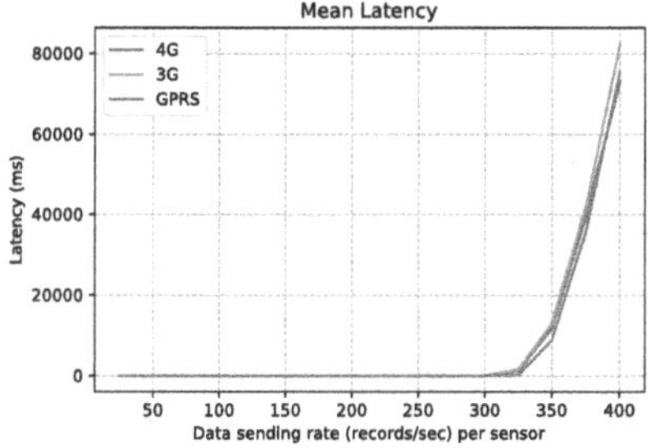

Fig. 8. Results of latency test for 4G, 3G and GPRS network

Table 3. Back pressure recovery time with AFC

Data rate (rec/sec)	Recovery time (seconds)
3250	~2
3500	~2.5
3750	~4
4000	~6
4500	~7

6 Summary and Future Work

The prototype system we developed enabled the edge devices to control the data rate it forwards to the cloud environment by dynamically reconfiguring the IoT devices. The AFC algorithm is effective for recovering the system from the backpressure in the data flow. This approach helps to improve the data freshness in a congested IoT network. Future work includes the integration of sampling algorithms into EGK to perform sampling of the incoming data keeping the data quality high. EGK also opens the possibility of load balancing between multiple edge devices to reduce the load while maintaining the data quality.

References

1. Abadi, D.J., et al.: Aurora: a new model and architecture for data stream management. VLDB J. **12**(2), 120–139 (2003)
2. Agarwal, S., Mozafari, B., Panda, A., Milner, H., Madden, S., Stoica, I.: BlinkDB: Queries with bounded errors and bounded response times on very large data. In: Proceedings of the 8th ACM European Conference on Computer Systems, pp. 29–42. ACM (2013)
3. Akidau, T., et al.: Millwheel: fault-tolerant stream processing at internet scale. Proc. VLDB Endowment **6**(11), 1033–1044 (2013)
4. Akidau, T., et al.: The dataflow model: a practical approach to balancing correctness, latency, and cost in massive-scale, unbounded, out-of-order data processing. Proc. VLDB Endowment **8**(12), 1792–1803 (2015)

5. Bahreini, T., Grosu, D.: Efficient placement of multi-component applications in edge computing systems. In: Proceedings of the Second ACM/IEEE Symposium on Edge Computing, p. 5. ACM (2017)
6. Beck, M., Bhatotia, P., Chen, R., Fetzer, C., Strufe, T., et al.: Privapprox: privacy-preserving stream analytics. In: 2017 {USENIX} Annual Technical Conference ({USENIX}{ATC} 17). pp. 659–672 (2017)
7. Boeing: Boeing 787s to create half a terabyte of data per flight, says virgin atlantic. https://www.computerworlduk.com/data/boeing-787s-create-half-terabyte-of-data-per-flight-says-virgin-atlantic-3433595/. Accessed 08 Apr 2019
8. Bonomi, F., Milito, R., Zhu, J., Addepalli, S.: Fog computing and its role in the internet of things. In: Proceedings of the First Edition of the MCC Workshop on Mobile Cloud Computing, MCC 2012, pp. 13–16. ACM, New York (2012). https://doi.org/10.1145/2342509.2342513
9. Carbone, P., Katsifodimos, A., Ewen, S., Markl, V., Haridi, S., Tzoumas, K.: Apache Flink: stream and batch processing in a single engine. Bull. IEEE Comput. Soc. Tech. Committee Data Eng. **36**(4), 28–38 (2015)
10. Chandrasekaran, S., et al.: TelegraphCQ: continuous dataflow processing for an uncertain world. In: CIDR, vol. 2, p. 4 (2003)
11. Cheng, B., Longo, S., Cirillo, F., Bauer, M., Kovacs, E.: Building a big data platform for smart cities: experience and lessons from Santander. In: IEEE International Congress on Big Data, pp. 592–599. IEEE (2015)
12. Chippa, V.K., Chakradhar, S.T., Roy, K., Raghunathan, A.: Analysis and characterization of inherent application resilience for approximate computing. In: Proceedings of the 50th Annual Design Automation Conference, p. 113. ACM (2013)
13. Goiri, I., Bianchini, R., Nagarakatte, S., Nguyen, T.D.: ApproxHadoop: bringing approximations to mapreduce frameworks. In: ACM SIGARCH Computer Architecture News, vol. 43, pp. 383–397. ACM (2015)
14. Hunkeler, U., Truong, H.L., Stanford-Clark, A.: MQTT-S - A publish/subscribe protocol for wireless sensor networks. In: 3rd International Conference on Communication Systems Software and Middleware and Workshops (COMSWARE 2008), pp. 791–798. IEEE (2008)
15. James, P.M., Dawson, R.J., Harris, N., Joncyzk, J.: Urban observatory environment. Newcastle University, pp. 154300–154319 (2014)
16. Kandula, S., et al.: Quickr: lazily approximating complex adhoc queries in bigdata clusters. In: Proceedings of the 2016 International Conference on Management of Data, pp. 631–646. ACM (2016)
17. Light, R.A., et al.: Mosquitto: server and client implementation of the MQTT protocol. J. Open Source Softw. **2**(13), 265 (2017)
18. Lin, W., Qian, Z., Xu, J., Yang, S., Zhou, J., Zhou, L.: Streamscope: continuous reliable distributed processing of big data streams. In: 13th {USENIX} Symposium on Networked Systems Design and Implementation ({NSDI} 2016), pp. 439–453 (2016)
19. Lukić, M., Mihajlović,, Mezei, I.: Data flow in low-power wide-area IoT applications. In: 2018 26th Telecommunications Forum (TELFOR). pp. 1–4 (Nov 2018). https://doi.org/10.1109/TELFOR.2018.8611848
20. Meyerson, J.: The go programming language. IEEE Softw. **31**(5), 104–104 (2014). https://doi.org/10.1109/MS.2014.127
21. Mohammadi, M., Al-Fuqaha, A., Sorour, S., Guizani, M.: Deep learning for IoT big data and streaming analytics: a survey. IEEE Commun. Surv. Tutorials **20**(4), 2923–2960 (2018)

22. Morabito, R., Beijar, N.: Enabling data processing at the network edge through lightweight virtualization technologies. In: IEEE International Conference on Sensing, Communication and Networking (SECON Workshops), pp. 1–6, June 2016. https://doi.org/10.1109/SECONW.2016.7746807
23. Murray, D.G., McSherry, F., Isaacs, R., Isard, M., Barham, P., Abadi, M.: Naiad: a timely dataflow system. In: Proceedings of the Twenty-Fourth ACM Symposium on Operating Systems Principles, pp. 439–455. ACM (2013)
24. Networking, C.V.: Cisco global cloud index: Forecast and methodology 2015–2020. White paper (2016)
25. O'Keeffe, D., Salonidis, T., Pietzuch, P.: Frontier: resilient edge processing for the internet of things. Proc. VLDB Endowment **11**(10), 1178–1191 (2018)
26. Quoc, D.L., Chen, R., Bhatotia, P., Fetze, C., Hilt, V., Strufe, T.: Approximate stream analytics in Apache Flink and Apache Spark streaming. arXiv preprint arXiv:1709.02946 (2017)
27. Ranjan, R., et al.: The next grand challenges: integrating the internet of things and data science. IEEE Cloud Comput. **5**(3), 12–26 (2018)
28. Sajjad, H.P., Danniswara, K., Al-Shishtawy, A., Vlassov, V.: Spanedge: towards unifying stream processing over central and near-the-edge data centers. In: 2016 IEEE/ACM Symposium on Edge Computing (SEC), pp. 168–178. IEEE (2016)
29. Szydlo, T., Brzoza-Woch, R., Sendorek, J., Windak, M., Gniady, C.: Flow-based programming for IoT leveraging fog computing. In: IEEE 26th International Conference on Enabling Technologies: Infrastructure for Collaborative Enterprises (WETICE), pp. 74–79, June 2017. https://doi.org/10.1109/WETICE.2017.17
30. Toshniwal, A., et al.: Storm@ Twitter. In: Proceedings of the 2014 ACM SIGMOD International Conference on Management of Data, pp. 147–156. ACM (2014)
31. Upton, E., Halfacree, G.: Raspberry Pi User Guide. Wiley, New York (2014)
32. Venkataraman, S., et al.: Drizzle: fast and adaptable stream processing at scale. In: Proceedings of the 26th Symposium on Operating Systems Principles, pp. 374–389. ACM (2017)
33. Wen, Z., Bhatotia, P., Chen, R., Lee, M., et al.: ApproxIoT: approximate analytics for edge computing. In: IEEE 38th International Conference on Distributed Computing Systems (ICDCS), pp. 411–421. IEEE (2018)
34. Zaharia, M., Das, T., Li, H., Hunter, T., Shenker, S., Stoica, I.: Discretized streams: Fault-tolerant streaming computation at scale. In: Proceedings of the Twenty-fourth ACM Symposium on Operating Systems Principles, pp. 423–438. ACM (2013)

A Monitoring System for Distributed Edge Infrastructures with Decentralized Coordination

Roger Pueyo Centelles[1], Mennan Selimi[1,2], Felix Freitag[1](✉), and Leandro Navarro[1]

[1] Universitat Politècnica de Catalunya, BarcelonaTech, Barcelona, Spain
{rpueyo,mselimi,felix,leandro}@ac.upc.edu

[2] Max van der Stoel Institute, South East European University, Tetovo, North Macedonia
m.selimi@seeu.edu.mk

Abstract. We present the case of monitoring a decentralized and crowd-sourced network infrastructure, that needs to be monitored over geographically distributed devices at the network edge. It is a characteristic of the target environment that both, the infrastructure to be monitored and the hosts where the monitoring system runs, change over time, and network partitions may happen. The proposed monitoring system is decentralized, and monitoring servers coordinate their actions through an eventually consistent data storage layer deployed at the network edge. We developed a proof-of-concept implementation, which leverages CRDT-based data types provided by AntidoteDB. Our evaluation focuses on the understanding of the continuously updated mapping of monitoring server to network devices, specifically on the effects of different policies for each individual monitoring server to decide on which and how many network devices to monitor. One of the policies is experimented by means of a deployment on 8 real nodes, leveraging the data replication of AntidoteDB in a realistic setting. The observed effects of the different policies are interpreted from the point of view of the trade-off between resource consumption and redundancy.

Keywords: Edge computing · Distributed monitoring · Decentralized coordination

1 Introduction

We aim to develop a monitoring system for decentralized and crowdsourced network infrastructures such as Guifi.net, a community network with more than 30,000 networking devices with IP addressing. The infrastructure of Guifi.net can be understood as a crowd-sourced, multi-tenant collection of heterogeneous network devices (wired and wireless) interconnected between them and forming a collective communication and computing system [1].

I. Brandic et al. (Eds.): ALGOCLOUD 2019, LNCS 12041, pp. 42–58, 2020.
https://doi.org/10.1007/978-3-030-58628-7_4

An edge cloud computing paradigm may initially be considered to build this monitoring system. In edge computing, cloud services running in data centers, e.g, data storage, are extended with the capacities of local processing at the edge. In such cloud-based services, which leverage edge devices, improved response time is achieved through local processing at the edge device and reduction of communication needs with remote data centers [2]. In the practical implementation of such a paradigm, the edge devices would be deployed as part of the vendor's monitoring application. They would need a suitable physical locations available in Guifi.net. In addition, the community network would need to assume the economic cost for the provision of the monitoring infrastructure.

Collaborative edge computing in Guifi.net started to be researched and developed in the last few years [3]. Currently in 2019 there are tenths of operational interconnected edge devices in the community network, which host diverse local services. These edge devices, such as mini-PCs or Single-Board-Computers (SBC), are located at the premises of some members of the community. Furthermore, the owners have system administrator permissions of the device, which enables them to install any required service. Differently, commercial edge gateways are typically locked and operate in a dedicated mode for the vendor's application. In fact, the edge computing model in community networks is radically different to the locked devices and application model of vendors: owners of edge devices in Guifi.net are encouraged to collaborate and actively contribute to the provision of network monitoring and end user-oriented services, and sustain edge micro-clouds [4,5].

The goal of the targeted monitoring system is to leverage the geographically-scattered low-capacity computing devices available at the premises of Guifi.net members to host the monitoring system software components. Since in the given context network partitions and failures of these servers may happen, and there is no traditional cloud data center infrastructure available in Guifi.net, we pursue a decentralized solution for the monitoring system. As a consequence, we envisioned to store monitoring data by means of a distributed replicated database. Furthermore, the software of the monitoring system will run as an additional service on the low-capacity computing devices that belong to Guifi.net members.

2 Needs for Monitoring System and Use Cases

The aim of a network monitoring system is to keep aware about the operational status of a network infrastructure, including the detection of anomalies and the collection of usage and performance data for every network component. We first describe the limitations of the current monitoring system, and we describe the requirements about economic compensation of network provision and usage.

2.1 Limitations of the Current Monitoring System

The current legacy monitoring system for the Guifi.net network aims at offering a public up-time and traffic accounting service. It consists of several independent, non-coordinated, crowd-sourced monitoring servers (built on several off-the-shelf Linux x86 low-end devices). Each server gets the list of nodes (i.e., network devices) to monitor from the Guifi.net website and, periodically, checks them for reachability/uptime (via ICMP pings) and measures network traffic (via SNMP). A limitation of this service is that each node in Guifi.net is assigned to only one monitoring instance/server. Therefore, if a monitor server fails, all the nodes under its supervision stop being monitored. Furthermore, monitoring data from a certain node is stored only by the assigned monitoring server, so data loss is prone to occur. Finally, the system is not self-adaptive to changes and requires manual intervention.

The current monitoring system impedes the implementation of relevant use cases, as sketched in the following subsection, and a more resilient, self-adaptive monitoring system is needed.

2.2 Needs of a Billing and Economic Compensations System

Currently, more than 20 companies operate their services professionally on top of the Guifi.net community network. For this, the project has put in practice a disruptive economic model [6] based on the commons and collaborative economy models, by means of the deployment of a common-pool network infrastructure and a fair and sustainable economic exploitation[1]. There is need for a comprehensive and reliable source of traffic data in the network.

The current billing system to balance the community effort and the commercial activity related to contribution of network capacity and consumption of connectivity mostly relies on the traffic accounting being performed at the core routers by the Guifi.net Foundation. However, this requires a considerable amount of manual intervention to combine, verify and validate not only the figures, but also the data reported by the ISPs themselves. An automated billing mechanism enabled by the retrieval of reliable monitoring information from a shared data layer would help in making the operation of the network more sustainable, both technically and economically. In addition, publicly-available traffic and resources usage data facilitated by a monitoring system would improve the transparency for the whole ecosystem, leading to less disputes between the Guifi.net Foundation and the ISPs.

3 An Edge Monitoring System for Network Infrastructures

The new monitoring system aims at solving the limitations of the legacy monitoring system and provide comprehensive and reliable monitoring data for all

[1] Guifi.net - The economic project - https://guifi.net/en/economic-project.

network devices despite network and server failures. We describe the system architecture and its implementation.

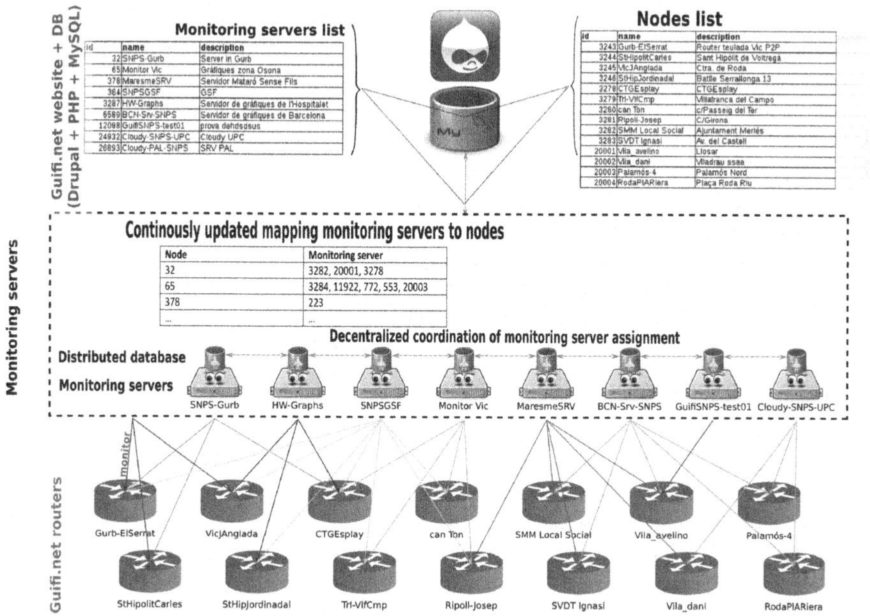

Fig. 1. Architecture of the monitoring system showing the different components.

3.1 Architecture

The architecture of the monitoring system, showing the monitoring servers and their integration with the Guifi.net website and network nodes, is depicted in Fig. 1. On the top of the picture appears the Guifi.net website and its central database, which contains the lists of network nodes and monitoring servers. These two lists are always provided by the website, and can be considered to be correct and available at any time. Compared to the current implementation (i.e., the legacy monitoring system) with a fixed mapping of network nodes to monitoring servers, the new monitoring system proposes a mapping, that is decentralized and autonomous, managed by the monitoring servers themselves, and dynamically updated to ensure sufficient coverage and balance in the monitoring.

Considering Algorithm 1, once the monitoring servers know the list of nodes to watch (Phase 1 - Monitor registration), they coordinate with each other (Phase 2 - Self-assignment) indirectly over the mutable data object given by the *monitoring servers* $\Leftrightarrow$ *network devices* mapping in order to perform the actual monitoring of all nodes. The objective is to assign every single network

Algorithm 1 Assign algorithm with policies, for node *id*

```
Require:
    dbhost          ▷ AntidoteDB hostname/IP address
    dbPort          ▷ AntidoteDB TCP port
    id              ▷ Unique ID of the monitor in the network
    minMonitors     ▷ Min # of monitors a device needs
    maxMonitors     ▷ Max # of monitors a device needs
    maxDevices      ▷ Max # of devices the monitor can watch
    policy          ▷ Network devices to monitoring servers assignation policy (1, 2, 3)

Phase 1 – Monitor registration

procedure REGISTRATION(G)
    monitorsList[] ← GetGlobalMonitorsList
    AddMonitorToList(id, monitorsList[])
    UpdateGlobalMonitorList(monitorsList[])
end procedure

Phase 2 – Monitor Self-assignment

procedure ASSIGN(id)
    numDevices ← 0
    devicesInAntidote[] ← getDevicesInAntidote()
    for each device in devicesInAntidote[] do
        if (id is in device.monitors[]) then
            numDevices++
        end if
    end for                    ▷ We find out the total numDevices this node monitors
    switch policy do
        case 1 ▷ Min: Assign if network device not enough covered (minMonitors)
            for each device in devicesInAntidote[] do
                if (sizeOf(device.monitors[]) < minMons)
                  && (numDevices < maxDevices)          then
                    assignMonitorToDevice(id, device), numDevices++
                end if
            end for
        case 2 ▷ Max: Assign if network device not fully covered (maxMonitors)
            for each device in devicesInAntidote[] do
                if (sizeOf(device.monitors[]) < maxMons)
                  && (numDevices < maxDevices)          then
                    assignMonitorToDevice(id, device), numDevices++
                end if
            end for
        case 3 ▷ Fair: Assign if device not well covered ([minMons, maxMons])
            maxMons ← minMons+1
            for each device in devicesInAntidote[] do       ▷ order by asc #mons
                if (sizeOf(device.monitors[]) ∈ [minMons, maxMons])
                  && (numDevices < maxDevices)                    then
                    assignMonitorToDevice(id, device), numDevices++
                end if
            end for
end procedure
```

device to –at least– a minimum number of monitoring servers. This task can be performed in different ways. Currently, three policies are implemented. Each policy leads to different properties of the monitoring system, elaborated in the following Sect. 4.

The data manipulated by the monitoring system draws from two sets of immutable objects and creates a mapping between these objects. The first set contains a list with all the network devices in Guifi.net that have to be monitored. The list of network devices in the whole Guifi.net contains more than 30,000 nodes. The data in this first set is only modified by authoritative updates issued from the Guifi.net website; the monitoring servers only read it but do not modify it.

The second set contains a list with all the active monitoring servers. Servers are also identified by a unique numeric ID, being the servers list a subset of the nodes list (a monitoring server is indeed a device inside the network, with its own IP address, etc. that must be monitored too). The data in this second set is only modified by authoritative updates issued from the Guifi.net website; again, the monitoring servers only read it but do not modify it.

In the *assign* operation (Phase 2 – Monitor Self-assignment), any monitoring server may modify the mapping between network devices and monitoring servers (add, update or remove these relations at any time).

The assignment in the *monitoring servers* ⇔ *network devices* mapping will change over time, as new network devices are added to the list, the network conditions change, workload is redistributed, monitoring servers join or exit the pool, etc. As a consequence, each monitoring server continuously and concurrently –not in synchronisation with the other servers– reads and writes to the shared distributed mapping object.

After conducting the *monitor self-assignment* procedure in Algorithm 1, in Algorithm 2 additional operations take place. Depending on policy, if the number of monitors for a device exceeds the requirement, a monitor may un-assign itself from the list of monitors of a device. With regards to un-assigning other unresponsive monitors, the sanitize function is performed. By means of outdated timestamps, disconnected monitors are detected and an active monitor erases them from the *monitoring servers* ⇔ *network devices* mapping. In case of a controlled disconnection of a monitor, it performs the de-registration function, in which a monitor un-assigns itself from the list of monitored devices before un-assigning itself from the list of available monitors.

In order to successfully deal with the required concurrent updates of the *monitoring servers* ⇔ *network devices* mapping shared among all monitors, the data consistency and integrity between the different database instances is needed. If these properties are kept, it can be ensured that all network nodes eventually end up being properly assigned to monitoring servers.

3.2 Implementation

We developed the monitoring system as a prototype implementation that uses the Go language. The system is composed of four components to conduct the

Algorithm 2 Algorithm for un-assign, sanitization and de-registration

Phase 1 – Monitor Self-unassignment

```
procedure UNASSIGN(id)
    devices[] ← getDevicesInAntidote()
    for each device in devices[] do
        if device.monitors[] > minMonitors then
            unassignMonitorFromDevice(id, device)
        end if
    end for
end procedure
```

Phase 2 – Global assignment sanitization

```
procedure SANITIZE
    monitorsList[] ← GetGlobalMonitorsList
    devices[] ← getDevicesInAntidote()
    for each device in devicesInAntidote[] do
        for each monitor in device.monitors[] do
            if (monitor is not in monitorsList[]) then
                unassignMonitorFromDevice(monitor,
                    device)
            end if
        end for
    end for
end procedure
```

Phase 3 – Monitor Self-deregistration

```
procedure DEREGISTRATION(id)
    monitorsList[] ← GetGlobalMonitorsList
    RemoveMonitorFromList(id, monitorsList[])
    UpdateGlobalMonitorList(monitorsList[])
end procedure
```

operations named fetch, assign, ping and snmp. The source code is available at our GitLab repository[2]. For the consistency of the data in the distributed database instances, the AntidoteDB database was chosen [7]. AntidoteDB implements Conflict-Free Replicated Data Types (CRDT), which offer strong eventual consistency [8]. The integration between the monitoring server component and AntidoteDB is done through AntidoteDB's Go client.[3]

4 Evaluation of the Assign Algorithm

Our objective is to study the *assign* component, specifically the algorithm of the assign operation, when using three different policies for assigning the monitors to network devices. For this purpose, we aim to observe the evolution of

[2] https://lightkone.guifi.net/lightkone.

[3] https://github.com/AntidoteDB/antidote-go-client.

the assignment of network devices, when monitoring servers perform the *assign* operation join and leave.

For conducting the experiments, first, using the *fetch* component of the monitoring system, a data file with 54 devices of a small region of Guifi.net infrastructure is stored in to the AntidoteDB storage service in order to have it for the monitors network devices to be assigned to these servers. For observing the *assign* operation in the experiments, a customized setting with shorter routine execution periods of 10 s is configured (instead of the default value of 150 s). The required minimum number of monitors per network device ($minMonitors$) is set to 3 monitors. The maximum number of network devices per monitor ($maxDevices$) is set to 50 devices. The assignment state is dumped every 5 s, which is half of the period of the assign operations. In the first half of the experiment duration, assign clients join one by one the monitoring system. In the second half of the experiment duration, the assign clients gradually leave the monitoring system.

The experiments for policy 1 and 2 are undertaken with a local AntidoteDB instance, to which during the experiment up to 10 assign client write. The experiment for policy 3 is conducted with 8 Minix devices and 7 assign clients in Guifi.net.

4.1 Assignment Policy 1 (min): Reach $minMons$ per Network Device

In policy 1 each monitoring server self-assigns those network devices that have less monitoring devices assigned than the minimum number specified by the $minMons$ parameter. Devices are picked randomly (no preference) until the server reaches its maximum number of monitored devices, specified by the $maxDevices$ parameter of the monitor.

In this experiment 10 assign clients join and leave the monitoring system during 7 min. In the first 3 min the assign servers join every 20 s, one by one, and after approximately 4 min, they gradually leave until having 0 clients at the end of the experiment.

Figure 2 shows the assigned devices with policy 1. The configuration has set the parameters $minMons = 3$, which requires a minimum of 3 monitors per device. With 54 devices in the dataset, the number of assigned devices must reach 162. Before 100 s, this number of assigned devices is reached. With a monitoring capacity configured as 50 devices per monitor, which 4 monitors the number of 162 assigned devices is reached. After 4 min, *one of assigned monitors* disconnects. When the other idle monitors periodically connect (unsynchronized with each other) to the system, they detect the under-monitoring of the system, and as a consequence, self-assign devices to be monitored as to their monitoring capacity ($maxDev = 50$). Since these operations are done concurrently among several monitors and while the local decision is not updated in the shared *monitoring servers* $\Leftrightarrow$ *network devices* mapping, the number of assigned devices raises. As the monitors get disconnected, down to 0 monitors, the number of assigned devices decreases correspondingly.

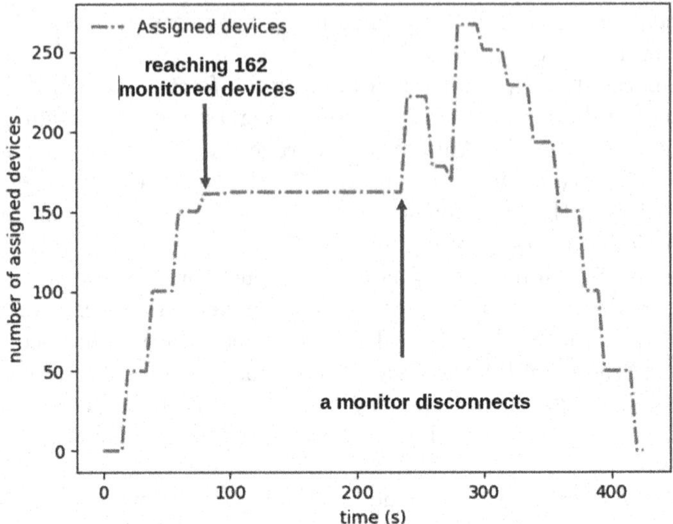

Fig. 2. Assigned devices with policy 1.

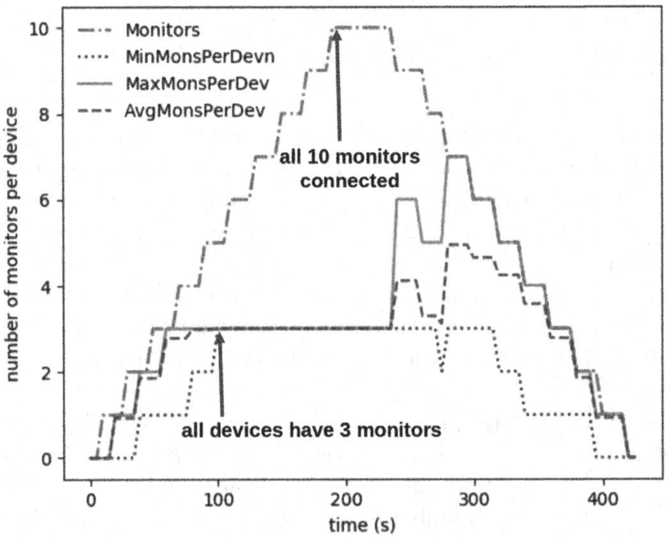

Fig. 3. Monitors per devices with policy 1.

Figure 3 shows the monitors per device with policy 1. It can be seen that after around 100 s, all devices have at least 3 monitors. This assignment corresponds to the configured system requirements and remains stable until the disconnection of one of the assigned monitors starts at minute 4. It can be seen that at some instant the maximum number of monitors per device (MaxMonPerDev) raises

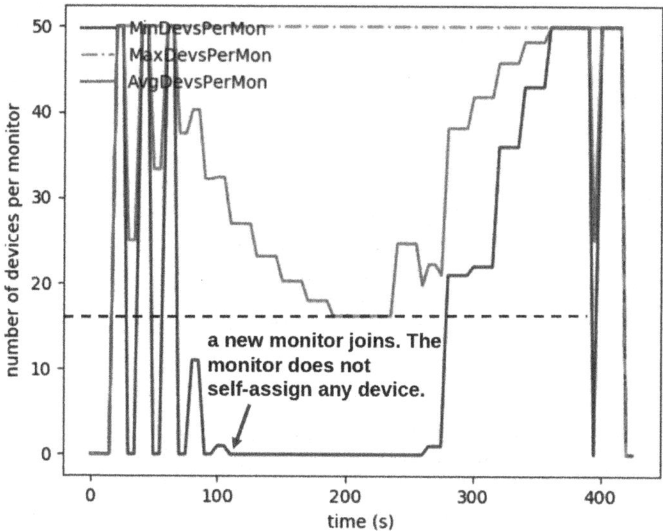

Fig. 4. Devices per monitor with policy 1.

up to 7, which corresponds to the concurrent responses of the idle monitors to take over the monitoring duties of the disconnected monitors.

Figure 4 shows the devices per monitor with policy 1. It can be seen that after around 100 s the value for the minimum number of devices per monitor stays at 0 during some time of the experiment. This can be explained since new joining monitors detect that the system requirements are satisfied and remain in idle state, without self-assigning any new devices to be monitored.

4.2 Assignment Policy 2 (max): Reach $maxMons$ per Network Device

In policy 2 the system uses *all* the possible monitoring resources. Devices are picked starting by the ones with the least monitors.

Figure 5 shows the sum of assigned devices with policy 2. Different to policy 1, policy 2 ignores any minimum number of monitors per device and the monitors self-assign devices to be monitored up to reaching its maximum monitoring capacity. It can be seen that a sum of up to 500 assigned devices is reached, which corresponds to the 10 monitoring servers and a capacity of 50 devices each to monitor.

Figure 6 shows the monitors per device with policy 2. Since all available monitors are assigned, devices obtain up to 10 monitors shortly before 200 s of the experiment, which corresponds to all 10 monitors connected.

In Fig. 7 it can be seen that at around 200 s the value for the minimum number of devices per monitor reaches 50, which corresponds to the fact that all

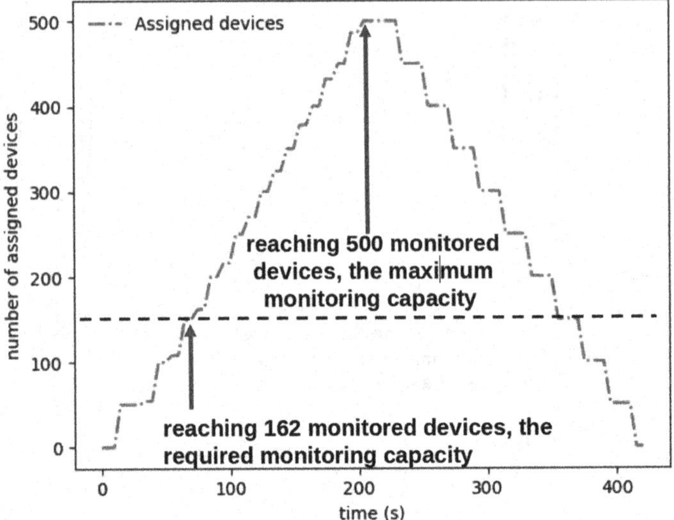

Fig. 5. Assigned devices with policy 2.

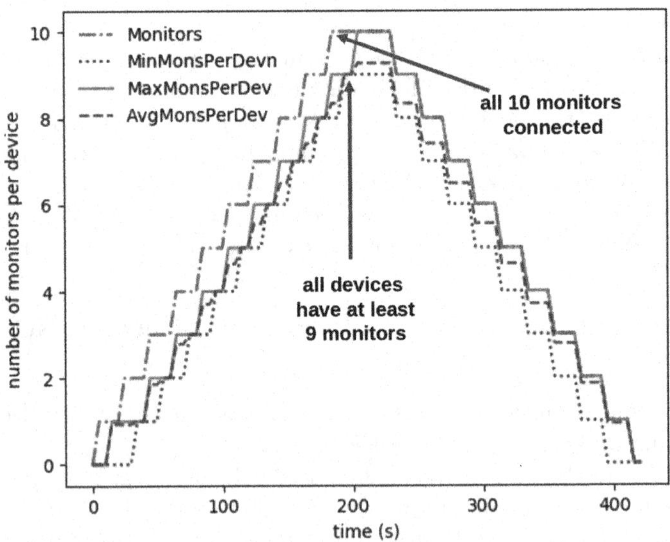

Fig. 6. Monitors per devices with policy 2.

joined monitors operate at the maximum monitoring capacity, corresponding to the behaviour expected from policy 2.

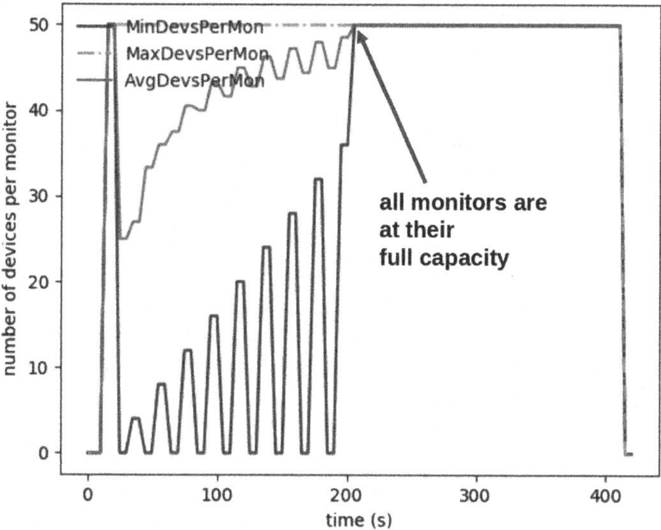

Fig. 7. Devices per monitor with policy 2.

4.3 Assignment Policy 3 (fair): Reach [$minMons, maxMons$] per Network Device

In policy 3, devices are picked starting by the ones with the least monitors until they are monitored by $minMons$ monitors. If there are still monitoring

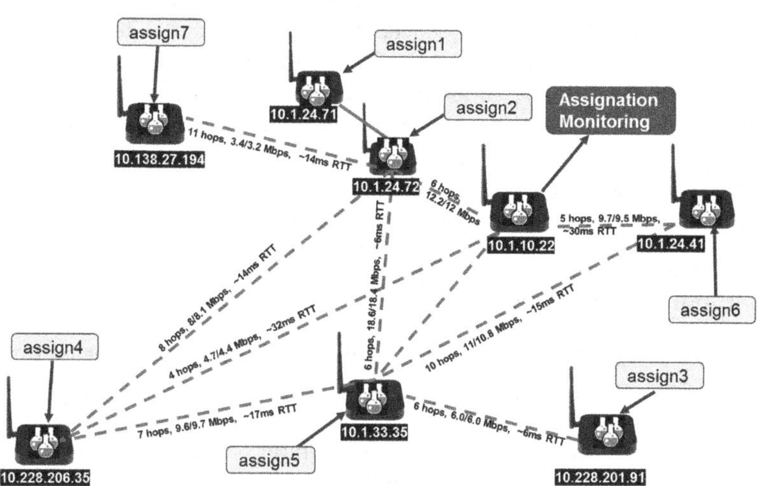

Fig. 8. Testbed for the assign operation with policy 3. The testbed is deployed in the GuifiSants wireless mesh network (see footnote 4).

capacities available, devices will be monitored by at most $maxMons$ (by default, $maxMons = minMons + 1$).

We conduct this evaluation by deploying the monitoring system on real nodes of Guifi.net. In the Guifi.net environment, monitoring servers consist of different hardware, which can range from resource-constraint SBCs to desktop computers. In order to represent this situation, we have have installed several x86 mini-PCs in a wireless mesh network part of Guifi.net (at users' homes) to form a testbed in which these devices operate as monitoring servers[4].

Figure 8 illustrates the deployed testbed and provides some information about the network characteristics (IP, bandwidth between nodes and RTT). The eight black nodes correspond to Minix devices (Intel Atom x5-Z8350 4-cores CPU @ 1.44 GHz, 4 GB of DDR3L RAM and 32 GB eMMC) running Debian Strech. Each Minix device hosts an AntidoteDB instance. Most of the Minix devices are geographically far from each other with a few hops of wireless links between them. As shown in the Fig. 8, we use 7 assign clients, which are hosted on the same Minix device they write to. On the $8th$ Minix device, we installed a component which reads the current assignments from the AntidoteDB instance every 5 s. Note that all 8 AntidoteDB instances are fully replicating the data.

Figure 9 shows the assigned devices with policy 3. The configuration has set the parameters $maxMons = minMons + 1$ ($minMons = 3$), which requires a minimum of 3 monitors per device, and 4 monitors if there are available monitoring capabilities in the system. With 54 devices in the dataset, the number of assigned devices can reach up to 216 for 4 monitors per device. At around 100 s, this capacity is reached. With a monitoring capacity configure as 50 devices per monitor, which 4 monitors the number of 162 assigned devices is reached, requiring 5 monitors for 216 assigned devices. After 4 min, *one of assigned monitors* disconnects. When the idle monitors periodically connect, they detect the under-monitoring, and as a consequence, self-assign devices as to their monitoring capacity ($maxDev = 50$). Since this operation is done concurrently among several monitors, the number of assigned devices raises. The local decisions are then communicated to the shared *monitoring servers* ⇔ *network devices* mapping to allow coordination in the next periodic assign operation of each monitor. As in the second half of the experiment the monitors become disconnected down to 0 monitors, the number or assigned devices decreases correspondingly.

4.4 Comparison of Policies

Table 1 compares the three assignment policies. Each of the policies target to achieve a certain property of the monitoring system. In policy 1 the joining monitors self-assign devices up to their maximum monitoring capacity. Once all devices are monitored by the minimum number of monitors, no additional assignment takes place. It can be considered that policy 1 is resource consumption efficient, by having the least number of monitors doing active monitoring at

[4] The wireless mesh network is GuifiSants; nodes and network topology can be found at http://dsg.ac.upc.edu/qmpsu/index.php.

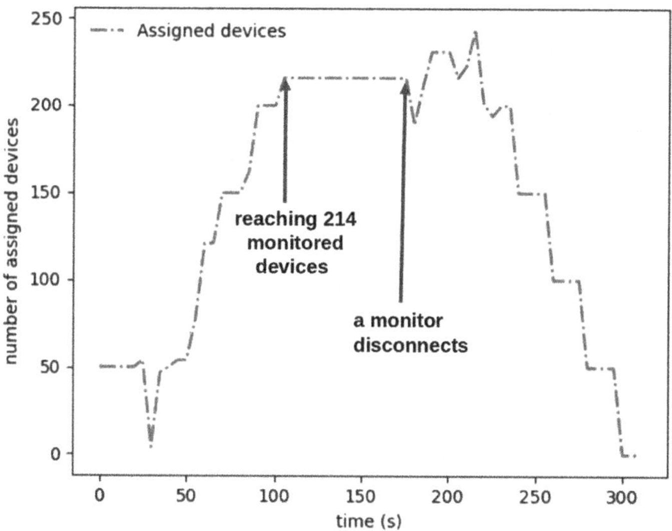

Fig. 9. Assigned devices with policy 3.

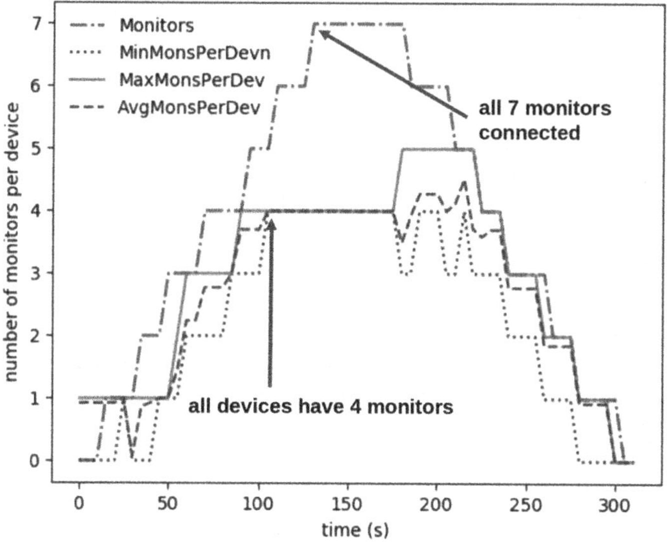

Fig. 10. Monitors per devices with policy 3.

their maximum capacity. In policy 2, the maximum redundancy for the monitoring task is pursued by assigning the total monitoring capacity of the monitors, even if the system requirements for the minimum number of monitors per device are exceeded. By activating all monitors, policy 2 is less resource consumption friendly. Policy 3 implements a trade-off between policy 1 and 2. By setting the

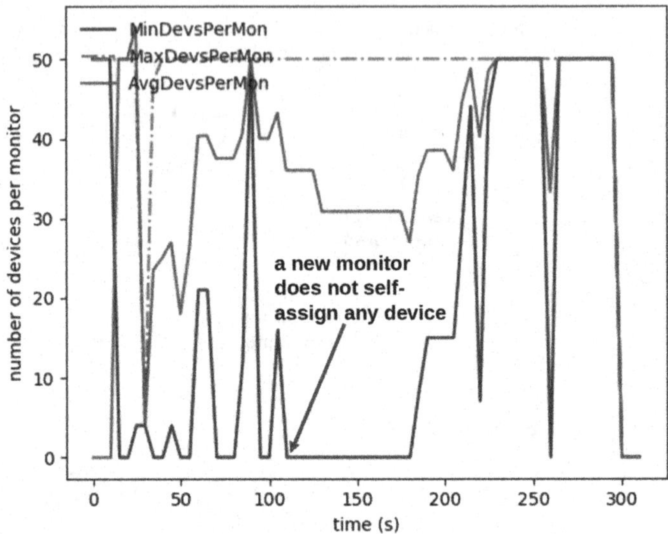

Fig. 11. Devices per monitor with policy 3.

Table 1. Comparison of the three assignment policies.

Policy	Pros	Cons
1	Once the system requirement are reached, additional monitors remain idle	In some corner cases, depending on the timing the servers joined the system, some devices could end up not being monitored even if there are enough resources available
2	Every device is overwatched. Increased redundancy	The more monitoring servers are available, the more waste of resources. No idle monitors
3	Exceeding slightly monitoring requirements if servers become available	Possibly idle monitors, not maximum redundancy

maxMons parameter, the minimum system requirement can be exceeded slightly, while if there is an excess of monitoring capacity available beyond the maxMons requirement, it will remain idle (Fig. 10).

5 Related Work

In the presented monitoring system, we focus on the control algorithm, how the distributed local monitors coordinate among them their actions. We consider that decisions are taken in a decentralized way by each local monitor, based on the information of the global state retrieved periodically from the distributed database, instead of retrieving the order for its monitoring actions from a centralized controller. We do not focus on the actual monitoring of network data, which corresponds to the actions of the monitors once the assignment is done. Differently, in [9] the lack of a centralized data storage is motivating a decentralized monitoring approach, where monitoring data is communicated among local monitors, which face the challenge of taking global decisions based on an incomplete view about the global monitoring data (Fig. 11).

In [10], targeting large-scale Software-Defined Networks (SDN), multiple monitoring entities that perform monitoring tasks autonomously and without maintaining a global view of the network run-time state are proposed. The goal is to enable these local managers to adaptively reconfigure the network resources under their scope of responsibility. The local managers, integrated in a so called monitoring module (MM), communicate northbound with a higher level management applications (MAs), and southbound with the SDN controller. The MAs change the monitoring requirements for the MMs. Differently, in our work there is no equivalent to the MA. Our monitors coordinate horizontally (over the shared database mapping object) with the other monitors their actions. The requirements for the monitoring that each monitor does are not obtained from a MA, but determined by each monitor from the actions of the other monitors.

Graphite [11] is monitoring tool able to run on low-cost hardware and cloud data centres. Graphite integrates with several other professional tools for data storage and visualization. While Graphite allows for many customization options, this flexibility is applied to the actual monitoring task. Context awareness to take into account in deciding about the monitoring operation, individual automatic re-configurations in response to a current situation in the network or monitoring system itself, seem to be less well supported.

Many other time series databases [12] exhibit centralization and the intrinsic problem of distributing writes while keeping full consistency, that depends on a data storage layer that ensures strong eventual consistency. This is the differentiating aspect of the monitoring system presented in this work, in the use of CRDT-based data structures to enable strong eventual consistency of the mapping object, which is used to by each monitor to decide on its individual monitoring duties, with concurrent writes to shared data structures.

6 Conclusions

A distributed monitoring system for a crowdsourced network infrastructure was presented. Situated in a dynamic edge environment in which failures and network partitions may happen, a decentralized approach was proposed to built the monitoring system. A key design was the shared distributed *monitoring servers* ⇔ *network devices* mapping to allow the coordination between the periodic assign operations of each monitor. The monitoring system was implemented and leverages the AntidoteDB database, which provides a strong eventually consistent data storage service for distributed replicas of data. The assign operation, decentrally conducted by all monitoring servers while they coordinate over a shared distributed data object, was evaluated. The functional performance of three assignment policies was analyzed. The different policies are interpreted from the point of view of the trade-off between resource consumption and redundancy, effects to be taken into account when determining the monitoring system requirements. Future work can consider enhancements of the assign policies, by becoming more context-aware, for instance by each monitor taking into account network conditions and network device attributes.

Acknowledgment. This work was supported by the European H2020 framework programme project LightKone (H2020-732505), by the Spanish government contract TIN2016-77836-C2-2-R and PID2019-106774RB-C21 by the Catalan government contract AGAUR SGR 990.

References

1. Baig, R., Roca, R., Freitag, F., Navarro, L.: Guifi.net, a crowdsourced network infrastructure held in common. Comput. Netw. **90**, 150–165 (2015)
2. Satyanarayanan, M.: The emergence of edge computing. Computer **50**(1), 30–39 (2017)
3. Baig, R., Freitag, F., Navarro, L.: Cloudy in guifi.net: establishing and sustaining a community cloud as open commons. Future Gener. Comput. Syst. **87**, 868–887 (2018)
4. Selimi, M., Cerdà-Alabern, L., Freitag, F., Veiga, L., Sathiaseelan, A., Crowcroft, J.: A lightweight service placement approach for community network micro-clouds. J. Grid Comput. **17**(1), 169–189 (2019)
5. Sathiaseelan, A., et al.: Towards decentralised resilient community clouds. In: Proceedings of the 2nd Workshop on Middleware for Edge Clouds & Cloudlets, MECC 2017, pp. 4:1–4:6. ACM, New York (2017)
6. Cerdà-Alabern, L., Baig, R., Navarro, L.: On the guifi.net community network economics. Comput. Netw. **168**, 107067 (2020)
7. AntidoteDB: A planet scale, highly available, transactional database (2019). https://www.antidotedb.eu/
8. Shapiro, M., Preguiça, N., Baquero, C., Zawirski, M.: Conflict-free replicated data types. In: Défago, X., Petit, F., Villain, V. (eds.) SSS 2011. LNCS, vol. 6976, pp. 386–400. Springer, Heidelberg (2011). https://doi.org/10.1007/978-3-642-24550-3_29
9. Falcone, Y., Cornebize, T., Fernandez, J.-C.: Efficient and generalized decentralized monitoring of regular languages. In: Ábrahám, E., Palamidessi, C. (eds.) FORTE 2014. LNCS, vol. 8461, pp. 66–83. Springer, Heidelberg (2014). https://doi.org/10.1007/978-3-662-43613-4_5
10. Tangari, G., Tuncer, D., Charalambides, M., Pavlou, G.: Decentralized monitoring for large-scale software-defined networks. In: 2017 IFIP/IEEE Symposium on Integrated Network and Service Management (IM), pp. 289–297, May 2017
11. Davis, C., contributors: Graphite: an enterprise-ready monitoring tool. https://graphiteapp.org/
12. Bader, A., Kopp, O., Falkenthal, M.: Survey and comparison of open source time series databases. Datenbanksysteme für Business, Technologie und Web (BTW 2017)-Workshopband (2017)

A Container-Driven Approach for Resource Provisioning in Edge-Fog Cloud

Hamid Mohammadi Fard[1](✉), Radu Prodan[2], and Felix Wolf[1]

[1] Department of Computer Science, Technical University of Darmstadt, Darmstadt, Germany
{fard,wolf}@cs.tu-darmstadt.de

[2] Alpen Adria-Universität Klagenfurt, Klagenfurt, Austria
radu@itec.aau.at

Abstract. With the emerging Internet of Things (IoT), distributed systems enter a new era. While pervasive and ubiquitous computing already became reality with the use of the cloud, IoT networks present new challenges because the ever growing number of IoT devices increases the latency of transferring data to central cloud data centers. Edge and fog computing represent practical solutions to counter the huge communication needs between IoT devices and the cloud. Considering the complexity and heterogeneity of edge and fog computing, however, resource provisioning remains the Achilles heel of efficiency for IoT applications. According to the importance of operating-system virtualization (so-called containerization), we propose an application-aware container scheduler that helps to orchestrate dynamic heterogeneous resources of edge and fog architectures. By considering available computational capacity, the proximity of computational resources to data producers and consumers, and the dynamic system status, our proposed scheduling mechanism selects the most adequate host to achieve the minimum response time for a given IoT service. We show how a hybrid use of containers and serverless microservices improves the performance of running IoT applications in fog-edge clouds and lowers usage fees. Moreover, our approach outperforms the scheduling mechanisms of Docker Swarm.

Keywords: Edge computing · Fog computing · Cloud computing · Resource provisioning · Containerization · Microservice · Orchestration · Scheduling

1 Introduction

The Internet of Things (IoT) has emerged by the rising number of connected smart technologies, which will remarkably affect the daily life of human beings in the near future. According to Cisco, 75 billion devices are expected to be connected to the Internet by 2025[1] in the future smart world. Nowadays, there

[1] https://www.cisco.com/c/en/us/solutions/internet-of-things/future-of-iot.html.

I. Brandic et al. (Eds.): ALGOCLOUD 2019, LNCS 12041, pp. 59–76, 2020.
https://doi.org/10.1007/978-3-030-58628-7_5

are countless IoT endpoints offloading their big data on the high performance resources of central clouds. In this traditional architecture, the raw data generated by IoT sensors are transferred to the cloud, which is in charge of filtering, processing, analyzing and persistently storing these data. After refining the data, the final results are transferred back to the IoT actuators to complete the cycle. The explosive amount of data produced by IoT sensors and the high computation demand for storing, transferring and analyzing these data are the new challenges of using centralized clouds that become a network and computational bottleneck.

A proposed solution to cover these challenges is a combination of edge, fog and cloud computing paradigms [4,11]. As shown in Fig. 1, the goal of this model, which we call it *edge-fog cloud* is to process and store data close to the producers and consumers instead of sending the entire traffic to the cloud resources. Therefore, the computation capacity for data analysis and application services will stay close to the end users, resulting in lower latency that is critically important for many types of real-time applications, such as augmented reality. As edge and fog computing are highly dynamic and increasingly complex distributed system paradigms with a high degree of heterogeneity [16], resource provisioning is one of the significant challenges in managing these architectures. Although edge and fog computing were suggested to deal with the response time and data latency of IoT applications, the edge and fog nodes are often not as strong as the cloud resources. Table 1 summarizes the main differences between edge, fog and cloud models by considering the features variations moving between the models.

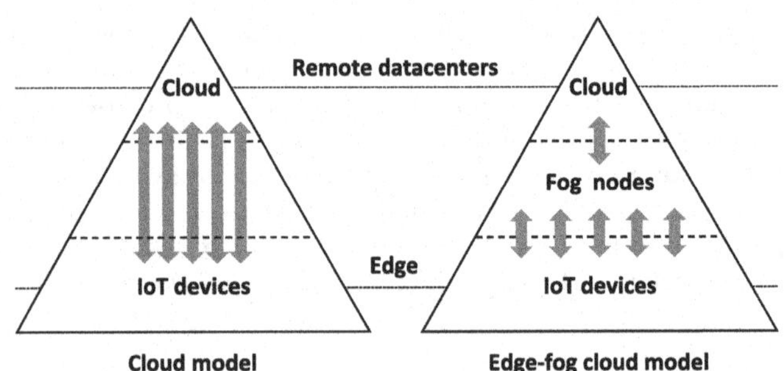

Fig. 1. Cloud vs. Edge-fog cloud: compared to the edge-fog cloud, execution of IoT applications in the cloud only causes much longer data transfer time.

In this paper, we discuss and analyze the efficiency of combining containers and serverless microservices compared to hardware virtualization for resource provisioning in an edge-fog cloud. We present that despite the limited resource capacity of edge and fog layers, the proximity of IoT nodes and computation resources in edge and fog computing reduces the communication cost of services and plays a remarkable role for achieving effective latency. By considering the available computation capacity, the proximity of these computation resources to

Table 1. Comparison of edge, fog and cloud models. Moving from cloud to IoT layer, node, network and data specications change considerably

	Specification	Change
Nodes	Number	Increasing
	Heterogeneity	Increasing
	Reliability	Decreasing
	Computation capability	Decreasing
	Mobility	Increasing
Network	Heterogeneity	Increasing
	Bandwidth	Decreasing
	Traffic	Increasing
Data	Volume	Increasing
	Persistence	Decreasing
	Distribution	Increasing

data producers and consumers and the dynamic nature of edge-fog cloud model, we propose a novel container orchestration mechanism to minimize the end-to-end latency of services. Our proposed mechanism selects the most adequate host to achieve the minimum response time for IoT services. Our scheduling mechanism can be implemented as a plugin module for any available orchestration framework such as Docker Swarm[2] and Kubernetes[3].

In Sect. 2, we first discuss how edge-fog cloud applications can benefit from containerization technology. Next in Sect. 3, we review the related work for resource provisioning problem in edge-fog cloud environment. We model the problem formally in Sect. 4. In Sect. 5, we propose our container orchestration approach, which is evaluated in Sect. 6. Finally, we conclude the paper in Sect. 7.

2 Containerization and Edge-Fog Cloud

Container as a service (CaaS) is relatively a new offering of almost all major cloud providers including Amazon Web Services, Microsoft Azure and Google Cloud Platform. Containerization is a lightweight kernel- or operating system (OS)-level virtualization technology [8]. A container is an isolated environment that includes its own process table structure, services, network adapters and mount points. As shown in Fig. 2, containers and virtual machines (VM) are two technologies for consolidation of hardware platforms. Containers are similar to VMs with a major difference that they run on a shared OS kernel. In contrast, traditional VMs (based on hardware-level virtualization) suffer from the overhead needed to separate the OS for individual VMs, which causes the waste of resources. Using the abstraction layer called containerization engine, libraries

[2] https://docs.docker.com/engine/swarm/.

[3] https://kubernetes.io/.

and application bundles no longer need complete and separated OS. Containers separate a single OS from isolated user spaces by using several OS features such as kernel namespaces and control group (cgroup). This type of isolation is more flexible and efficient than using hypervisor virtualized hardware (such as vCPU and vRAM) [5].

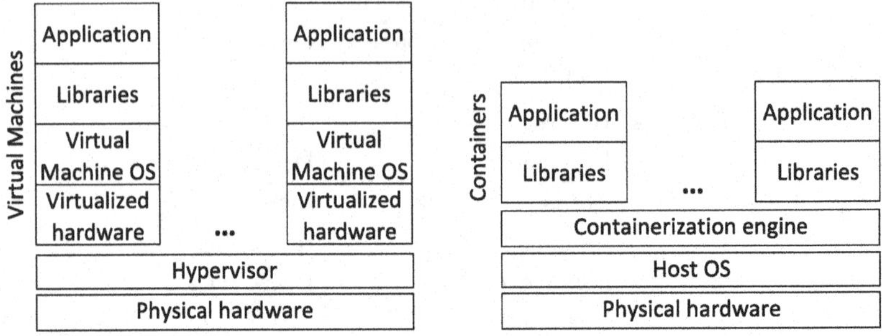

Fig. 2. Containers versus virtual machines architectural comparison.

In comparison to hardware-level virtualization, kernel-level virtualization benefits from several remarkable advantages:

- containers can be deployed faster;
- containers are more scalable than VMs;
- booting containers takes few seconds (or even milliseconds for cached images) instead of tens of seconds for VMs;
- containers are more portable across infrastructures;
- because of sharing kernel services, containers consume and waste less resources;
- images of containers are smaller and can be transferred or migrated faster;
- containers are usable in limited bandwidth environments;
- containerized services are cheaper than leasing VMs in public clouds.

Container technologies, such as LXC and LXD[4], have been around for more than a decade, but they got popularized by Docker[5], which proposed in 2013 a simple to use framework. Docker is an API around several open source Linux containers projects that wraps up a piece of software in a complete file system including code, runtime system tools and libraries.

Orchestration tools are responsible for placement and state management of containers in a cluster. Swarm is the native clustering solution in the Docker ecosystem and there are several third-party orchestration tools usable for Docker containers like Kubernetes and Apache Memos[6]. In fact, the main task of orchestrator is to choose a node out of all available cluster nodes for deploying a container, considering all its requirements (e.g. fast storage).

[4] https://www.linuxcontainers.org/.
[5] https://www.docker.com/.
[6] http://mesos.apache.org/.

Containerization is the major backbone technology used for microservice architectures. A *serverless microservice* is a package that consists of the entire environment required to run an application, including the application and its dependencies. This technology is not new either and has been promoted by the Heroku[7] as the initiator of this kind of services. A serverless microservice is a fine-grained service that can be run on demand on the cloud and has several features such as auto-scaling, pay-per-execution, short-lived, stateless functions and event-driven workflow. To gain these features, we need to transform monolithic applications into a microservices-oriented architecture, which is not always easy because of its complexity and the need of redesign in most cases.

The limited computation capability of edge and fog nodes forces the applications to be designed and decomposed as less resource-intensive and more lightweight services. Moreover, the mobility of the endpoints [3] in IoT networks (e.g. wearable devices, smart phones, car cameras) needs lightweight migration of services. Infrastructure agnosticism provided by containerization covers the ultra heterogeneity of resources in complex environments like edge-fog cloud. Using containers, the infrastructure becomes an application platform rather than plain data center hardware. Considering the advantages of containers and microservices, particularly their single-service, short-lived and lightweight nature and their ultra scalability, we motivated to use their combination efficiently for resource provisioning in an edge-fog cloud environment.

3 Related Work

IoT devices are usually simple sensors and embedded systems with low battery, low computation capacity and low bandwidth level. To efficiently execute IoT applications in an edge-fog cloud, resource provisioning and scheduling of services are of highest importance [3,14].

Because of dynamic nature of the IoT network, static scheduling and dynamic rescheduling of resources are not efficiently applicable in an edge-fog cloud that requires fully dynamic approaches [1]. Although the fog is assumed as a new distributed system extending the cloud, scheduling approaches such as [7] are inefficient and need to be customized to deal with the new challenges of an edge-fog cloud environment.

In [17], the authors proposed a time-shared provisioning approach for services. The main simplification in their model is neglecting the dynamic nature of fog environments.

In [15], the authors assumed that the edge and fog devices are powerful enough for hardware virtualization which is not always true. We discuss the inefficiency of hardware virtualization in our results in Sect. 6.

Fog computing extends the cloud boundaries such that the fog nodes can play the providers' role. An example implementation of a new cloud is the iExec project[8]. FogSpot [18] is a spot pricing approach for service provisioning of IoT

[7] https://www.heroku.com/.

[8] https://iex.ec/.

applications in fog computing, but ignores many challenges in such a market. For these new commercial computation models, we need to deal with many issues like reliability of resources and selfishness of the providers. Using game theory, we proposed a truthful market model [6] for execution of scientific applications in a cloud federation that can be extended easily for edge-fog cloud market.

Different models have been proposed for edge and fog computing [19,21] and all have the same crucial constraints for resource provisioning. Some works such as [17] miss implementation details. The authors of [20] proposed a container-based task scheduling model considering assembly lines in smart manufacturing.

The idea of using containerization is a controversial subject too. Some researches use containerization as a proper and efficient approach [12,13], while other works [2] claim that containers are inefficient in fog computing. In this paper we propose an edge-fog cloud model and a container orchestration approach, efficiently usable in such an environment.

4 System Model

In this section, we formally define our model including platform, application and problem models.

4.1 Platform Model

Usually two approaches are followed for implementing edge and fog computing models. In the first approach called cloud-edge, the public cloud providers with the help of internet and telecommunication service providers, extend their data centers in multiple point-of-presence (PoP) locations. Although this approach is widely used, it is costly and limited to special locations and services. In the second approach called device-edge, different organizations emulate the cloud services by running a custom software stack on their existing geo-distributed hardware. Any device including computation power and storage with connected network could be a fog or edge node. This approach is more affordable in many scenarios and can efficiently utilize the organizational in-house infrastructure. Inspired by these models, we propose our general Edge-Fog Cloud model, which is a hybrid combination of both cloud-edge and device-edge models and involves all other new computation models in this domain, such as dew and mist computing.

We assume a set of m geographically distributed non-mobile IoT devices (on the edge) denoted as $D = \{d_1, \ldots, d_m\}$, belonging to an organization. The fog layer contains a range of devices including network equipment (e.g. Cisco IOx routers), geo-distributed personal computers, cloudlets and micro- and mini-data centers. We model the fog layer by the set of n geo-distributed nodes, denoted as $F = \{f_1, \ldots, f_n\}$. The set of p leased virtual machines in different availability zones provided by the cloud federation providers is denoted by $C = \{c_1, \ldots, c_p\}$. In this model, we assume that $m \gg n \gg p$.

We assume that F is the in-house IT infrastructure of the organization (e.g. routers and local distributed data centers) and C is the public cloud infrastructure that needs to be leased by the organization on demand. An abstraction of our model is shown in Fig. 3. Based on this model, using the local IT infrastructure has no extra cost for the organization, but it needs to pay for using public infrastructure, which includes the cost of data transfer to and from the cloud and the cost of using cloud computation capacities.

The cloud resources in C can be used in two different ways; reserved in advance (by leasing virtual machine instances for example) or by calling serverless microservices. Therefore, to implement our edge-fog cloud model (cluster), we follow two approaches:

(a) model_a clusters all nodes available in $V = D \cup F \cup C$.
(b) model_b clusters only the nodes in $D \cup F$ (in other words $V - C$) and the cloud resources are used as serverless microservice calls.

In model_a, we need to regularly lease the cloud resources based on the cloud pay-as-you-go model (e.g. hourly-based virtual machines) and then to add the leased nodes to the cluster. In model_b we do not lease and reserve any resource in advance, but pay based on the number of service calls. We evaluate both implementations in Sect. 6 and compare their differences.

The network topology, connecting three layers (see Fig. 3), is modeled as a weighted directed graph $G(V, E)$ such that the set of all available nodes is the vector set V and the network links available between the nodes denotes the edge set E.

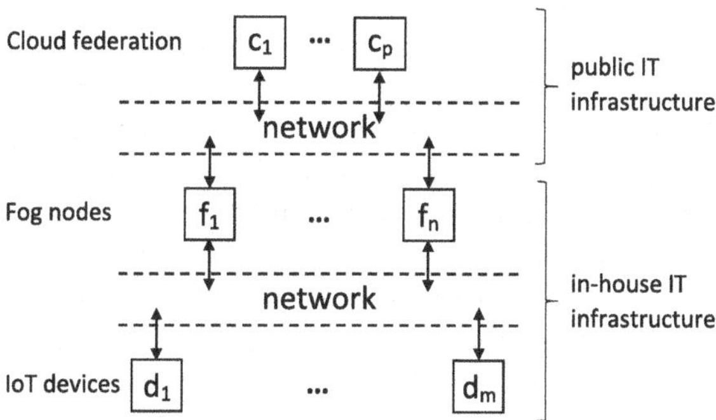

Fig. 3. Edge-fog cloud model: IoT, edge and fog nodes are in-house assets and the cloud data centers belong to an enterprise public cloud federation.

4.2 Application Model

Each IoT device $d_i \in D$ calls a set of services, denoted by $s_i = \{s_i^1, ..., s_i^{l_i}\}$ such that l_i is the number of services that might be called by d_i. The services are modeled as stateless containerized services on the edge. The set of all services required by D is $S = \{s_1, ..., s_m\}$. To sake of precise modeling, we need to notice that while there can be services shared by two devices d_i and d_j such that $s_i \cap s_j \neq \emptyset$, sharing stateless services has no impact on the model.

Theoretically, each service of S can run on cloud, fog and even IoT devices (edge), which have enough hardware to run the containerized services. Therefore each node $v_i \in V$ can be potentially a container host in this model.

Each service $s_i^j \in s_i$ is initiated by the IoT device d_i. To run the service s_i^j on a node $v_k \in V$, we need to transfer the required input data from d_i to v_k that will last $timeIn(s_i^j, v_k)$. After the execution, we need to transfer the output data from v_k to d_i that takes $timeOut(s_i^j, v_k)$. Consequently, the entire data transfer time between the device and the service's host is $timeInOut(s_i^j, v_k) = timeIn(s_i^j, v_k) + timeOut(s_i^j, v_k)$.

The service processing time for s_i^j on v_k lasts $timeProcess(s_i^j, v_k)$. If the service s_i^j cannot physically run on v_k, for instance because of need to special hardware or privacy issues, we define $timeProcess(s_i^j, v_k) = \infty$.

Because the services running on the cluster are containerized, we need to model the image transfer time of each container from a locally-implemented image repository by $timeImage(s_i^j, v_k)$. Depending on the service used frequency and the amount of available storage per host, the image may be cached on the host and thus, $timeImage(s_i^j, v_k) = 0$. To keep the model simple, however, we ignore this situation without loss of generality.

4.3 Problem Model

To place a service s_i^j called by the IoT device d_i on a cluster node v_k, we define the orchestration as the function $orchestration(s_i^j, v_k) : S \mapsto V$. Since the services are dynamically initiated by the IoT devices, we cannot assume a predefined and static communication network graph between S and V. In other words, the network graph for assigning each service to the cluster is a subgraph of G. A single and static network graph allows us to benefit from techniques such as *betweenness centrality* from graph theory to find the best placement of services [10]. However, considering the dynamic complexity and variety of the network graph, we need to apply other dynamic heuristic- or greedy-based approaches.

5 Minimizing End-to-End Latency Algorithm

In this section, we propose a novel resource provisioning approach for our proposed edge-fog cloud architecture based on a dynamic application-aware container orchestration called *Minimizing End-to-End Latency (METEL)*. The main goal of METEL is to run the services S on the cluster nodes V to minimize the round-trip time of each single service. Since scheduling of containers in serverless microservices provided by commercial public clouds (e.g. AWS Lambda) are controlled by the providers, we concentrate in METEL only on the user-level orchestration.

Transferring multi-hop distance for each chunk of data is timely and costly inefficient. On the other hand, clearly one cannot always expect that processing data on the adjacent nodes reduces the service delivery latency. Of course, the proximity of IoT nodes and computation resources reduces the network traffic and communication cost, however, a major challenge in the edge-fog cloud provisioning is the lack of powerful resources compared to the cloud data centers. To minimize the end-to-end latency, one should not simply rely on the proximity of nodes and minimize the data movement only. For container orchestration, in addition to the proximity, we need to define the effective latency by considering the processing time and the image transfer delay of each service. Since the edge and fog nodes are not rich capacity resources, there is always a tradeoff between the available capacity and the proximity of data producers and consumers to the computational resources.

Our scheduling mechanism needs least modification in the available orchestration frameworks such as Docker Swarm and Kubernetes and can be implemented as a plugin besides any orchestration module. For instance, as displayed in Fig. 4, using Docker APIs, METEL extracts the cluster information from the discovery service in Swarm and, after making the decision about the most adequate worker node, can justify the constraints in Swarm (e.g. by using affinity filters, placement constraints or host labels) such that the container is hosted on the selected node.

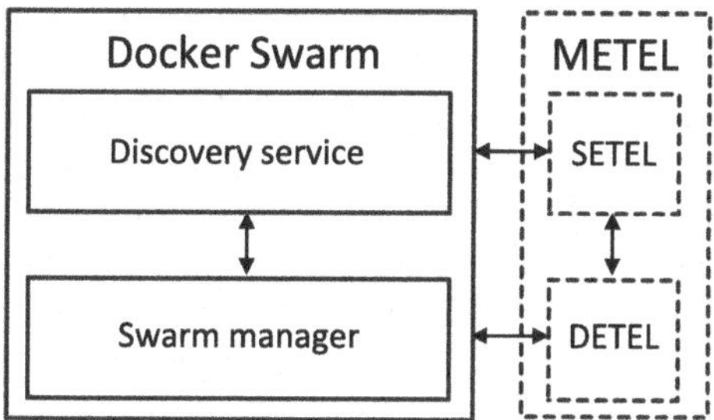

Fig. 4. METEL implementation in the Docker Swarm mode.

METEL includes two main modules: Algorithm 1, called SETEL, to calculate the *static end-to-end-latency* and Algorithm 2, called DETEL, to select the most adequate worker nodes for running the services, based on *dynamic end-to-end-latency*. The role of these two modules in METEL algorithm and their relation are shown in Fig. 5.

We declare a global two-dimensional matrix $setelMatrix$ to store the static end-to-end latency of each service $s_i^j \in S$ to each $v_k \in V$. The static end-to-end latency is the latency of running a service ignoring the dynamic load and availability of the resources, calculated offline based on the static available information. Algorithm 1 calculates the static end-to-end latency of services on each cluster node. In lines 2–6, the Dijkstra's algorithm calculates the shortest cycle from and to each IoT endpoint $d_i \in D$ which must pass through $v_k \in V$. Because of different up- and down-links between the devices, the send and

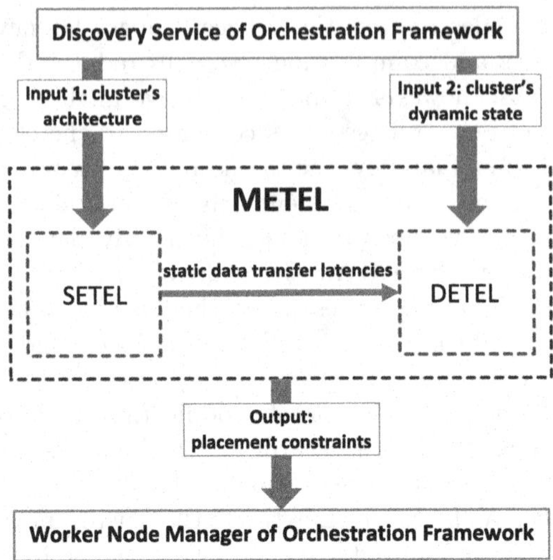

Fig. 5. METEL's inside. SETEL (Static End-to-End Latency) calculates the static latency. It runs once at launch time and is triggered and run by cluster changes. DETEL (Dynamic End-to-End Latency) adjusts the placement constraints to select the worker node for containers and runs in each orchestration decision.

receive communication paths between the IoT devices and fog nodes may not be the same. The three nested loops in lines 7–13 calculate the static-end-to-end latency of the services. The algorithm returns the calculated static end-to-end latency of all services on all nodes in $setelMatrix$. The matrix is updated whenever the resource discovery module in the container orchestration detects an infrastructure change, such as adding a new node or failing an already available node.

Dynamic end-to-end latency of each service is calculated by considering the static end-to-end latency and the dynamic status of the worker node. Algorithm 2 makes the final orchestration decision for each service s_i^j using $setelMatrix$ calculated by Algorithm 1, and returning the cluster node which provides the minimum effective latency for the service s_i^j. The function $delay(s_i^j, v_k)$ in line 4 returns the dynamic delay of the service s_i^j on the worker node v_k, obtained from runtime status of the nodes. Lines 3–10 find the host which provides the lowest completion time of the service s_i^j, and line 11 returns the selected host v_{min} as the final schedule decision.

The sequence diagram of launching a service is shown in Fig. 6. Upon requesting a service by an IoT device, the scheduler finds the proper host based on METEL, which justifies the builtin orchestrator constraints such that the service is hosted on the selected node. The rest of the container life-cycle is monitored and controlled by the orchestrator.

Algorithm 1: Static End-to-End Latency (SETEL).

Input: Set of services: S; Set of worker nodes: V
Output: Static end-to-end latency matrix: $setelMatrix$

begin
  for $i \leftarrow 1$ **to** m **do**
    /* Iterate over IoT devices */
    for $k \leftarrow 1$ **to** $|V|$ **do**
      /* Iterate over the cluster nodes */
      $spf(d_i, v_k) \leftarrow Dijkstra(\textbf{from} : d_i, \textbf{to} : d_i, \textbf{must\_pass} : v_k)$ /* Find shortest cycle from d_i through v_k */
    end
  end
  for $i \leftarrow 1$ **to** m **do**
    /* Iterate over IoT devices */
    for $j \leftarrow 1$ **to** l_i **do**
      /* Iterate over IoT device services */
      for $k \leftarrow 1$ **to** $|V|$ **do**
        /* Iterate over cluster nodes */
        $setelMatrix(s_i^j, v_k) \leftarrow timeProcess(s_i^j, v_k) + timeInOut(s_i^j, v_k) + Image(s_i^j, v_k)$
        /* Calculate static latency of each service s_i^j on each node v_k */
      end
    end
  end
  return $setelMatrix$
end

Algorithm 2: Dynamic End-to-End Latency (DETEL).

Input: Service called by d_i: s_i^j; Set of worker nodes: V; Static end-to-end latency matrix: $setelMatrix$
Output: Worker node for running s_i^j: $v_{\min}$

begin
  $detel_{\min} \leftarrow \infty$ /* Dynamic latency of running service s_i^j */
  for $k \leftarrow 1$ **to** $|V|$ **do**
    /* Iterate over cluster nodes */
    $detel \leftarrow setelMatrix(s_i^j, v_k) + delay(s_i^j, v_k)$ /* Calculate dynamic latency of running service s_i^j on node v_k */
    if $detel < detel_{\min}$ **then**
      /* Find node with lowest dynamic latency */
      $detel_{\min} \leftarrow detel$
      $v_{\min} \leftarrow v_k$
    else
    end
  end
  return $v_{\min}$
end

5.1 Time Complexity Analysis

To analyze the time complexity of METEL, we need to analyze SETEL and DETEL algorithms separately.

As shown in Fig. 5, DETEL runs dynamically at each orchestration decision. The time complexity of Algorithm 2 is $\mathcal{O}(|V|)$, which is simply linear (as discussed in Sect. 4.1, $|V| = m + n + p$).

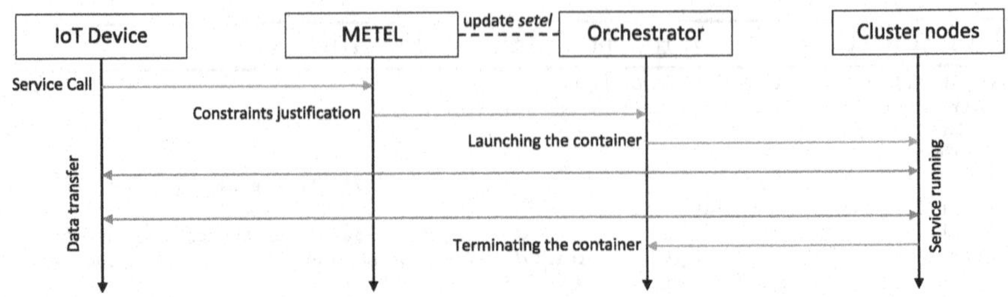

Fig. 6. METEL service orchestration timeline based on the sense-process-actuate model.

The complex part of METEL is SETEL module. As shown in Fig. 5, Algorithm 1 runs once at launch time and is triggered and run by cluster changes. Algorithm 1 includes two nested loops. Respecting the time complexity of Dijkstra's algorithm, which is $\mathcal{O}(|E| + |V| \cdot \log |V|)$, the time complexity of the first loop (2–6) is $\mathcal{O}(m \cdot |V| \cdot (|E| + |V| \cdot \log |V|))$. As discussed in Sect. 4.1, if we assume a fully connected network between all nodes in two adjacent layers of the graph G (between IoT and fog nodes and between fog and cloud nodes) then $|E| = n \cdot (m + p)$. The time complexity of the second loop (lines 7–13) is $\mathcal{O}(m \cdot \max_{1 \leq i \leq m}(l_i) \cdot |V|)$, which will be dominated by the time complexity of the first loop.

About the time complexity of the first loop in SETEL, we need to notice several important facts in the real world problems:

- $|E| \ll n \cdot (m + p)$ because the nodes in two adjacent layers are not fully connected;
- as discussed in Sect. 4.2, for all nodes with $timeProcess(s_i^j, v_k) = \infty$, we do not need to run Dijkstra's algorithm.

Consequently, the final time complexity of Algorithm 1 is much lower than $\mathcal{O}(m \cdot |V| \cdot (|E| + |V| \cdot \log |V|))$. Moreover, we need to notice that the calculated time complexity for SETEL is for the first run of the algorithm at lunch time. Algorithm 1 will be also triggered and run by cluster changes but in this case, the update of *setelMatrix* is only calculated for the cluster changes not for the whole cluster. In other words, the time complexity of Algorithm 1 to update *setelMatrix* is much lower than the time complexity of first run of the algorithm. Therefore, in practice we could observe that METEL is really well scalable, even for enterprise organizations with large number of IoT devices and services.

6 Evaluation

Considering the variety and the number of resources in edge, fog and cloud layers, resource management in the edge-fog cloud is a complex task. The real-time need of many IoT applications makes this problem even more complicated.

Running comprehensive empirical analysis for the resource management algorithms in such a problem would be very costly, therefore, we rely on simulation environment.

For evaluating our approach, we ran an extensive set of experiments, based on the iFogSim [9] simulator for sense-process-actuate modeling of IoT applications. However, we needed to extend iFogSim to overcome some of its limitations required by our experiments. First, iFogSim implements a tree network structure (a hierarchical topology with direct communication possible only between a parent-child pair). To create a flexible network topology, we needed to replicate IoT devices for each gateway by extending the `Tuple` class. Second, iFogSim does not support containerization. To cover this, we extended the `AppModule` class, which is the entity scheduled on the fog devices. The simulation setup used in our experiments is summarized in Table 2.

Table 2. Experimental simulation setup.

Entity	Entity specification
IoT devices	$m = 500$
	$10000 \leq computation\ capacity\ (MIPS^{a}) \leq 20000$
IoT services	$1 \leq \lvert s_i \rvert \leq 5$
	$3000 \leq service\ size\ (MI^{b}) \leq 30000$
	$20 \leq container\ image\ size\ (MB) \leq 100$
	$1 \leq data\ rate\ (MB/s) \leq 10$
Fog nodes	$n = 50$
	$15000 \leq computation\ capacity\ (MIPS) \leq 30000$
Cloud zones	$p = 5$
	$20000 \leq computation\ capacity\ (MIPS) \leq 80000$
Network	$1 \leq bandwidth(Mb/s) \leq 100$
	$1 \leq hops\ to\ fog \leq 5$
	$10 \leq hops\ to\ cloud \leq 15$

[a] MIPS: Million Instructions Per Second
[b] MI: Million Instructions

6.1 Containers Versus VMs

In the first part of the experiments (see Fig. 7), we analyzed the efficiency of containerization in edge-fog cloud resource provisioning and compared METEL with a VM-based provisioning approach using no containers. In the VM-based approach we launched separated VMs for isolated services, while for shared services we used a single shared VM. The VMs including services are launched at the start of the simulation and kept running across the entire evaluation time, which avoids the overhead of launching services. For launching VMs, we defined three priority levels: IoT devices, fog nodes and cloud. To launch a service, we first search in the IoT device layer. If there is no possibility to launch an IoT service, we search in the fog layer. Finally in case of not enough resources in the fog, we launch a VM in the cloud.

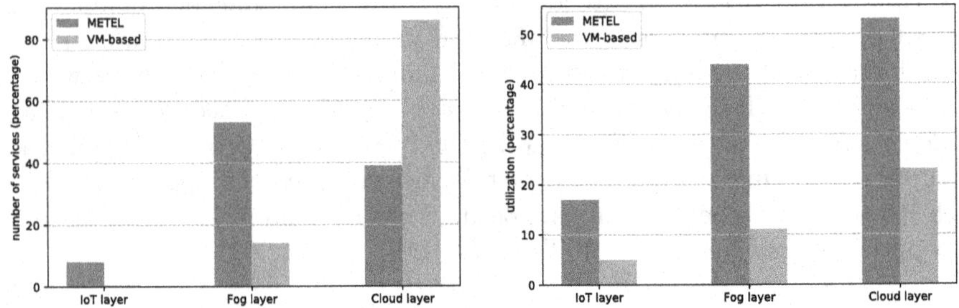

(a) Number of services running in different layers. (b) Average utilization of different layers.

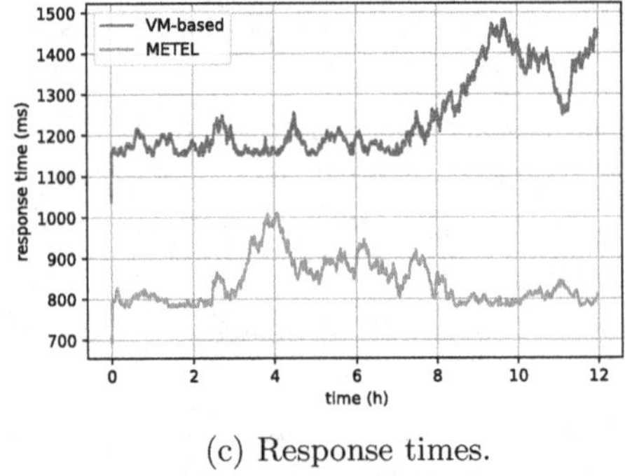

(c) Response times.

Fig. 7. Experimental comparison of METEL against a pure VM-based approach.

Figure 7a compares the number of services distributed across different edge-fog cloud layers. First, we observe that in a pure VM-based approach, the IoT resources are not rich enough to launch the VMs and no IoT device can provide a service. Because of the lightweight containers, METEL was able to run around 8% of the services on the IoT layer. Similarly, we observed that METEL executed around 57% of the services in the fog, in comparison to 10% by VM-based approach. In contrast, the pure VM-based approach run close to 90% of the services in the cloud layer, against around 40% run by METEL. Using no containerization, we not only spend a higher cost for leasing cloud resources, but also increase the latency. As we discussed before, the response time is important in comparing the final results, not the latency time.

Figure 7b represents the average utilization of nodes on the IoT, fog and cloud layers, which is considerably lower using a VM-based approach compared to METEL. As expected, the lightweight containers improve the consolidation of the resources and increase the average utilization in all three layers.

Figure 7c shows that METEL attains much better response time compared to the VM-based approach because of lower latency time and close proximity of producers and consumers.

6.2 Serverless Versus Containers

In the next experiments, we compare two implementations of METEL based on the two proposed models $model_a$ and $model_b$, discussed in Sect. 4, for a period of 12 h. The motivation for this analysis is to evaluate the efficiency of using serverless microservice implementation of services compared to calling remote containerized services on the leased cloud VMs. For this experiment, we simulated the service prices based on the AWS EC2[9] and AWS Lambda pricing[10] models.

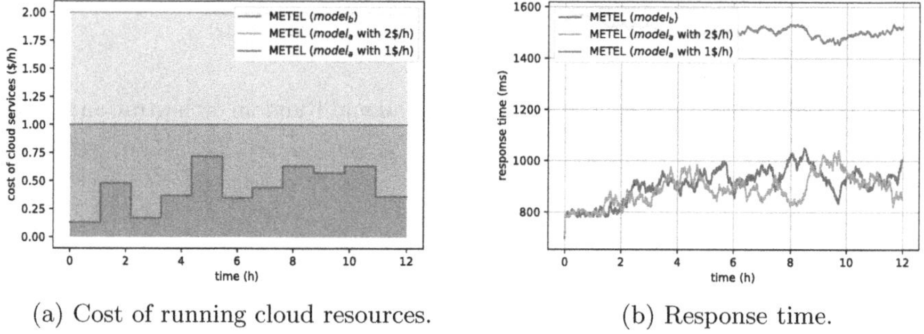

(a) Cost of running cloud resources.

(b) Response time.

Fig. 8. Experimental comparison of $model_a$ and $model_b$.

Figure 8a shows the monetary cost of our two implementations of METEL. For $model_a$, we present the results of running the cloud services with \$1 and \$2 per hour (or \$12 and \$24 for 12 h). The services run as containerized services on these leased cloud resources. In the $model_b$, we do not lease VMs on the cloud, but use serverless microservice calls instead. As shown in Fig. 8a, $model_b$ has remarkably lower cloud expenses using serverless microservice calls. Furthermore, the total cost in $model_a$ is even higher than the measured cost because we ignored the data transfer cost in our model. As shown in Fig. 8b, serverless microservices do not have a remarkable overhead in response time compared to calling services directly on leased VMs. In addition, not leasing enough resources in $model_b$ dramatically increases the response times due to over-utilizing the VMs.

[9] https://aws.amazon.com/ec2/pricing/.
[10] https://aws.amazon.com/lambda/pricing/.

Figure 9 compares METEL with the two native orchestration strategies implemented by Docker Swarm: Random and Spread. In the random strategy, the containers are placed randomly on the cluster nodes and the Spread strategy balances the cluster nodes by selecting the nodes with the least container load. As indicated in the figure, METEL outperforms both Random and Spread strategies.

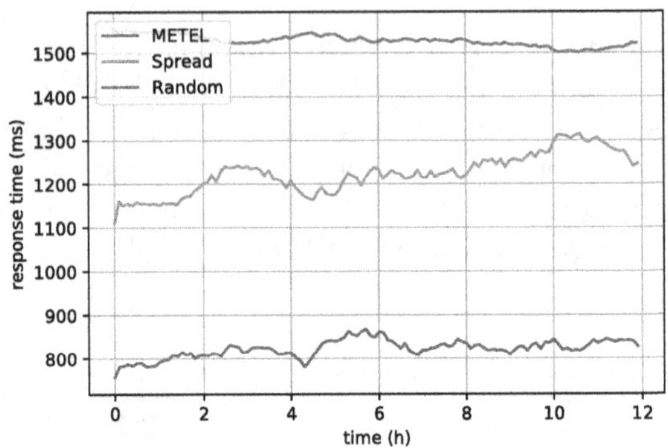

Fig. 9. Experimental comparison of METEL, Spread and Random orchestration strategies.

7 Conclusion

Although cloud computing can deliver scalable services for IoT network, the latency of data communication between ever increasing IoT devices and centralized cloud data centers can not be easily ignored and might be the bottleneck for many IoT applications. The edge-fog cloud promises to overcome the high amount of traffic generated by IoT devices, by bringing the cloud capabilities closer to the IoT endpoints.

In this paper, we introduced a minimizing end-to-end latency algorithm to provide the computation demand of IoT services in edge-fog cloud model. We also presented that serverless microservices provided by public clouds can be efficiently used in combination with in-house containerized services by our proposed mechanism. Moreover, our approach can be implemented as a complementary plugin in any container orchestration too.

In our experiments, we first showed that using traditional virtualization of resources is not scalable in an edge-fog cloud and containerization properly fits in such environments. Then, we analyzed how our application-aware scheduling mechanism can dramatically improve the utilization of fog resources to improve the response time, considering both proximity and compute capacity of edge, fog and cloud nodes. Finally, we observed that our results outperform the builtin Spread and Random scheduling mechanisms of Docker Swarm.

Considering the mobility of IoT nodes, migration of services is a major need. Although the lightweight containerization technology seems to be a proper choice for resource provisioning, its efficiency and applicability needs to be evaluated as future work.

Acknowledgement. This research has been funded by the European Union's Horizon 2020 Framework Programme for Research and Innovation under Grant Agreement No. 785907 (Human Brain Project SGA2).

References

1. Aazam, M., Huh, E.N.: Dynamic resource provisioning through fog micro datacenter. In: IEEE International Conference on Pervasive Computing and Communication Workshops (PerCom Workshops), pp. 105–110, March 2015. https://doi.org/10.1109/PERCOMW.2015.7134002
2. Ahmed, A., Pierre, G.: Docker container deployment in fog computing infrastructures. In: IEEE International Conference on Edge Computing (EDGE), pp. 1–8, July 2018. https://doi.org/10.1109/EDGE.2018.00008
3. Bittencourt, L.F., Diaz-Montes, J., Buyya, R., Rana, O.F., Parashar, M.: Mobility-aware application scheduling in fog computing. IEEE Cloud Comput. **4**(2), 26–35 (2017). https://doi.org/10.1109/MCC.2017.27
4. Bonomi, F., Milito, R., Zhu, J., Addepalli, S.: Fog computing and its role in the internet of things. In: Proceedings of the First Edition of the MCC Workshop on Mobile Cloud Computing, MCC 2012, pp. 13–16. ACM, New York (2012). https://doi.org/10.1145/2342509.2342513
5. Dua, R., Raja, A.R., Kakadia, D.: Virtualization vs. containerization to support PaaS. In: Proceedings of the 2014 IEEE International Conference on Cloud Engineering, IC2E 2014, Washington, DC, USA, pp. 610–614. IEEE Computer Society (2014). https://doi.org/10.1109/IC2E.2014.41
6. Fard, H.M., Prodan, R., Moser, G., Fahringer, T.: A bi-criteria truthful mechanism for scheduling of workflows in clouds. In: IEEE Third International Conference on Cloud Computing Technology and Science, pp. 599–605, November 2011. https://doi.org/10.1109/CloudCom.2011.92
7. Fard, H.M., Ristov, S., Prodan, R.: Handling the uncertainty in resource performance for executing workflow applications in clouds. In: IEEE/ACM 9th International Conference on Utility and Cloud Computing (UCC), pp. 89–98, December 2016. https://doi.org/10.1145/2996890.2996902
8. Felter, W., Ferreira, A., Rajamony, R., Rubio, J.: An updated performance comparison of virtual machines and linux containers. In: IEEE International Symposium on Performance Analysis of Systems and Software (ISPASS), pp. 171–172, March 2015. https://doi.org/10.1109/ISPASS.2015.7095802
9. Gupta, H., Dastjerdi, A.V., Ghosh, S.K., Buyya, R.: ifogsim: A toolkit for modeling and simulation of resource management techniques in internet of things, edge and fog computing environments. Softw. Pract. Exp. (SPE) **47**(9), 1275–1296 (2017)
10. Kimovski, D., Ijaz, H., Surabh, N., Prodan, R.: Adaptive nature-inspired fog architecture. In: IEEE 2nd International Conference on Fog and Edge Computing (ICFEC), pp. 1–8, May 2018. https://doi.org/10.1109/CFEC.2018.8358723

11. Masip-Bruin, X., Marín-Tordera, E., Tashakor, G., Jukan, A., Ren, G.J.: Foggy clouds and cloudy fogs: a real need for coordinated management of fog-to-cloud computing systems. IEEE Wirel. Commun. **23**(5), 120–128 (2016). https://doi.org/10.1109/MWC.2016.7721750
12. Morabito, R., Cozzolino, V., Ding, A.Y., Beijar, N., Ott, J.: Consolidate IoT edge computing with lightweight virtualization. IEEE Network **32**(1), 102–111 (2018). https://doi.org/10.1109/MNET.2018.1700175
13. Pahl, C., Lee, B.: Containers and clusters for edge cloud architectures - a technology review. In: 3rd International Conference on Future Internet of Things and Cloud, pp. 379–386, August 2015. https://doi.org/10.1109/FiCloud.2015.35
14. Pham, X.Q., Huh, E.N.: Towards task scheduling in a cloud-fog computing system. In: 18th Asia-Pacific Network Operations and Management Symposium (APNOMS), pp. 1–4, October 2016
15. Scoca, V., Aral, A., Brandic, I., Nicola, R.D., Uriarte, R.B.: Scheduling latency-sensitive applications in edge computing. In: CLOSER (2018)
16. Shi, W., Cao, J., Zhang, Q., Li, Y., Xu, L.: Edge computing: vision and challenges. IEEE Internet Things J. **3**(5), 637–646 (2016). https://doi.org/10.1109/JIOT.2016.2579198
17. Skarlat, O., Schulte, S., Borkowski, M., Leitner, P.: Resource provisioning for IoT services in the fog. In: IEEE 9th International Conference on Service-Oriented Computing and Applications (SOCA), pp. 32–39, November 2016. https://doi.org/10.1109/SOCA.2016.10
18. Tasiopoulos, A., Ascigil, O., Psaras, I., Toumpis, S., Pavlou, G.: Fogspot: spot pricing for application provisioning in edge/fog computing. IEEE Trans. Serv. Comput. 1 (2019). https://doi.org/10.1109/TSC.2019.2895037
19. Villari, M., Fazio, M., Dustdar, S., Rana, O., Ranjan, R.: Osmotic computing: a new paradigm for edge/cloud integration. IEEE Cloud Comput. **3**(6), 76–83 (2016). https://doi.org/10.1109/MCC.2016.124
20. Yin, L., Luo, J., Luo, H.: Tasks scheduling and resource allocation in fog computing based on containers for smart manufacturing. IEEE Trans. Ind. Inf. **14**(10), 4712–4721 (2018). https://doi.org/10.1109/TII.2018.2851241
21. Yousefpour, A., Ishigaki, G., Jue, J.P.: Fog computing: Towards minimizing delay in the internet of things. In: IEEE International Conference on Edge Computing (EDGE), pp. 17–24, June 2017. https://doi.org/10.1109/IEEE.EDGE.2017.12

Self-adaptive Container Deployment in the Fog: A Survey

Valeria Cardellini[(✉)], Francesco Lo Presti, Matteo Nardelli, and Fabiana Rossi

Department of Civil Engineering and Computer Science Engineering, University of Rome Tor Vergata, Rome, Italy
{cardellini,nardelli,f.rossi}@ing.uniroma2.it, lopresti@info.uniroma2.it

Abstract. The fast increasing presence of Internet-of-Things and fog computing resources exposes new challenges due to heterogeneity and non-negligible network delays among resources as well as the dynamism of operating conditions. Such a variable computing environment leads the applications to adopt an elastic and decentralized execution. To simplify the application deployment and run-time management, containers are widely used nowadays. The deployment of a container-based application over a geo-distributed computing infrastructure is a key task that has a significant impact on the application non-functional requirements (e.g., performance, security, cost). In this survey, we first develop a taxonomy based on the goals, the scope, the actions, and the methodologies considered to adapt at run-time the application deployment. Then, we use it to classify some of the existing research results. Finally, we identify some open challenges that arise for the application deployment in the fog. In literature, we can find many different approaches for adapting the containers deployment, each tailored for optimizing a specific objective, such as the application response time, its deployment cost, or the efficient utilization of the available computing resources. However, although several solutions for deploying containers exist, those explicitly considering the distinctive features of fog computing are at the early stages: indeed, existing solutions scale containers without considering their placement, or do not consider the heterogeneity, the geographic distribution, and mobility of fog resources.

Keywords: Containers · Elasticity · Fog computing · Placement · Self-adaptive systems

1 Introduction

Fog computing promises to extend cloud computing exploiting the ever increasing presence of resources located at the edges of the network (e.g., single-board computers, wearable devices, smartphones). However, it introduces new challenges that mainly result from the heterogeneity of computing and networking resources as well as from their decentralized distribution. Differently from cloud

I. Brandic et al. (Eds.): ALGOCLOUD 2019, LNCS 12041, pp. 77–102, 2020.
https://doi.org/10.1007/978-3-030-58628-7_6

resources, fog resources typically offer a constrained environment, where changes in resource availability, efficiency, and energy consumption play a critical role in determining a successful computing platform. The presence of different Internet connectivity and bandwidth, as well as the dispersed resource distribution, calls for the study of deployment strategies that explicitly take into account at least the presence of heterogeneous resources and non-negligible network delays.

Extending cloud computing towards network edges, fog computing is well suited to manage Internet-of-Things (IoT) applications, whose data are generated and consumed at the network periphery. When interacting with IoT applications, the user requires the application to run with strict quality requirements (e.g., low latency response requirements), often expressed by means of Service Level Agreements (SLAs). In particular, IoT applications usually require reduced response time and high throughput, that should be obtained even in face of highly changing operating conditions. To satisfy these performance goals, the application deployment should be promptly adapted at run-time by conveniently acting according to two control directions: the *placement* and *elasticity* of the application. The application placement addresses the mapping of each application instance to a specific computing resource, while the elasticity feature aims at scaling at run-time the number of application instances and/or the amount of computing resources assigned to each of them. To simplify the deployment and run-time adaptation of applications, we can use software containers. Exploiting a lightweight operating system-level virtualization, software containers (e.g., Docker) have rapidly become a popular technology to run applications on any machine, physical or virtual. Containers enable to bundle together applications and their dependencies (i.e., libraries, code). Differently from virtual machines (VMs), they allow a faster start-up time and a reduced computational overhead.

In this paper, we survey existing solutions to adapt the deployment of container-based applications on fog and cloud computing resources, focusing on the algorithms used to control the adaptation. Different surveys (e.g., [16,26,46,60,77]) have recently investigated the challenges that arise in fog computing environments. Mahmud et al. [46] analyze the challenges in fog computing and discuss its differences with respect to other computing paradigms. Yi et al. [77] identify security and privacy as critical points that should be considered in every stage of fog computing platform design. Specifically, the authors believe that, in a fog environment, general application programming interfaces (APIs) should be provided to cope with existing protocols and APIs. Puliafito et al. [60] analyze the applicability of existing technologies in the fog computing environment in order to support IoT devices and services. Gedeon et al. [26] focus on the application perspective and present a classification and analysis of use cases of edge/fog computing. The survey by Brogi et al. [16] is the one most related to our work since they explore the existing methodologies and algorithms to place applications on fog resources. Differently from these works and in particular from [16], we focus on the runtime execution of fog applications, since their deployment should also efficiently self-adapt with respect to workload changes and dynamism of the fog computing environment (e.g., fog resource constraints, network constraints in term of latency and bandwidth, fog resources that join or leave the system). Therefore, not only an effective application placement should be enacted as initial deployment, but it should be also conveniently modified at run-time so to be dynamism-aware and deal with the heterogeneity of the underlying fog resources. To this end, the application elasticity plays a key role. Indeed, fog-native applications should be able to adapt to workload changes by provisioning and de-provisioning resources in an autonomic manner, thus coping with the environment dynamism. While the elasticity issue has been well investigated in the cloud environment, as surveyed in [4], as well as in specific domains such as data stream processing [62], to the best of our knowledge it has not yet been analyzed and categorized in the fog context, especially from an algorithmic perspective. Moreover, in this work we aim to identify fully-fledged deployment solutions that can jointly address the elasticity and placement of applications in fog computing environments. When the managed applications are geo-distributed, a fully centralized controller introduces a single point of failure and a bottleneck for scalability. Indeed, a centralized controller may be able to efficiently control the adaptation of only a limited number of entities, and its efficacy may be negatively affected by the presence of network latencies among the application components. Considering the new emerging environment, in this work we want to identify the existing solutions that can be used in practice to decentralize the self-adaptation functionalities.

The rest of the paper is organized as follows. First, we discuss the specific challenges of fog computing environments and their fundamental differences with cloud computing environments (Sect. 2). Second, we present a taxonomy on the existing approaches and deployment controllers used to adapt at run-time the deployment of applications on fog and cloud resources (Sect. 3). Then, in Sects. 4 and 5, we describe some container orchestration tools used to simplify the deployment and management of container-based applications, as well as some simulation tools proposed and used by the research community to perform experiments. We conclude by identifying open research challenges that can be explored to improve the deployment effectiveness in fog environments (Sect. 6).

2 Fog Environment Challenges

Fog computing extends the cloud computing paradigm by expanding computational and storage resources at the edge of the network, in a close proximity to where data are generated. As such, fog environment exposes many old and new challenges. In accordance with previous surveys on fog computing [16,26,46,60,77], we can identify the following most relevant challenges: heterogeneity, scale and complexity, dynamism and mobility, fault tolerance, and security.

Fog and cloud computing infrastructures provide computing resources with different characteristics. Cloud computing offers powerful and general purpose computing (and storage) resources on-demand. Conversely, fog computing usually exposes heterogeneous resources, with reduced computing and energy capacity, that can also change location at run-time. Also, fog computing can provide storage resources, usually of reduced capacity, that can be used to collect and distribute data from/to edge devices (e.g., AWS Snowball Edge). Being of limited capacity, fog computing resources are cheaper and more constrained than traditional cloud computing resources (e.g., Raspberry Pi); therefore, we assist to a large proliferation of devices standing at the network periphery [17]. As regards the connectivity among resources, we observe that cloud resources reside in a single data center or can be distributed among multiple data centers; either way, they rely on very a fast inter-connectivity that results in negligible communication delays. Conversely, fog resources can communicate using different (and mixed) technologies (e.g., wired, wireless, Bluetooth) that may introduce non-negligible network latency. Such a delay can impact on performance, and be detrimental for latency-sensitive applications.

To rule the complexity of the emerging fog computing environment, efficient algorithms to drive the application deployment are needed. They should explicitly address its heterogeneity and dynamism, which also include the presence of mobile resources (e.g., smartphones). Due to these features and the increased number of constraints, deploying application in a fog computing environment is challenging. As such, many fog computing architectures and platforms have been proposed in literature, aiming to simplify the application distribution and execution (e.g., [30,41]). Most of them resort on lightweight virtualization technologies, i.e., software containers, to simplify the application management (e.g., [12,81]).

Similarly to cloud applications, the user wants to obtain specified levels of Quality of Service (QoS), e.g., in terms of response time, or Quality of Experience (QoE). In cloud computing, the user and the service provider often stipulate a contract referred as SLA. It represents an agreement between the customer and service provider, and is characterized by quantified objectives and metrics (Service Level Objectives, SLOs) which the provider undertakes to respect during service delivery. Defining such kind of agreement is particularly challenging in the fog computing environment, because the SLOs satisfaction is often affected by many factors, which might also be out of the provider's control (e.g., connectivity, mobility).

In the past few years, cloud applications stressed the importance of fault tolerance, and the key role it plays when the application requires a distributed execution. Although many mechanisms can be used to increase fault tolerance (e.g., check-pointing, replication), their implementation in a fog environment is not trivial due to the increased scale, heterogeneity, and complexity with respect to a cloud scenario. However, fault tolerance is a key enabler for the deployment of applications in the fog environment. So far, only a limited number of works explore fault tolerance in the emerging scenario, resulting in an important open challenge to be addressed in the near future [13]. For example, Javed et al. [33] propose a fault-tolerant architecture for IoT applications in edge and cloud infrastructure. Specifically, the proposed solution replicates the processing instancing using the fault-tolerance functionality by Kubernetes; to transfer data with no loss, the architecture includes a fault-tolerant message broker, implemented using Apache Kafka.

When distributed applications, possibly with IoT sensors and actuators, are deployed on fog resources, the overall system may expose a large number of vulnerabilities, which can represent security threats. Geographically distributed computing and storage resources, that communicate through Internet, might not be easily controlled by a single provider. This further exposes the system to attacks, data leaks, impersonations, and hijacking. So far, many fog platforms and their deployment algorithms have been designed without considering security as a first-class pillar. Moreover, the limited capabilities of fog resources may compromise the applicability of widely adopted security mechanisms [67].

Considering the dynamism and heterogeneity of the fog environment, the discussed challenges and the (unpredictable) changes in the application workload make of primary importance the run-time self-adaption of the deployment of container-based applications. In the next section, we therefore survey existing models and algorithms that explore, possibly in a joint manner, the placement and elasticity control dimensions in a fog computing environment.

3 Approaches for Container-Based Application Deployment

In this section, we analyze existing approaches that deal with the deployment of container-based applications on cloud and fog computing resources. We broaden the view also to the cloud environment because, so far, only few research works have specifically targeted the fog environment, especially with regards to the elasticity issue. As we will see, the different research efforts address a wide range of challenges that arise when applications with stringent QoS requirements run in a dynamic and geo-distributed environment. We can classify the existing research works according to: (1) the deployment goals, (2) the scope, (3) the deployment actions, (4) the methodologies used to adapt the deployment, and (5) the deployment controllers. Figure 1 illustrates a taxonomy of the design choices to control the container deployment, whereas Table 1 classifies with respect to the taxonomy the application deployment approaches in literature.

3.1 Deployment Goals

The deployment adaptation of applications is carried out in order to satisfy a variety of QoS requirements. To quantify the deployment objective, several metrics have been adopted in literature; we can broadly distinguish them in user-oriented and system-oriented metrics. A *user-oriented* metric models a specific aspect of the application performance, as can be perceived by the user: e.g., throughput, response time, cost. A *system-oriented* metric aims to quantify a specific aspect of the system, following the service provider's viewpoint who wants to efficiently use the available resources. Considering the Cloud service stack, an IaaS provider wants to maximize profits, minimize resource utilization, while fulfilling the SLA agreed with its customers. A PaaS provider can be interested in minimizing the cost associated to the infrastructure utilization. A SaaS

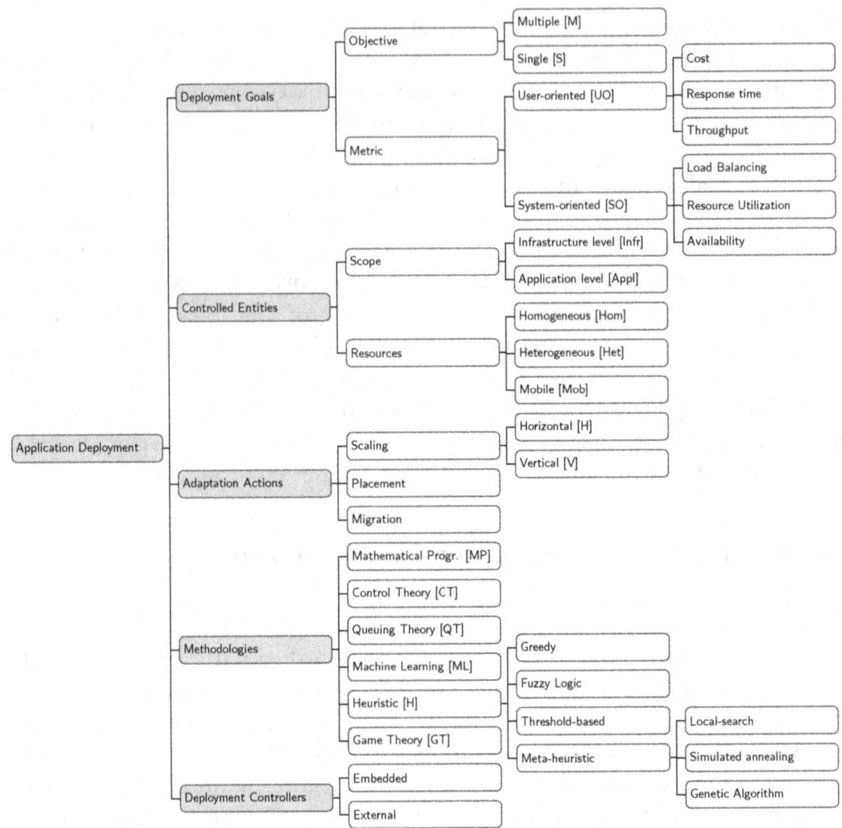

Fig. 1. Taxonomy of existing container deployment solutions

customer aims at minimizing the service costs, while achieving a satisfactory QoE level. Deployment policies in literature aim to reduce the application response time (e.g., [10,31,64]), its deployment costs (e.g., [3,11,16,27,53,54]), and/or to save energy consumption (e.g., [9,27,36,37]). To better exploit the on-demand resource allocation, several approaches aim to optimize load balance and resource utilization (e.g., [1,28,35,47]), or to improve system availability (e.g., [39,40,47]). In the context of fog computing, most works consider user-oriented metrics. On the other hand, few works (e.g., [19,23,27,51,63,79]) consider a combination of deployment goals. Casalicchio et al. [19] aim to improve the resource allocation and fulfill application response time constraints. Zhao et al. [79] aim to improve data locality and load balance. Mseddi et al. [51] goal is to optimize the number of served end-users and resource utilization taking into account storage demands. Rossi et al. [63] propose a container-based application deployment strategy to jointly optimize the 95th percentile of application response time and resource utilization. De Maio et al. [23] propose a hybrid approach for task offloading in

Table 1. Classification of existing solutions for deploying applications in geo-distributed computing environments according to the taxonomy in Fig. 1.

Ref.	*Depl. goals*		*Controlled entity*		*Adaptation actions*			*Methodologies*
	Objective	Metric	Scope	Resources	Scaling	Placement	Migration	
Abdelbaky et al. [1]	M	UO + SO	Appl.	Het.	No	Yes	No	MP
Addya et al. [2]	M	SO	Infr.	Hom.	No	Yes	No	H
AlDhuraibi et al. [3]	M	UO + SO	Appl.	Hom.	V	No	Yes	H
Ali-Eldin et al. [6]	S	SO	Infr.	Hom.	H	No	No	CT + QT
Arabnejad et al. [7]	M	UO + SO	Infr.	Hom.	H	No	No	ML + H
Arkian et al. [8]	M	UO	Infr.	Het.	No	Yes	No	MP
Asnaghi et al. [9]	S	SO	Appl.	Hom.	V	No	No	CT + H
Baresi et al. [10]	S	UO	Appl.	Hom.	H+V	No	No	CT
Barna et al. [11]	S	SO	Infr. + Appl.	Hom.	H	No	No	QT + H
Brogi et al. [15]	M	UO + SO	Appl.	Het.	No	Yes	No	ML + H
Casalicchio et al. [19]	M	UO + SO	Appl.	Hom.	H	No	No	H
Garefalakis et al. [25]	M	SO	Appl.	Hom.	No	Yes	No	MP
Guan et al. [27]	M	SO	Appl.	Hom.	H	Yes	No	MP
Guerrero et al. [28]	M	SO	Appl.	Het.	H	Yes	No	H
Horovitz et al. [31]	S	UO	Appl.	Hom.	H	No	No	ML + H
Huang et al. [32]	S	SO	Appl.	Hom.	No	Yes	No	MP
Kaewkasi et al. [35]	S	SO	Appl.	Hom.	No	Yes	No	H
Kaur et al. [36]	M	SO	Appl.	Hom.	No	Yes	Yes	H + GT
Kayal et al. [37]	M	SO	Appl.	Het.	No	Yes	No	MP
Khazaei et al. [39]	M	SO	Appl.	Hom.	H	No	No	H
Khazaei et al. [40]	M	SO	Appl.	Hom.	H	No	No	H
Mahmud et al. [45]	M	UO	Appl.	Het.	No	Yes	No	H
Mao et al. [47]	M	SO	Appl.	Het.	No	Yes	Yes	QT + H
Mennes et al. [49]	S	SO	Appl.	Het.	No	Yes	No	H
Mouradian et al. [50]	M	UO	Appl.	Het. + Mob.	No	Yes	No	MP + H
Mseddi et al. [51]	M	UO + SO	Appl.	Het. + Mob.	No	Yes	Yes	H
Naas et al. [52]	M	UO	Appl.	Het.	No	Yes	No	MP + H
Nardelli et al. [53]	M	UO + SO	Infr. + Appl.	Het.	H	Yes	No	MP
Nardelli et al. [54]	M	UO	Infr. + Appl.	Het.	H	Yes	No	MP
Nouri et al. [56]	M	SO	Appl.	Hom.	H	No	No	ML
Rossi et al. [63]	M	UO + SO	Appl.	Het.	H + V	Yes	No	MP + ML
Rossi et al. [64]	M	UO + SO	Appl.	Hom.	H + V	No	No	ML
Santos et al. [65]	S	UO	Appl.	Het.	No	Yes	No	H
Souza et al. [66]	S	UO	Appl.	Hom.	No	Yes	No	H
Tan et al. [69]	S	SO	Infr. + Appl.	Hom.	No	Yes	No	H
Tang et al. [70]	M	SO	Appl.	Het. + Mob.	No	No	Yes	MP + ML
Tesauro et al. [71]	S	UO	Infr.	Hom.	No	Yes	No	QT + ML
Townend et al. [72]	S	SO	Appl.	Hom.	No	Yes	No	H
Wu et al. [75]	S	SO	Appl.	Hom.	H	No	No	H
Yigitoglu et al. [78]	M	UO + SO	Appl.	Het. + Mob.	No	Yes	No	H
Zhao et al. [79]	M	UO + SO	Appl.	Het.	No	Yes	No	H
Zhu et al. [82]	M	UO + SO	Infr.	Hom.	V	No	No	CT + ML

mobile edge computing scenarios which jointly maximize user-oriented (i.e., user QoE) and system-oriented (i.e., provider profit) metrics.

3.2 Controlled Entities

To identify the *scope*, we observe that adaptation actions can be applied either at the *infrastructure level* [4] or at the *application level* [44]. At the *infrastructure level*, the elasticity controller changes the number of computing resources, usually by acquiring and releasing VMs, e.g., [6,54,71]. At the *application level*, the controller adjusts the computing resources directly assigned to the application (e.g., changing their parallelism degree [3,27,64]).

Fog environments can include resources with different computing and storage capacity as well as network connectivity. Therefore, some deployment solutions explicitly consider *resource heterogeneity*, i.e., they take into account specific features of computing and networking resources, such as processing or storage capacity of resources, available resources, or network delay (e.g., [28,53,63,70]). Nonetheless, a large number of solutions model only a homogeneous computing infrastructure (e.g., [6,7,9,64,66,82]). Moreover, user devices and/or fog resources (e.g., smart cars, drones) can be *mobile*. Most works consider only user mobility and address the application migration among multiple resources (e.g. [58]) or the placement of static edge nodes in a cellular network [23] with the goal to satisfy the application SLOs. To the best of our knowledge, only the work by Mouradian et al. tackles the mobility of fog nodes [50], while there are more efforts in the research area of vehicle cloud computing (e.g., [80]).

Software containers offer a lightweight virtualization solution, which is often adopted in the context of fog computing (e.g., [30]), even in extremely constrained nodes as fog gateways [12]. Souza et al. [66] analyze the challenges of fog computing environments and propose containers as a possible solution to smoothly deploy application across geo-distributed fog nodes. When applications are containerized, a *single-level deployment* regards the container placement on the underlying (physical or virtual) resources. In addition, depending on the virtualization layering, a double-level deployment can involve the placement of virtual resources (i.e., VMs) onto physical computing resources. Most works consider a single level of deployment (e.g., [2,3,27,64,79]), while only a few solve a *multi-level deployment* problem [11,53,69].

3.3 Adaptation Actions

The *adaptation actions* to control at run-time the deployment of container-based applications include the application placement, the application elasticity according to two possible directions (i.e., horizontal and vertical scaling), and the migration of some application components. The *elasticity problem* determines *how* and *when* to perform scaling operations, thus enabling elastic applications that can dynamically adapt in face of workload variations. Horizontal scaling allows to increase (scale-out) and decrease (scale-in) the number of application instances (e.g., containers or VMs). Vertical scaling allows to increase (scale-up) and decrease (scale-down) the amount of computing resources assigned to each application instance. A fine-grained vertical scaling is preferred to more quickly react to small workload changes, while a horizontal scaling operation makes easier to react to sudden workload peaks. However, most of the existing solutions consider either horizontal or vertical scaling operations to change at run-time the application deployment (e.g., [3,7,9,11,31,53,54]).

Differently from cloud computing environment, the presence of heterogeneous fog resources emphasizes the importance of the application *placement problem*. Its goal is to define the computing resources that will host and execute each application instance. Most of the existing solutions consider the two problems separately and focus either on the placement or on the elasticity of application instances (e.g., [8,10,71]). So far, only a limited number of works have studied how to jointly solve the two problems (e.g., [27,28,53,63]).

When the application placement is updated at run-time, it results in (stateless or stateful) migrations of virtualized resources (i.e., containers or VMs), that can be moved from one location to another. *Migration* is used to improve system performance, seeking to balance load or to maximize resource utilization. In addition, it allows to cope with user and/or resource movement across different geographical locations. For example, Kaur et al. [36] propose a technique that allows task scheduling on lightweight containers and supports container migration within or between the VMs. Elliott et al. [24] present a novel approach that enables the rapid live migration of stateful containers between hosts belonging to different cloud infrastructures. However, migration has a cost, because the application downtime during migration, although minimal, cannot be avoided. Therefore, a trade-off between migration benefits and cost should be considered.

3.4 Methodologies

The methodology identifies the class of algorithms used to plan how the application deployment should be changed so to achieve the deployment goals. Elasticity and placement are often considered as two orthogonal problems [9,32,66]. Nonetheless, few research efforts propose policies that jointly address the two problems (e.g., [27,63]). Considering that scaling in the fog environment take place in a geo-distributed context, where network latencies among computing resources cannot be neglected as when scaling inside a data center, we believe that the two issues cannot be separately solved.

We classify the methodologies in the following categories: mathematical programming, control theory, queuing theory, machine learning, and heuristics.

Mathematical Programming. *Mathematical programming* approaches exploit methods from operational research in order to determine or adapt at run-time the placement of application instances, to change the application parallelism, or a combination thereof (e.g., [8,27,47,52]). The formulation and resolution of Integer Programming (IP) problems belongs to this category.

When the deployment problem is formulated as an IP optimization problem, its most general definition can be described as follows. Given an application with n instances, a deployment strategy can be modeled by associating to each application instance $i = 1, \ldots, n$ a vector $\mathbf{x}^i = (x_1^i, \ldots, x_R^i)$, with R the set of fog resources, where $x_r^i = 1$ if an application instance is placed on the fog resource $r \in R$, 0 otherwise. The deployment problem can be expressed as:

$$\begin{aligned} \textbf{min } & F(\mathbf{x}) \\ \textbf{subject to}: & Q^\alpha(\mathbf{x}) \le Q^\alpha_{\max} \\ & Q^\beta(\mathbf{x}) \ge Q^\beta_{\min} \\ & \mathbf{x} \in D \end{aligned} \tag{1}$$

where $\mathbf{x} = (\mathbf{x}^1, \ldots, \mathbf{x}^n)$ is the vector of the application instances deployment variables. $F(\mathbf{x})$ is a suitable deployment objective function to be optimized. $Q^\alpha(\mathbf{x})$ and $Q^\beta(\mathbf{x})$ are, respectively, those QoS attributes whose values are bounded by a maximum and a minimum, respectively, and $\mathbf{x} \in D$ is a set of functional constraints.

Most of the existing solutions use IP formulations to solve (only) the placement problem of application instances. Mao et al. [47] present an IP formulation of the initial container placement aiming to maximize the available resources in each hosting machine. Garefalakis et al. [25] propose Medea, a new cluster scheduler based on Apache Hadoop YARN. Medea solves an Integer Linear Programming (ILP) placement problem to meet global cluster objectives, such as to minimize the number of application constraint violations, reduce resource fragmentation, balance node load, and minimize number of active computing nodes. However, fog-based deployment goals are not considered. Arkian et al. [8] solve a Mixed-ILP (MILP) problem to deploy application components (i.e., VMs) on fog nodes to satisfy end-to-end delay constraints. Huang et al. [32] model the mapping of IoT services to edge/fog devices as a quadratic programming problem, that, although simplified into an ILP formulation, may suffer from scalability issues. To reduce the resolution time that limits the system size scalability, Naas et al. [52] exploit the geographic distribution of fog resources so to identify subproblems that are then solved separately. Zhao et al. [79] deal with the scheduling of containerized cloud applications with the goal to make them more aware of their data locality. To address the limited scalability of the proposed mathematical optimization problem (which is a variant of the Multiple Knapsack Problem and therefore NP-hard), they devise heuristic algorithms, tackling the problem in a bottom-up fashion. Such a resolution approach is well rooted in the fog environment, characterized by a hierarchical architecture. Kayal et al. [37] present an autonomic service placement strategy based on Markov approximation to map microservices to fog resources without any central coordination.

In literature there are some works that consider mathematical approaches not only to address the application placement problem but also to jointly solve the elasticity problem (e.g., [27,53,63]). For example, Guan et al. [27] present a LP formulation to determine the number of containers and their placement on a static pool of physical resources; nevertheless, vertical scaling operations are not considered. Nardelli et al. [53] propose an optimization problem formulation of the elastic provisioning of VMs for container deployment taking into account the time needed for the deployment reconfiguration. A multi-level optimization problem is defined: at the first level, it deals with the elastic adaptation of the number and type of application instances (i.e., containers); at the second level, it defines the container placement on a set of VMs that can be elastically acquired and released on demand. Rossi et al. [63] propose a two-step approach that manages the run-time adaptation of container-based applications deployed over geo-distributed VMs. An ILP problem is formulated to place containers on VM, with the aim of minimizing adaptation time and VM cost.

Some works have addressed the problem of offloading computation in a fog environment, For example, Liu et al. [42] formulate a multi-objective optimization problem, which involves minimizing the energy consumption, delay, and payment cost. Chang et al. [21] propose an energy-efficient optimization problem to find the optimal offloading probability and transmission power. By using the method of multipliers [14], they allow to deal with it in a distributed manner.

The main drawback of the mathematical programming approaches is scalability. Indeed, the deployment problem is NP-hard and resolving the exact formulation may require prohibitive time when the problem size grows.

Control Theory. A deployment policy based on *control theory* usually identifies three main entities: decision variables, disturbance, system configuration. Then, it adapts consolidate theory to determine the next system configuration that satisfies the deployment objectives. The decision variables identify the placement or replication of each application instance. The disturbances represent the events that cannot be controlled, e.g., incoming data rate, load distribution, and processing time; nevertheless, it is usually assumed that their future value can be predicted, at least in the short term. By combining the decision variables, alternative configurations of the application deployment can be obtained, which result in different performance, e.g., in terms of application latency or throughput. There are three types of control systems: open-loop, feedback and feed-forward. Open-loop controllers (without feedback) are based exclusively on system input, not being able to analyze the output. Feedback controllers, on the other hand, monitor the output of the system in order to correct any deviations from the final goal. Feed-forward controllers can be used to implement a proactive approach as they predict, using a model, the behavior of the system and react before the error is produced.

Baresi et al. [10] model a control system for horizontal and vertical scaling of applications. They combine infrastructure and application adaptation using a novel deployment planner that consists of a discrete-time feedback controller. In their work, a nonlinear, time-invariant dynamic system controls the application response time as a function of the assigned CPU cores (decision variables) and the request rate (disturbance). Zhu et al. [82] use control theory combined with reinforcement learning techniques to adapt the applications deployment in cloud computing environments. To dynamically add or remove VMs of cloud services, Ali-Eldin et al. [6] propose two adaptive reactive/proactive controllers. They model a cloud service and estimate the future load using queuing theory.

Queuing Theory. *Queuing theory* is often used to estimate the application response time. The key idea is to model the application as a queuing network with inter-arrival times and service times having general statistical distributions (e.g., M/M/1, M/M/k, Gi/G/k). To simplify the analytical investigation, the application is considered to satisfy the Markovian property, thus leading to approximated system behavior (and performance metrics).

Since queuing theory allows to predict the application performance under different conditions of load and number of replicas, it is often used to drive scaling operations (e.g., [11,47]), also in combination with other techniques (e.g., [6,66,71]). Mao et al. [47] model a four-tier application using queuing theory. A centralized deployment controller takes scaling decisions using the queuing model of each application layer. Using a Layered Queuing Network, Barna et al. [11] use the number of user requests and the application topology to estimate the resource utilization and application response time. Ali-Eldin et al. [6] and Tesauro et al. [71] combine queuing theory with control theory and machine learning, respectively.

Machine Learning. In the field of *machine learning*, reinforcement learning (RL) is a special technique that has been used to adapt the application deployment at run-time. RL refers to a collection of trial-and-error methods by which an agent can learn to make good decisions through a sequence of interactions with a system or environment. As such, the agent learns from experience the adaptation policy, i.e., the best adaptation action to take with respect to the current system state. The system state can consider the amount of incoming workload, the current application deployment, or its performance (e.g., [64]). When the agent applies an action, the system transits in a new state and the agent receives a reward, that indicates the action goodness. The received reward and the next state transition usually depend on external unknown factors. One of the challenges that arise in RL is the trade-off between exploration and exploitation. To maximize the obtained reward, the RL agent must prefer actions known to provide high reward (exploitation). However, in order to discover such actions, it has to try actions not selected before (exploration). The dilemma is that neither exploration nor exploitation can be pursued exclusively without failing at the task. To maximize the expected long-term reward, the agent estimates the so-called Q-function. It represents the expected long-term reward that follows the execution of an action in a specific system state. Different strategies can be used to estimate the Q-function, ranging from model-free (e.g., Q-learning, SARSA) to model-based solutions; these solutions exploit different degrees of system knowledge to approximate its behavior [68].

RL has mostly been applied to devise policies for VM allocation and provisioning (e.g., [7,71]) and, in a limited way, to manage containers (e.g., [31,64]). Horovitz et al. [31] propose a threshold-based policy for horizontal container elasticity using Q-learning to adapt the thresholds. Nouri et al. [56] describe a decentralized RL-based controller to scale a web application running on cloud computing resources. Interestingly, they design a decentralized architecture, where each server is responsible for maintaining the performance of its own-hosted applications, while fulfilling the requirements of the whole system. This decentralized approach is well suited to rule complexity of nowadays fog computing environments.

Being model-free solutions, Q-learning and SARSA may suffer from slow convergence rate. To overcome this issue, Tesauro et al. [71] propose a hybrid RL method to dynamically allocate homogeneous servers to multiple applications. They combine the advantages of both explicit model-based methods and tabula rasa RL. Instead of training a RL module online, they propose to train offline the RL agent using collected data, while an initial policy (based on a queuing model) drives management decisions in the system. Arabnejad et al. [7] combine Q-learning and SARSA RL algorithms with a fuzzy inference system that drives VM auto-scaling. Rossi et al. [64] present RL policies to control (horizontal and vertical) elasticity of containers so to satisfy the average application response time. To speed-up the learning phase, they propose a model-based RL approach that exploits the (known or estimate) system dynamics.

Another approach to solve the slow convergence rate of RL consists in approximating the system state or the action-value function; as such, the agent can explore a reduced number of system configurations [68]. Tang et al. [70] propose a RL algorithm that controls the migration of containers in a fog environment. In particular, they define a multi-dimensional Markov Decision Process aimed to minimize communication delay, power consumption and migration costs; interestingly, to deal with the large number of system states, the authors integrate a deep neural network within the Q-learning algorithm.

Recently, RL approaches have also been used to drive the decision of offloading computation from mobile devices to cloud resources (e.g., [5,76]). Alam et al. [5] propose a deep Q-learning based offloading policy suited for mobile fog environments. To minimize the service latency, offloading decisions are taken by considering resource demand and availability as well as the geographical distribution of mobile devices. Xu et al. [76] present a post-decision state solution for managing computing resources, which learns on-the-fly the optimal policy of dynamic workload offloading and edge resource provisioning.

Heuristics. Different *heuristics* have been proposed to solve the placement and elasticity of container-based applications. The most popular heuristics include: greedy heuristics (e.g., [66,78]), fuzzy logic (e.g., [7,46]), threshold-based heuristics (e.g., [11,40]), meta-heuristics (e.g., [28,35]), and specifically designed solutions (e.g., [55]).

Due to their design simplicity, *greedy heuristics* are often adopted to allocate containers. Yigitoglu et al. [78] propose to place the application containers on the available fog resources in a greedy first-fit manner. Souza et al. [66] propose a greedy best-fit heuristic that first sorts the applications according to their processing demand, and then allocates them on the available fog resources; if there is not enough processing capacity available, cloud computing resources are used. Along with the simple best-fit solution, the authors also propose a "best-fit with queue" heuristic that offloads applications to the cloud, exploiting the estimated application response time.

The purpose of *fuzzy logic* is to model human knowledge; it allows to convert knowledge in rules, that can be applied to the system to identify suitable deployment actions. The fuzzy logic usually includes three phases: fuzzification, fuzzy inference, and defuzzification. In fuzzification, system states or metrics are converted into equivalent fuzzy dimensions by using a membership function. During fuzzy inference, fuzzy inputs are mutually compared to determine the corresponding fuzzy output. A set of fuzzy rules assists in this case. Fuzzy rules are collections of *if-then* rules that represent how to take decisions and control a system according to human knowledge. In a fuzzy inference, any number of fuzzy rules can be triggered. Then, the fuzzy outputs are combined through a defuzzification function so to derive a metric related to the application placement request. Mahmud et al. [45] propose a QoE-aware placement policy based on fuzzy logic, which prioritizes different application placement requests and classifies fog computing resources. Arabnejad et al. [7] combine the fuzzy controller with a model-free RL algorithm to horizontally scale VMs at run-time.

Many solutions exploit best-effort *threshold-based policies* to change the application replication degree or to recompute the application instance placement at run-time. Threshold-based policies represent the most popular approach to scale at run-time application instances (i.e., containers) also for the cloud infrastructure layer. Orchestration frameworks that support container scaling (e.g., Kubernetes, Docker Swarm, Amazon ECS) usually rely on best-effort threshold-based policies based on some load metrics (e.g., CPU utilization). The main idea is to increase (or reduce) the application parallelism degree or to change the application instance placement as soon as a QoS metric is above (or below) a critical value. Several works use as QoS metric the utilization of either the system nodes or the application replicas. Most of works use policies based on the definition of static thresholds. Barna et al. [11] propose a static threshold-based algorithm which determines the scaling action taking into account the average CPU utilization of the containers in a cluster. Static thresholds are also used for planning the adaptation of container deployment (e.g., [3,36,39,40]). Khazaei et al. [39,40] take into account CPU, memory, network utilization to determine the scaling action of container-based application. Al-Dhuraibi et al. [3] propose ElasticDocker, which employs a threshold-based policy to vertically scale CPU and memory resources assigned to each container. Kaur et al. [36] use a static threshold-based approach to enable container migration. The migration would be initiated whenever the utilization of the computing nodes exceeds or falls behind the predefined upper and lower threshold limits, respectively. All these approaches require a manual tuning of the thresholds, which can be cumbersome and application-dependent. To overcome this limitation, Horovitz et al. [31], for example, propose a threshold-based policy for horizontal container elasticity that uses Q-learning to dynamically adapt the thresholds at run-time.

Among *meta-heuristics*, we can include local search, simulated annealing, and genetic algorithms. Greedy approaches or *local search* solutions that greedily explore local changes may get stuck in local optima and miss the identification of global optimum configurations. Conversely, *simulated annealing* is a popular meta-heuristic that first aims to find the region containing the global optimum configuration, and then moves with small steps towards the optimum. To the best of our knowledge, simulated annealing has not been yet used in the context of fog computing. Starting from initial configuration, this technique randomly generates a new neighbouring configuration, aiming to find a better deployment solution. If the best computed solution does not improve the previous one, it can be accepted with a certain probability (referred as temperature), which decreases over time (e.g., [2]).

A *genetic algorithm* generates a random population of chromosomes, which represent deployment configurations. Then, it performs genetic operations, such as crossover and mutations, to obtain successive generations of these chromosomes. A crossover operator takes a pair of parent chromosomes and generates an offspring chromosome by crossing over individual genes from each parent. A mutation operator randomly alters some parts of a given chromosome so to avoid to get stuck in a local optimum. Afterwards, the genetic algorithm picks the best chromosomes from the entire population based on their fitness values and eliminates the rest. This process is repeated until a stopping criterion is met. Guerrero et al. [28] present a genetic algorithm for container horizontal scaling and allocation on physical machines; however, this solution does not take explicitly into account the characteristics of a geo-distributed environment (i.e., network delay between fog resources). To solve the fog placement problem, Tan et al. [69], Wen et al. [73], and Mennes et al. [49] propose service placement solutions based on genetic algorithms. Tan et al. [69] provide a novel problem definition of the two-level container allocation problem. Specifically, they design a genetic algorithm to automatically generate rules for allocating VMs to physical nodes. Even though genetic algorithms considerably reduce the need of systematically exploring large solution space (thus reducing the resolution time), they are not well suited to quickly react to the dynamism of a fog computing environment. To overcome this issue, recent approaches combine genetic algorithms with Monte Carlo simulations (e.g., [15,23]). De Maio et al. [23] focus on offloading application tasks in a mobile edge computing scenario, whereas Brogi et al. [15] target the multi-service application placement in the Fog.

Kaur et al. [36] consider a multi-layer computing infrastructure that allows to process tasks on fog and cloud computing resources. The scheduling problem maps tasks to broker and, then, from broker to containers across VMs. To solve the task scheduling problem, the authors propose a *game theoretical* solution. The primary objective of the cooperative game is to schedule the set of task requests to containers so that the overall energy utilization of VMs and response time of tasks are minimized. In the game, each player (i.e., broker) attempts to reduce the overall communication cost based on its current bandwidth and load status. The utility function of brokers is formulated using weighted contributions of these two metrics (i.e., bandwidth and load).

3.5 Deployment Controllers

The deployment controller is the software component in charge of controlling the deployment of applications or computing resources. In the context of fog computing, deployment controllers usually manage the execution of (containerized) applications on heterogeneous and geo-distributed computing resources. Besides determining the initial deployment, this controller can be used to adapt the application deployment at run-time so to respond to system or workload changes. The deployment controller usually provides deployment mechanism, so it can be equipped with centralized or decentralized deployment policies. Few solutions integrate the deployment controller within the application code (e.g., embedded elasticity [4]). Having no separation of concerns, the application itself should also implement mechanisms and policies steering the adaptation. Although this approach enables optimized scaling policies, it complicates the application design.

Conversely, most research efforts use an *external deployment controller* to carry out the adaptation actions (e.g., [9,11,22,30,31,40,41,64]). Such approach improves software modularity and flexibility. Kimoviski et al. [41], for example, propose SmartFog, a nature-inspired fog architecture. Modeling the fog environment as the human brain, SmartFog is capable of providing low-latency decision making and adaptive resource management. The fog nodes are modeled as neurons, while the communication channels as synapses. Fog nodes are capable of self-clustering into multiple functional areas. IoT devices and sensors are represented as the sensory nervous system. Cloud computing resources support communication between the different functional areas.

Extending the existing orchestration tools (see Sect. 4), the external controllers usually implement a MAPE control loop [38]. The latter includes four main components (Monitor, Analyze, Plan and Execute) that manage the self-adaptation functions. The Monitor collects data about the application and the execution environment. The Analyze component uses the collected data to determine whether an adaptation is beneficial. If so, the Plan component determines an adaptation plan for the application, which is enacted through the Execute component. Different patterns to design multiple MAPE loops have been used in practice by decentralizing the self-adaptation components [74], being the *master-worker* the most used one. In the master-worker decentralization pattern, the system includes a single master, which runs the centralized Analyze and Plan phases, and multiple independent workers, which run the decentralized Monitor and Execute phases. To manage services in a fog environment, De Brito et al. [22] propose an architecture that includes a multitude of decentralized agents, coordinated by a single orchestrator (which could be elected among the agents). For container deployment in a fog computing environment, Hoque et al. [30] extend an existing orchestration tool (i.e., Docker Swarm) according to a master-worker decentralization pattern. No fog-aware orchestration policy is provided. A centralized master component allows to more easily design the self-adaptation policies and compute globally optimal reconfiguration strategies. However, it may easily become the system bottleneck when it has to control a great number of entities in a large-scale geo-distributed system.

4 Container Orchestration Tools

To simplify the deployment and management of applications over fog and cloud computing resources, most of the existing solutions exploit software containers. A software container allows to tie an application with all the dependencies required for its execution, such as libraries, configurations, and data. Docker is the most popular container management system, which allows to create, distribute, and run applications inside containers. Although it is easy to manually deploy a single container, managing a complex application (or multiple applications) during its whole lifetime requires a container orchestration tool. The latter automatizes the container provisioning, management, communication, and fault-tolerance. Although several container orchestration tools exist [20,61], nowadays the most used ones in the academic and industrial scenarios are Docker Swarm, Apache Mesos, and Kubernetes.

Docker Swarm is an open-source platform that enables to simplify the execution and management of containers across multiple computing nodes[1]. There are two types of nodes: managers and workers. The manager nodes perform the orchestration and management functions required to maintain the desired cluster state; they elect a single leader to conduct orchestration and scheduling tasks. The worker nodes execute tasks received from the leader node; they do not participate in taking scheduling decisions and in maintaining the cluster state. To manage the global cluster state, the manager nodes implement the Raft algorithm for distributed consensus [57]. Let n be the number of managers, Raft tolerates up to $(n-1)/2$ failures and requires a quorum of $(n/2)+1$ managers to agree on the cluster state. Having the same consistent state across the cluster means that, in case of unexpectedly leader failure, any other manager can restore the services to a stable state.

Apache Mesos allows to share resources in a cluster between multiple frameworks ensuring resource isolation[2]. Mesos can be considered as a kernel for the data center: it provides a unified view of all node resources and shares the available capacity among heterogeneous frameworks. The main components of Mesos are the master, the workers and the (external) frameworks. The master is responsible for mediating between the worker resources and the frameworks. At any point, Mesos has only one active master, which is elected through distributed consensus using Zookeper. The master offers worker resources to frameworks, and launches tasks on workers for the accepted offers. The workers manage various resources (e.g., CPU, memory, storage), and can execute tasks submitted by the frameworks. A framework is an application to run on Mesos and consists of, at least, a scheduler and an executor. The framework scheduler is responsible for

[1] https://docs.docker.com/engine/swarm/.
[2] http://mesos.apache.org.

accepting or rejecting resources offered by Mesos, while the executors consume resources to run application-specific tasks.

Kubernetes[3] is an open-source platform developed and released by Google to manage container-based applications in an autonomic manner. Kubernetes architecture also follows the master-worker decentralization pattern, where the master uses worker nodes to manage resources and orchestrate applications (using pods). Multiple master nodes provide a highly-available replicated cluster state through the Raft consensus algorithm. A worker node is a physical or virtual machine that offers its computational capability for executing pods in a distributed manner. A pod is the smallest deployment unit in Kubernetes, which consists of a single container or a reduced number of tightly coupled containers. When multiple containers run within a pod, they are co-located and scaled as an atomic entity. To provide a specific service, Kubernetes can ensure that a given number of pods are up and running using a ReplicaSet. To further simplify the deployment of applications, Kubernetes exposes DeploymentControllers, a higher-level abstraction built upon the ReplicaSet concept. Kubernetes includes Horizontal Pod Autoscaler, which automatically scales the number of pods in a DeploymentController by monitoring, as default metric, CPU utilization. Experimental results in [34] demonstrate that, for complex application deployments, Kubernetes performs better than other orchestration tools.

We observe that all the above-mentioned orchestration tools have been specifically designed for clustered environments, so they are not well-suited for managing applications in a geographically distributed environment. Indeed, their placement policies do not take into account the heterogeneity and geographic distribution of the available computing resources. For example, Kubernetes' default scheduler spreads containers on cluster's worker nodes, while Docker Swarm distributes containers so to optimize for the node with the least number of containers. We also note that, as regards elasticity, these orchestration tools are usually equipped with basic policies, such as static threshold-based policies on system-oriented metrics. As discussed in Sect. 3.4, setting such thresholds is a cumbersome and error-prone task and may require knowledge of the application's resource usage to be effective. To address these limitations, some research works aim to improve existing orchestration tools (e.g., [55,65,72,75]). Wu et al. [75] modify Kubernetes Horizontal Pod Autoscaler to adapt at run-time the deployment of containerized data stream processing applications according to the predicted load arrival rate. Netto et al. [55] propose a state machine approach to scale Docker containers in Kubernetes. Santos et al. [65] extend the default Kubernetes scheduler so to select nodes using a policy that minimizes the round trip time between the node and a target location (labels are used to statically assign the round trip time to each node).

[3] https://kubernetes.io.

5 Simulation Tools

A large number of research works resort on simulation to evaluate application performance in distributed computing environments (e.g., [2,27,32,45,66,69]). On the one hand, simulators enable to more easily evaluate deployment policies under different configurations and workload conditions. On the other hand, it is not often clear how accurately they capture the dynamism of distributed computing environments. Fog simulators allow to model the heterogeneity of computing resources, which can be geographically distributed. Fog resources are often organized as a graph; some simulators allow to further aggregate resources in groups (also called cloudlets or micro-data centers). Although most recent simulators model both cloud and fog computing resources, few existing solutions offer the possibility to simulate mobility.

ContainerCloudSim [59] is a discrete-event-based simulator that supports the evaluation of different container placement policies in cloud environments. Extending CloudSim [18], ContainerCloudSim allows to model hosts, VMs, containers, and tasks. For each host, its processing, memory, and storage capacity, as well as the belonging data center should be specified. Each host can run one or more VMs where containers can be deployed. For each container, it should be specified the required CPU and memory resources, needed to execute tasks.

EmuFog [48] is a framework for emulating a fog environment. In EmuFog, a network is modeled as an undirected graph of devices (switches and routers) connected together through communication channels (links). To create a fog environment, the first step is to translate the network topology (generated or imported) in a network topology supported by EmuFog. The second step consists in defining the type and location of nodes. Although EmuFog allows to easily create fog environments, it does not support application modeling.

iFogSim [29] provides a platform to simulate a fog environment and to deploy applications. Based on CloudSim, it supports elasticity and migration of VMs. The fog network topology structure should be tree-like: the deployment of application instances starts from tree leaves (fog nodes) and proceeds up to the tree root (usually, the cloud). iFogSim allows to monitor latency, network congestion, energy consumption and resource utilization of the application instances. The application is modeled as a directed graph: vertices represent the processing units (i.e., modules), whereas edges are the data flow between the modules. The communication between the different application modules occurs by sequentially sending tuples. With respect to the other simulators, iFogSim allows to model realistic multi-component applications. Nevertheless, it is not possible to express network topologies different from tree-like. Furthermore, it does not support node mobility. To overcome this limitation, Lopes et al. [43] proposed MyiFogSim, an extension that supports mobility.

6 Open Challenges and Research Directions

Extending cloud computing, fog computing promises to improve scalability of distributed applications and to reduce their response time. Nevertheless, the fog environment presents several key features (e.g., large-scale distribution, resource heterogeneity) that introduce new challenges. The research community has been dealing with these challenges in the last years; however, we are still at the first stages, and there are several open issues and research directions to investigate.

Among all the interesting challenges, we identify a few of them that we consider to be of utmost importance: elasticity and placement of multi-component applications, mobility, scalability, fault-tolerance, security, and SLA definition.

The existing deployment algorithms usually consider single-component applications. However, modern applications often result by composing multiple microservices, where the adaptation of an application component is likely to affect other components. In a fog environment, the limitation of computing resources further stresses the need of optimized adaptation actions that pro-actively change the multi-component application deployment.

Today's applications exploit elasticity to efficiently use resources and react to dynamic working conditions. The fog environment comes with a high number of heterogeneous resources, which often rely on a poor Internet connection. These features call for efficient solutions for determining an application placement, which should efficiently deal with the uncertainty of computing resources and incoming workloads. So far, there is only a limited number of fog-specific and mobility-aware solutions (e.g., [50]); most of the existing approaches solve the application deployment problem in a centralized manner. Moreover, mobility of fog resources have been so far scarcely studied, notwithstanding that it can lead to new applications and research directions, where mobile resources are opportunistically exploited to reduce the dependence over geographically bounded fixed fog resources.

Nowadays, orchestration tools present only a partially decentralized architecture, which could not be suitable to manage complex applications in a geographically distributed environment. In a master-worker architecture, collecting monitoring data on the master and dispatching the subsequent adaptation actions to the decentralized executors may introduce significant communication overhead. Furthermore, the master may easily become the system bottleneck when it has to control a multitude of entities scattered in a large-scale geo-distributed environment. To increase scalability, a hierarchical architecture could be investigated: exploiting the benefits of both centralized and decentralized architectures and policies, it could be well suited for controlling applications in a fog environment. The hierarchical control pattern revolves around the idea of a layered architecture, where each layer works with time scales and concerns separation. Given the great amount of interconnected devices and the system dynamism, also the deployment algorithms should be as scalable as possible.

The definition of multi-component applications that run on edge devices also exposes new security risks and trustiness issues, which should be addressed to boost the utilization of fog computing. Most of the existing deployment solutions neglect security-related issues. However, security is a first-class citizen in the fog environment: while allocating containers on fog resources, privacy constraints should be taken into account, as well as the security of the communication channels among the fog resources. The limited energy, network, and computing capacity of fog resources also requires to investigate whether existing fault-tolerance mechanisms can be adopted in the fog. Processing data at the network periphery, device (or connectivity) failures can easily compromise the application availability and integrity. Considerations should be also made observing that nearby fog resources are more likely to fail simultaneously (e.g., due to connectivity outage).

Also monitoring and enforcing the QoS of multi-component applications is challenging in a fog environment. SLAs as defined today do not fit well in the emerging environment, where applications can exchange data across multiple service providers and, most importantly, can run on resources under different administrative domains. In a fog environment, it could be also difficult to collect application and service provisioning metrics, needed to evaluate the SLA fulfillment. The dynamism and heterogeneity of fog resources further increase the difficulty of controlling the application performance.

To conclude, we can observe that deployment solutions for fog environments are at their early stages; therefore, novel solutions that account for the distinctive fog computing features are needed. Methodologies that have been successfully adopted for cloud resources can be considered for the fog environments. For example, it would be interesting to further investigate the applicability of evolutionary algorithms, e.g., deep learning, genetic algorithms, and game theory, for adapting the deployment of microservice-based applications.

References

1. Abdelbaky, M., Diaz-Montes, J., Parashar, M., Unuvar, M., Steinder, M.: Docker containers across multiple clouds and data centers. In: Proceedings of IEEE/ACM UCC 2015, pp. 368–371 (2015). https://doi.org/10.1109/UCC.2015.58
2. Addya, S.K., Turuk, A.K., Sahoo, B., Sarkar, M., Biswash, S.K.: Simulated annealing based VM placement strategy to maximize the profit for cloud service providers. Eng. Sci. Technol. Int J. **20**(4), 1249–1259 (2017)
3. Al-Dhuraibi, Y., Paraiso, F., Djarallah, N., Merle, P.: Autonomic vertical elasticity of Docker containers with ElasticDocker. In: Proceedings of IEEE CLOUD 2017, pp. 472–479 (2017). https://doi.org/10.1109/CLOUD.2017.67
4. Al-Dhuraibi, Y., Paraiso, F., Djarallah, N., Merle, P.: Elasticity in cloud computing: state of the art and research challenges. IEEE Trans. Serv. Comput. **11**, 430–447 (2018). https://doi.org/10.1109/TSC.2017.2711009
5. Alam, M.G.R., Hassan, M.M., Uddin, M.Z., Almogren, A., Fortino, G.: Autonomic computation offloading in mobile edge for IoT applications. Future Gener. Comput. Syst. **90**, 149–157 (2019). https://doi.org/10.1016/j.future.2018.07.050
6. Ali-Eldin, A., Tordsson, J., Elmroth, E.: An adaptive hybrid elasticity controller for cloud infrastructures. In: Proceedings of IEEE NOMS 2012, pp. 204–212 (2012)
7. Arabnejad, H., Pahl, C., Jamshidi, P., Estrada, G.: A comparison of reinforcement learning techniques for fuzzy cloud auto-scaling. In: Proceedings of IEEE/ACM CCGrid 2017, pp. 64–73 (2017). https://doi.org/10.1109/CCGRID.2017.15
8. Arkian, H.R., Diyanat, A., Pourkhalili, A.: MIST: fog-based data analytics scheme with cost-efficient resource provisioning for IoT crowdsensing applications. J. Netw. Comput. Appl. **82**, 152–165 (2017). https://doi.org/10.1016/j.jnca.2017.01.012

9. Asnaghi, A., Ferroni, M., Santambrogio, M.D.: DockerCap: a software-level power capping orchestrator for Docker containers. In: Proceedings of IEEE EUC 2016 (2016)
10. Baresi, L., Guinea, S., Leva, A., Quattrocchi, G.: A discrete-time feedback controller for containerized cloud applications. In: Proceedings of ACM SIGSOFT FSE 2016, pp. 217–228 (2016). https://doi.org/10.1145/2950290.2950328
11. Barna, C., Khazaei, H., Fokaefs, M., Litoiu, M.: Delivering elastic containerized cloud applications to enable DevOps. In: Proceedings of SEAMS 2017, pp. 65–75 (2017)
12. Bellavista, P., Zanni, A.: Feasibility of fog computing deployment based on Docker containerization over RaspberryPi. In: Proceedings of ICDCN 2017. ACM (2017)
13. Bermbach, D., et al.: A research perspective on fog computing. In: Braubach, L., et al. (eds.) ICSOC 2017. LNCS, vol. 10797, pp. 198–210. Springer, Cham (2018). https://doi.org/10.1007/978-3-319-91764-1_16
14. Boyd, S., Parikh, N., Chu, E., Peleato, B., Eckstein, J.: Distributed optimization and statistical learning via the alternating direction method of multipliers. Found. Trends Mach. Learn. **3**(1), 1–122 (2011)
15. Brogi, A., Forti, S., Guerrero, C., Lera, I.: Meet genetic algorithms in Monte Carlo: optimised placement of multi-service applications in the fog. In: Proceedings of IEEE EDGE 2019, pp. 13–17 (2019). https://doi.org/10.1109/EDGE.2019.00016
16. Brogi, A., Forti, S., Guerrero, C., Lera, I.: How to place your apps in the fog: state of the art and open challenges. Softw. Pract. Exp. (2019). https://doi.org/10.1002/spe.2766
17. Buyya, R., et al.: A manifesto for future generation cloud computing: research directions for the next decade. ACM Comput. Surv. **51**(5), 105:1–105:38 (2019)
18. Calheiros, R.N., Ranjan, R., Beloglazov, A., De Rose, C., Buyya, R.: CloudSim: a toolkit for modeling and simulation of cloud computing environments and evaluation of resource provisioning algorithms. Softw. Pract. Exp. **41**(1), 23–50 (2011)
19. Casalicchio, E., Perciballi, V.: Auto-scaling of containers: the impact of relative and absolute metrics. In: Proceedings of IEEE FAS*W 2017, pp. 207–214 (2017)
20. Casalicchio, E.: Container orchestration: a survey. In: Puliafito, A., Trivedi, K.S. (eds.) Systems Modeling: Methodologies and Tools. EICC, pp. 221–235. Springer, Cham (2019). https://doi.org/10.1007/978-3-319-92378-9_14
21. Chang, Z., Zhou, Z., Ristaniemi, T., Niu, Z.: Energy efficient optimization for computation offloading in fog computing system. In: Proceedings of IEEE GLOBECOM 2017 (2017). https://doi.org/10.1109/GLOCOM.2017.8254207
22. de Brito, M.S., et al.: A service orchestration architecture for fog-enabled infrastructures. In: Proceedings of FMEC 2017, pp. 127–132. IEEE (2017)
23. De Maio, V., Brandic, I.: Multi-objective mobile edge provisioning in small cell clouds. In: Proceedings of ACM/SPEC ICPE 2019, pp. 127–138. ACM (2019)
24. Elliott, D., Otero, C., Ridley, M., Merino, X.: A cloud-agnostic container orchestrator for improving interoperability. In: Proceedings of IEEE CLOUD 2018, pp. 958–961 (2018). https://doi.org/10.1109/CLOUD.2018.00145
25. Garefalakis, P., Karanasos, K., Pietzuch, P., Suresh, A., Rao, S.: Medea: scheduling of long running applications in shared production clusters. In: Proceedings of EuroSys 2018, pp. 4:1–4:13. ACM (2018). https://doi.org/10.1145/3190508.3190549
26. Gedeon, J., Brandherm, F., Egert, R., Grube, T., Mühlhäuser, M.: What the fog? Edge computing revisited: promises, applications and future challenges. IEEE Access **7**, 152847–152878 (2019). https://doi.org/10.1109/ACCESS.2019.2948399

27. Guan, X., Wan, X., Choi, B.Y., Song, S., Zhu, J.: Application oriented dynamic resource allocation for data centers using Docker containers. IEEE Commun. Lett. **21**(3), 504–507 (2017). https://doi.org/10.1109/LCOMM.2016.2644658
28. Guerrero, C., Lera, I., Juiz, C.: Genetic algorithm for multi-objective optimization of container allocation in cloud architecture. J. Grid Comput. **16**(1), 113–135 (2018). https://doi.org/10.1007/s10723-017-9419-x
29. Gupta, H., Vahid Dastjerdi, A., Ghosh, S.K., Buyya, R.: iFogSim: a toolkit for modeling and simulation of resource management techniques in the internet of things, edge and fog computing environments. Softw. Pract. Exp. **47**(9), 1275–1296 (2017). https://doi.org/10.1002/spe.2509
30. Hoque, S., d. Brito, M.S., Willner, A., Keil, O., Magedanz, T.: Towards container orchestration in fog computing infrastructures. In: Proceedings of IEEE COMPSAC 2017, vol. 2, pp. 294–299 (2017). https://doi.org/10.1109/COMPSAC.2017.248
31. Horovitz, S., Arian, Y.: Efficient cloud auto-scaling with SLA objective using Q-learning. In: Proceedings of IEEE FiCloud 2018, pp. 85–92 (2018)
32. Huang, Z., Lin, K.J., Yu, S.Y., Hsu, J.Y.J.: Co-locating services in IoT systems to minimize the communication energy cost. J. Innov. Digit. Ecosyst. **1**(1), 47–57 (2014). https://doi.org/10.1016/j.jides.2015.02.005
33. Javed, A., Heljanko, K., Buda, A., Främling, K.: Cefiot: a fault-tolerant IoT architecture for edge and cloud. In: Proceedings of IEEE WF-IoT 2018, pp. 813–818 (2018)
34. Jawarneh, I.M.A., et al.: Container orchestration engines: a thorough functional and performance comparison. In: Proceedings of IEEE ICC 2019, pp. 1–6 (2019)
35. Kaewkasi, C., Chuenmuneewong, K.: Improvement of container scheduling for Docker using ant colony optimization. In: Proceedings of KST 2017. IEEE (2017)
36. Kaur, K., Dhand, T., Kumar, N., Zeadally, S.: Container-as-a-service at the edge: trade-off between energy efficiency and service availability at fog nano data centers. IEEE Wirel. Commun. **24**(3), 48–56 (2017)
37. Kayal, P., Liebeherr, J.: Autonomic service placement in fog computing. In: Proceedings of IEEE WoWMoM 2019, pp. 1–9 (2019)
38. Kephart, J.O., Chess, D.M.: The vision of autonomic computing. IEEE Comput. **36**(1), 41–50 (2003). https://doi.org/10.1109/MC.2003.1160055
39. Khazaei, H., Bannazadeh, H., Leon-Garcia, A.: SAVI-IoT: a self-managing containerized IoT platform. In: Proc. of IEEE FiCloud 2017, pp. 227–234 (2017)
40. Khazaei, H., Ravichandiran, R., Park, B., Bannazadeh, H., Tizghadam, A., Leon-Garcia, A.: Elascale: autoscaling and monitoring as a service. In: Proceedings of CASCON 2017, pp. 234–240 (2017)
41. Kimovski, D., Ijaz, H., Saurabh, N., Prodan, R.: Adaptive nature-inspired fog architecture. In: Proceedings of IEEE ICFEC 2018, pp. 1–8 (2018)
42. Liu, L., Chang, Z., Guo, X., Mao, S., Ristaniemi, T.: Multiobjective optimization for computation offloading in fog computing. IEEE Internet Things J. **5**(1), 283–294 (2018). https://doi.org/10.1109/JIOT.2017.2780236
43. Lopes, M.M., Higashino, W.A., Capretz, M.A., Bittencourt, L.F.: MyiFogSim: a simulator for virtual machine migration in fog computing. In: Proceedings of IEEE/ACM UCC 2017 Companion, pp. 47–52. ACM (2017)
44. Lorido-Botran, T., Miguel-Alonso, J., Lozano, J.A.: A review of auto-scaling techniques for elastic applications in cloud environments. J. Grid Comput. **12**(4), 559–592 (2014). https://doi.org/10.1007/s10723-014-9314-7

45. Mahmud, M., Srirama, S., Ramamohanarao, K., Buyya, R.: Quality of experience (QoE)-aware placement of applications in fog computing environments. J. Parallel Distrib. Comput. **123**, 190–203 (2018)
46. Mahmud, R., Kotagiri, R., Buyya, R.: Fog computing: a taxonomy, survey and future directions. In: Di Martino, B., Li, K.-C., Yang, L.T., Esposito, A. (eds.) Internet of Everything. IT, pp. 103–130. Springer, Singapore (2018). https://doi.org/10.1007/978-981-10-5861-5_5
47. Mao, Y., Oak, J., Pompili, A., Beer, D., Han, T., Hu, P.: DRAPS: dynamic and resource-aware placement scheme for Docker containers in a heterogeneous cluster. In: Proceedings of IEEE IPCCC 2017 (2017). https://doi.org/10.1109/PCCC.2017.8280474
48. Mayer, R., Graser, L., Gupta, H., Saurez, E., Ramachandran, U.: EmuFog: extensible and scalable emulation of large-scale fog computing infrastructures. In: Proceedings of IEEE FWC 2017, pp. 1–6 (2017). https://doi.org/10.1109/FWC.2017.8368525
49. Mennes, R., Spinnewyn, B., Latré, S., Botero, J.F.: GRECO: a distributed genetic algorithm for reliable application placement in hybrid clouds. In: Proceedings of IEEE CloudNet 2016, pp. 14–20 (2016). https://doi.org/10.1109/CloudNet.2016.45
50. Mouradian, C., Kianpisheh, S., Abu-Lebdeh, M., Ebrahimnezhad, F., Jahromi, N.T., Glitho, R.H.: Application component placement in NFV-based hybrid cloud/fog systems with mobile fog nodes. IEEE J. Sel. Areas in Commun. **37**(5), 1130–1143 (2019). https://doi.org/10.1109/JSAC.2019.2906790
51. Mseddi, A., Jaafar, W., Elbiaze, H., Ajib, W.: Joint container placement and task provisioning in dynamic fog computing. IEEE Internet Things J. **6**, 10028–10040 (2019)
52. Naas, M.I., Parvedy, P.R., Boukhobza, J., Lemarchand, L.: iFogStor: an IoT data placement strategy for fog infrastructure. In: Proceedings of IEEE ICFEC 2017, pp. 97–104 (2017). https://doi.org/10.1109/ICFEC.2017.15
53. Nardelli, M., Cardellini, V., Casalicchio, E.: Multi-level elastic deployment of containerized applications in geo-distributed environments. In: Proceedings of IEEE FiCloud 2018, pp. 1–8 (2018). https://doi.org/10.1109/FiCloud.2018.00009
54. Nardelli, M., Hochreiner, C., Schulte, S.: Elastic provisioning of virtual machines for container deployment. In: Proceedings of ACM/SPEC ICPE 2017 Companion, pp. 5–10 (2017). https://doi.org/10.1145/3053600.3053602
55. Netto, H.V., Luiz, A.F., Correia, M., de Oliveira Rech, L., Oliveira, C.P.: Koordinator: a service approach for replicating Docker containers in Kubernetes. In: Proceedings of IEEE ISCC 2018, pp. 58–63 (2018)
56. Nouri, S.M.R., Li, H., Venugopal, S., Guo, W., He, M., Tian, W.: Autonomic decentralized elasticity based on a reinforcement learning controller for cloud applications. Future Gener. Comput. Syst. **94**, 765–780 (2019)
57. Ongaro, D., Ousterhout, J.: In search of an understandable consensus algorithm. In: Proceedings of USENIX ATC 2014, pp. 305–319 (2014)
58. Ouyang, T., Zhou, Z., Chen, X.: Follow me at the edge: mobility-aware dynamic service placement for mobile edge computing. IEEE J. Sel. Area Comm. **36**(10), 2333–2345 (2018). https://doi.org/10.1109/JSAC.2018.2869954
59. Piraghaj, S.F., Dastjerdi, A.V., Calheiros, R.N., Buyya, R.: ContainerCloudSim: an environment for modeling and simulation of containers in cloud data centers. Softw. Pract. Exp. **47**(4), 505–521 (2017)

60. Puliafito, C., Mingozzi, E., Longo, F., Puliafito, A., Rana, O.: Fog computing for the internet of things: a survey. ACM Trans. Internet Technol. **19**(2), 18:1–18:41 (2019). https://doi.org/10.1145/3301443
61. Rodriguez, M.A., Buyya, R.: Container-based cluster orchestration systems: a taxonomy and future directions. Softw. Pract. Exp. **49**(5), 698–719 (2019)
62. Röger, H., Mayer, R.: A comprehensive survey on parallelization and elasticity in stream processing. ACM Comput. Surv. **52**(2), 36:1–36:37 (2019)
63. Rossi, F., Cardellini, V., Lo Presti, F.: Elastic deployment of software containers in geo-distributed computing environments. In: Proceedings of IEEE ISCC 2019 (2019). https://doi.org/10.1109/ISCC47284.2019.8969607
64. Rossi, F., Nardelli, M., Cardellini, V.: Horizontal and vertical scaling of container-based applications using reinforcement learning. In: Proceedings of IEEE CLOUD 2019, pp. 329–338 (2019). https://doi.org/10.1109/CLOUD.2019.00061
65. Santos, J., Wauters, T., Volckaert, B., De Turck, F.: Towards network-aware resource provisioning in Kubernetes for fog computing applications. In: Proceedings of IEEE NetSoft 2019, pp. 351–359 (2019). https://doi.org/10.1109/NETSOFT.2019.8806671
66. Souza, V., et al.: Towards a proper service placement in combined fog-to-cloud (F2C) architectures. Future Gener. Comput. Syst. **87**, 1–15 (2018)
67. Subashini, S., Kavitha, V.: A survey on security issues in service delivery models of cloud computing. J. Netw. Comput. Appl. **34**(1), 1–11 (2011)
68. Sutton, R.S., Barto, A.G.: Reinforcement Learning: An Introduction, 2nd edn. MIT Press, Cambridge (2018)
69. Tan, B., Ma, H., Mei, Y.: A hybrid genetic programming hyper-heuristic approach for online two-level resource allocation in container-based clouds. In: Proceedings of IEEE CEC 2019, pp. 2681–2688 (2019). https://doi.org/10.1109/CEC.2019.8790220
70. Tang, Z., Zhou, X., Zhang, F., Jia, W., Zhao, W.: Migration modeling and learning algorithms for containers in fog computing. IEEE Trans. Serv. Comput. **12**(5), 712–725 (2019). https://doi.org/10.1109/TSC.2018.2827070
71. Tesauro, G., Jong, N.K., Das, R., Bennani, M.N.: A hybrid reinforcement learning approach to autonomic resource allocation. In: Proceedings of IEEE ICAC 2006, pp. 65–73 (2006). https://doi.org/10.1109/ICAC.2006.1662383
72. Townend, P., et al.: Improving data center efficiency through holistic scheduling in Kubernetes. In: Proceedings of IEEE SOSE 2019, pp. 156–166 (2019)
73. Wen, Z., Yang, R., Garraghan, P., Lin, T., Xu, J., Rovatsos, M.: Fog orchestration for internet of things services. IEEE Internet Comput. **21**(2), 16–24 (2017)
74. Weyns, D., et al.: On patterns for decentralized control in self-adaptive systems. In: de Lemos, R., Giese, H., Müller, H.A., Shaw, M. (eds.) Software Engineering for Self-Adaptive Systems II. LNCS, vol. 7475, pp. 76–107. Springer, Heidelberg (2013). https://doi.org/10.1007/978-3-642-35813-5_4
75. Wu, Y., Rao, R., Hong, P., Ma, J.: FAS: a flow aware scaling mechanism for stream processing platform service based on LMS. In: Proceedings of ICMSS 2017, pp. 280–284. ACM (2017). https://doi.org/10.1145/3034950.3034965
76. Xu, J., Chen, L., Ren, S.: Online learning for offloading and autoscaling in energy harvesting mobile edge computing. IEEE Trans. Cogn. Commun. Netw. **3**(3), 361–373 (2017). https://doi.org/10.1109/TCCN.2017.2725277
77. Yi, S., Hao, Z., Qin, Z., Li, Q.: Fog computing: platform and applications. In: Proceedings of HotWeb 2015, pp. 73–78. IEEE (2015). https://doi.org/10.1109/HotWeb.2015.22

78. Yigitoglu, E., Mohamed, M., Liu, L., Ludwig, H.: Foggy: a framework for continuous automated IoT application deployment in fog computing. In: Proceedings of IEEE AIMS 2017, pp. 38–45 (2017). https://doi.org/10.1109/AIMS.2017.14
79. Zhao, D., Mohamed, M., Ludwig, H.: Locality-aware scheduling for containers in cloud computing. IEEE Trans. Cloud Comput. **8**(2), 635–646 (2020)
80. Zhou, Z., Liu, P., Feng, J., Zhang, Y., Mumtaz, S., Rodriguez, J.: Computation resource allocation and task assignment optimization in vehicular fog computing: a contract-matching approach. IEEE Trans. Veh. Technol. **68**(4), 3113–3125 (2019)
81. Zhu, J., Chan, D.S., Prabhu, M.S., Natarajan, P., Hu, H., Bonomi, F.: Improving web sites performance using edge servers in fog computing architecture. In: Proceedings of IEEE SOSE 2013, pp. 320–323 (2013)
82. Zhu, Q., Agrawal, G.: Resource provisioning with budget constraints for adaptive applications in cloud environments. IEEE Trans. Serv. Comput. **5**(4), 497–511 (2012). https://doi.org/10.1109/TSC.2011.61

Security-Aware Database Migration Planning

K. Subramani[1(✉)], Bugra Caskurlu[2], and Utku Umur Acikalin[2]

[1] LDCSEE, West Virginia University, Morgantown, WV, USA
k.subramani@mail.wvu.edu
[2] Department of Computer Engineering,
TOBB University of Economics and Technology, Ankara, Turkey
{bcaskurlu,uacikalin}@etu.edu.tr

Abstract. Database migration is an important problem faced by companies dealing with big data. Not only is migration a costly procedure, it involves serious security risks as well. For some institutions, the primary focus is on reducing the cost of the migration operation, which manifests itself in application testing. For other institutions, minimizing security risks is the most important goal, especially if the data involved is of a sensitive nature. In the literature, the database migration problem has been studied from a test cost minimization perspective. In this paper, we focus on an orthogonal measure, i.e., security risk minimization. We associate security with the *number of shifts* needed to complete the migration task. Ideally, we want to complete the migration in as few shifts as possible, so that the risk of data exposure is minimized. In this paper, we provide a formal framework for studying the database migration problem from the perspective of security risk minimization (shift minimization) and establish the computational complexities of several models in the same. We present experimental results for various intractable models and show that our heuristic methods produce solutions that are within 3.67% of the optimal in more than 85% of the cases.

1 Introduction

The process of transferring data between storage types, formats, or computer systems is usually referred to as data migration [8,11]. Software solutions are preferred for the data migration operation [2] in order to automate the migration process [21] and free up human resources [22]. Data migration is required when organizations or individuals change their computer systems or upgrade their existing systems to new computer systems, or when two or more computer systems merge. The latter usually takes place when two companies merge. The data migration operation [14–16] may involve several phases, but at the very minimum it includes the following two phases [12,28]: *data extraction* [23], and *data loading*. In order to accomplish data migration effectively, the data from the old system must be mapped onto the new system [1]. This mapping provides a design for data extraction [30] and data loading [19]. The procedure usually

I. Brandic et al. (Eds.): ALGOCLOUD 2019, LNCS 12041, pp. 103–121, 2020.
https://doi.org/10.1007/978-3-030-58628-7_7

involves complex data manipulation [3], especially if the new system is not an upgrade of the old system, but software produced by a different vendor. This is because different vendors typically use different data formats.

Storage migration [17,24] is the data migration method that is used most often. In the event that more efficient storage technologies become available, a business may choose to upgrade its physical media to take advantage of it. This results in having to move physical blocks of data from one tape or disk to a more efficient media by using virtualization techniques. The data format and content itself are usually unchanged since the same database management system (or file system if the data is stored as a collection of files) is used before and after the operation. Since the storage migration operation does not affect the applications, we do not need to test these applications.

The database migration operation is performed when a company moves from one database vendor to another, or when the database software being used is upgraded to a newer version [4,10]. In the former case, a physical migration of data is required. Along with data extraction and data loading, the migration operation may involve complex data manipulation since different database management systems store data in different formats. Upgrading the existing system to a newer version is less likely to require a physical data migration, but this can occur with major upgrades.

When we migrate databases, we also need to consider how the migration will affect the behavior of the database applications. The change in behavior depends heavily on whether or not the data manipulation language or protocol has changed. Modern application software is designed for all commonly used database management systems. This means if we change the application software for a database, we should not have to worry about testing the software itself. However, we must test the database performance to make sure that it has not been adversely affected. Scheduling the migration so as to minimize testing costs has been studied in the literature [29]. We focus on an orthogonal concern in this paper, viz., minimization of security risks [18]. Greater the period over which the data is exposed, greater is the risk of security violations. We therefore focus our efforts in minimizing data exposure, which in turn is achieved by minimizing the number of shifts that are used in the process.

The principal contributions of this paper are as follows:

1. A modeling framework for capturing a host of specifications in database migration. This model is similar to the framework in [29], but is different in that it considers different objective functions and allows the specification of inter-database timing constraints.
2. Identifying tractable and **NP-hard** models within the above-mentioned framework.
3. Developing efficient heuristic algorithms that find near-optimal solutions for most instances of the intractable models.

The rest of this paper is organized as follows: Sect. 2 formally describes the models and problems that are analyzed in this paper. We commence our analysis in Sect. 3 by establishing the computational complexities of various models.

The experimental results are presented in Sect. 4. We conclude in Sect. 5, by summarizing our contributions and identifying avenues for future research.

2 Notations and Problem Formulation

We have a collection of n databases $\mathcal{B} = \{B_1, B_2, \ldots, B_n\}$, the sizes of which are given by the size-vector $\mathbf{w} = [w_1, w_2, \ldots, w_n]^T$ with w_i representing the size of database B_i.

In the database migration process, the set of databases are clustered so that the databases in the same cluster are migrated at the same time. The migration of the databases is carried out in shifts. The cumulative size of the databases that may migrate in shift i (i.e., the capacity of shift i) is denoted by l_i. The shift capacity-vector $\mathbf{l} = [l_1, l_2, \ldots, l_n]^T$ is also part of the input. In the worst case, we may have to assign each database to a separate shift.

Associated with each database B_i is a schedule-time variable s_i, which specifies the shift B_i is scheduled to be moved. There exist temporal relationships between pairs of databases which constrain their schedules. Typical constraints are of the following form:

(i) Database B_5 must be scheduled in one of the first 4 shifts. This is represented as: $s_5 \le 4$.
(ii) Database B_3 must be scheduled to migrate no earlier than database B_1. This is represented as: $s_3 \ge s_1$.

The temporal relationships, given as a list $\mathbf{C}$ of m constraints, are also part of the input. If a constraint involves only one variable, it is called an *absolute* constraint, whereas if a constraint involves two variables, it is called a *relative* timing constraint. In our framework, we allow absolute constraints of the form $s_i \le k$ and $s_i \ge k$ for some integer k. Within relative constraints, our framework supports both strict inequality constraints of the form $s_i < s_j$ and non-strict inequality constraints of the form $s_i \le s_j$.

Thus, the input to the Security-Aware Database Migration (SADM) problem is the following triple: $\langle \mathbf{w}, \mathbf{l}, \mathbf{C} \rangle$. Example 1 illustrates a potential input.

Example 1: Consider the following input:

$$\langle (\mathbf{1}, \mathbf{2}, \mathbf{2}, \mathbf{3})^{\mathbf{T}}, (\mathbf{5}, \mathbf{7}, \mathbf{10}, \mathbf{12})^{\mathbf{T}}, [\mathbf{s_1} < \mathbf{s_2}, \mathbf{s_2} \le \mathbf{s_3}, \mathbf{s_4} \le \mathbf{3}, \mathbf{s_4} \ge \mathbf{3}] \rangle.$$

In this example, there are four databases with sizes $1, 2, 2$, and 3 respectively. The $\mathbf{l}$ vector gives the capacities of the four shifts, i.e., the total size of the databases that can migrate in each shift, as $5, 7, 10, 12$. The $\mathbf{C}$ list gives the four temporal constraints. The first constraint is a strict inequality relative timing constraint, whereas the second is a non-strict inequality relative timing constraint. The third and the fourth constraints are absolute constraints and they together imply that database B_4 must be scheduled to migrate in the third shift.

There are several parameters associated with the SADM problem:

(i) Size of Databases (α) - The size of a database is a factor in the amount of time required for its migration. This is because the database migration operation must read the database at the original location, write it at the new location, and then delete the original database. This means the size of the database affects the number of databases that are migrated in the same shift. It is always a good practice for companies to have databases with the same size, but this is not always possible for every organization. This means we need two size models associated with the databases.
   (a) Constant (*const*) - In this model, all databases have the same size and are equal to some fixed constant W.
   (b) Arbitrary (*arb*) - In this model, the sizes of the databases are arbitrary.

(ii) Shift capacity (β) - During the database migration operation, some parts of the database will be inaccessible. For some companies, there is no ideal time to make a database unavailable. For instance, Facebook and Youtube have users all over the world which means the database access rate is roughly uniform. In this case, regardless when a database becomes inaccessible, there will be a subset of users who cannot access the database until the migration is complete. It is critical for these companies to perform the database migration operation in small shifts to minimize user dissatisfaction. For companies that operate during regular business hours (for instance, banks), it is preferable for the databases to be unavailable when the companies are closed rather than when they are open. In order to model the needs of several different companies, we use two capacity models associated with shifts.
   (a) Uniform (*unif*) - In this model, the capacity of each shift is the same and is equal to a constant L, for all shifts (i.e., $\mathbf{l} = \langle L, L, \ldots, L \rangle$). We note that this model suits better for the database migration needs of companies that have uniform database access rates.
   (b) Non-uniform (*non-unif*) - In this model, the total size of the databases that may migrate in each shift is arbitrary. We note that this model would be more suitable for the database migration needs of companies that have non-uniform database access rates.

(iii) Inter-database relationship (γ) - The data entries of a database B_i and another database B_j may be complementary in nature. In this situation, the company would prefer databases B_i and B_j migrate in the same shift. Consider a company, such as Youtube, that stores various media uploaded by its users. A typical user of Youtube will search for some keywords and want to see relevant videos. Two distinct databases B_i and B_j are substitutable to the users if the databases store data (e.g., videos) with similar content. In this case, the company will prefer these two databases to migrate in different shifts, so that the information content of at least one of them is available at all times. As far as temporal inter-database relationships are concerned, we have the following three models:
   (a) $\mathbf{R} = \phi$ - In this model, we consider the scenario where there are no temporal constraints (i.e., each database can migrate in any shift).
   (b) $\mathbf{R} = abs$ - In this model, only absolute constraints are permitted.

(c) $\mathbf{R} = rel$ - In this model, we consider the most general form of inter-database relationships, where both absolute and relative timing constraints are permitted. If the data contents of the databases B_i and B_j are complementary for the users of a company, the company may prefer to schedule the migration of B_i and B_j to the same shift by using the relative timing constraints $s_i \leq s_j$ and $s_j \leq s_i$. If the data content of B_i and B_j can be considered as substitutable for the users of a company, the company may prefer to have one of the relative timing constraints $s_i < s_j$ or $s_i > s_j$ to ensure that both B_i and B_j are not unavailable simultaneously.

(iv) Optimization function (Θ) - There are two optimization functions that are of interest in minimizing the security risks involved during database migration.

(a) The number of actually used shifts (*used*) - The SADM problem with the objective of minimizing the number of actually used shifts addresses an important vulnerability of data security. The database migration operation enables technical personnel to access all contents of the database that will be migrated. Although the technical personnel will have proper training to perform the database migration operation using the highest possible level of security measures, performing the operation will eventually become routine. When this occurs, there is a potential risk that the personnel will become careless and fail to ensure that all security measures are properly handled before performing the database migration operation. Since accidentally leaking information content can have severe repercussions, the database migration operation should not be performed often. This optimization function aims to prevent potential adverse consequences by minimizing the number of times the database migration occurs. Notice that in this model, if the migrator assigns databases to the first and the third shifts, but not to the second shift, the total number of shifts actually used is 2.

(b) The index of the last shift used (*last*) - This optimization function is designed to accommodate corporations that aim to finish the database migration process as soon as possible. This is true in situations where the companies have to pay for blocks of contiguous time. In this case, the companies are charged for shifts whether or not they are used. Accordingly, the goal is to finish the migration process as quickly as is feasible. In the SADM problem in which the goal is to minimize the index of the last shift used, if the migrator assigns databases to the first and the third shifts, but not to the second shift, then the index of the last shift used is 3.

Thus, a model of the security-aware database migration (SADM) problem has four parameters, and it is specified as a 4-tuple $\langle \alpha \mid \beta \mid \gamma \mid \Theta \rangle$. For instance, $\langle const \mid unif \mid \phi \mid used \rangle$ refers to the SADM problem in which all databases have the same size, the shift capacities are uniform, there are no inter-database timing relationships, and the goal is to minimize the number of shifts actually used. For notational convenience we use $*$ as an entry of the 4-tuple when we present a statement that is true for all the models for that entry. For instance, the notation $\langle * \mid * \mid \phi \mid last \rangle$ refers to all 4 models of the SADM problem in which there are no inter-database timing relationships, and the goal is to minimize the index of the last shift used. The following is formal definition of the SADM problem:

SADM: *Given a triple* $\langle \mathbf{w}, \mathbf{l}, \mathbf{C} \rangle$ *and a 4-tuple* $\langle \alpha \mid \beta \mid \gamma \mid \Theta \rangle$, *the goal is to organize the migration of the databases in accordance with the size, capacity and timing constraints given by* $\langle \mathbf{w}, \mathbf{l}, \mathbf{C} \rangle$ *under the model* $\langle \alpha \mid \beta \mid \gamma \mid \Theta \rangle$.

Given that we have 2 different models for sizes of databases, 2 different models for shift capacities, 3 different models for inter-database timing relationships, and 2 different models for optimization functions; the SADM problem formulation gives us a framework with a total of 24 different models, each of which is suitable for database migration needs of different companies.

3 Computational Complexity Results

This section is devoted to establishing the computational complexities of the models of the SADM problem. We first show by Theorem 1 that the SADM problem is **NP-hard** for all the 12 models with arbitrary database sizes.

Theorem 1. *The SADM problem is* **NP-hard** *for all the* 12 *models captured by the notation* $\langle arb \mid * \mid * \mid * \rangle$.

Proof. Notice that the models $\langle arb \mid unif \mid \phi \mid last \rangle$ and $\langle arb \mid unif \mid \phi \mid used \rangle$ are the most restricted models of $\langle arb \mid * \mid * \mid last \rangle$ and $\langle arb \mid * \mid * \mid used \rangle$, respectively. Moreover, $\langle arb \mid unif \mid \phi \mid last \rangle$ and $\langle arb \mid unif \mid \phi \mid used \rangle$ are equivalent in the sense that the optimal value of the optimization functions *last* and *used* are the same when shift capacities are uniform and timing constraints are absent. Thus, all we need to complete the proof is to give a strict reduction from the optimization version of the BIN-PACKING problem to the SADM problem under the model $\langle arb \mid * \mid * \mid used \rangle$.

In the optimization version of the BIN-PACKING problem, we are given a bin size V and a list $a_1, \ldots, a_n$ of sizes of the items to pack. The goal is to find the smallest integer C such that there exists a C-partition $S_1 \cup \ldots \cup S_C$ of $\{1, 2, \ldots, n\}$ subject to the constraint that $\sum_{i \in S_k} a_i \leq V$, for all $k = 1, \ldots C$. Given an instance x of BIN-PACKING, we construct an instance y of the SADM problem under the model $\langle arb \mid * \mid * \mid used \rangle$ as follows:

- The size of the databases in instance y are equal to the size of the items in instance x, i.e., $\mathbf{w} = [a_1, a_2, \ldots, a_n]^T$.
- The size of each shift in instance y is equal to the bin size in instance x, i.e., $\mathbf{l} = [V, V, \ldots, V]^T$.

The reduction given above is a strict reduction, since any feasible solution to instance y is mapped to a feasible solution to instance x with the same objective function value. □

Corollary 1 follows since the reduction given in the proof of Theorem 1 is an approximation-preserving strict reduction, and BIN-PACKING admits an asymptotic PTAS while it does not admit a PTAS.

Corollary 1. *The SADM problem does not admit a PTAS for any of the models* $\langle arb \mid * \mid * \mid * \rangle$, *unless* $\mathbf{P} = \mathbf{NP}$. *Furthermore, there is an asymptotic PTAS for the SADM problem for the models captured by the notation* $\langle arb \mid unif \mid \phi \mid * \rangle$.

Due to Theorem 1, we focus on the models with uniform database sizes in the rest of the section. We show by Theorem 2 that the optimal solution can be found in $O(n)$-time for the 4 models with uniform databases sizes and no temporal constraints.

Theorem 2. *The SADM problem can be solved in* $O(n)$ *time for all the* 4 *models captured by the notation* $\langle const \mid * \mid \phi \mid * \rangle$.

Proof. We prove the result by giving an $O(n)$ algorithm for the 4 models captured by the notation $\langle const \mid * \mid \phi \mid * \rangle$ (see Algorithm 3.1). Since the models under consideration have no temporal constraints, the list $\mathbf{C}$ is dropped from the parameter list of Algorithm 3.1. All the databases in these models have the same size, and W denotes the size of each database. If the optimization function is *used*, shifts are renumbered with respect to their capacities in descending order (with the COUNTING-SORT algorithm [5] in $O(n)$-time). They are left as they are, if the optimization function is *last*. Algorithm 3.1 is a greedy algorithm that assigns the maximum number of databases that can be assigned to each shift. In particular, it assigns $\lfloor \frac{l_1}{W} \rfloor$ databases to the first shift, $\lfloor \frac{l_2}{W} \rfloor$ databases to the second shift, and so on until all databases are assigned to a shift. It is easy to see that Algorithm 3.1 runs in $O(n)$-time.

Function MODELS $\langle const \mid * \mid \phi \mid * \rangle(\langle \mathbf{w}, \mathbf{l} \rangle)$

Let W denote the size of each database.
Let U, initialized to B, denote the set of unscheduled databases.
if The optimization function Θ is *used* **then**
    Renumber the shifts with respect to their sizes in descending order.
end if
Initialize counter $i = 0$.
while $(U \neq \emptyset)$ **do**
    $i = i + 1$.
    Let D be a subset of $\lfloor \frac{l_i}{W} \rfloor$ databases of U.
    Assign the set of databases D to shift i.
    $U = U - D$.
end while

Algorithm 3.1: Polynomial Time Algorithm for the models $\langle const \mid * \mid \phi \mid * \rangle$.

Correctness: First assume that the optimization function Θ is *used*. Let s be the number of shifts used by the schedule constructed by Algorithm 3.1. For the purpose of contradiction, assume the optimal schedule uses $k < s$ shifts. But then there should be an optimal schedule that only uses the first k shifts since the shifts are ordered with respect to their sizes in descending order. However, no schedule can assign all the databases to the first k shifts, since otherwise, that is what Algorithm 3.1 would do. Thus, the schedule returned by Algorithm 3.1 is optimal.

Let us now assume that the optimization function Θ is *last*. Let s be the largest index of the shift used by the schedule constructed by Algorithm 3.1. For the purpose of contradiction, assume the largest index of the shift used in the optimal schedule is k for some $k < s$. No schedule can assign all the databases to the first k shifts, since otherwise, Algorithm 3.1 that assigned as many databases as can be assigned to the first k shifts would suffice. Thus, the schedule returned by Algorithm 3.1 is optimal. □

3.1 Models with Timing Constraints

In this section, we consider the 8 models with uniform database sizes and inter-database timing constraints. We show that the SADM problem is **NP-hard** in all the models with relative timing constraints. For the models with only absolute constraints, we show that there is an $O(m+n \lg n)$ algorithm for the *last* optimization function. The computational complexity, however, is not resolved if the optimization function is *used* and there are only absolute constraints. Before we proceed, we make the following definitions.

Definition 1. *We define r_i, the* **release-time** *of the database B_i, as k if the most stringent lower-bounding absolute timing constraint for B_i is $s_i \geq k$. If no such constraint exists for B_i then its release-time is* 1.

Definition 2. *We define d_i, the* **deadline** *of the database B_i, as k if the most stringent upper-bounding absolute timing constraint for B_i is $s_i \leq k$. If no such constraint exists for B_i then its deadline is n.*

Notice that the release-time (deadline) of a database is defined as the earliest (latest) shift it can be assigned without violating the absolute timing constraints.

Theorem 3 establishes that for the 2 models with *last* objective function, optimal solution can be found in $O(m + n \cdot \lg n)$-time, where m is the number of constraints and n is the number of databases.

Theorem 3. *The SADM problem can be solved in $O(m + n \cdot \lg n)$ time for the* 2 *models captured by the notation $\langle const \mid * \mid abs \mid last \rangle$.*

Proof Sketch: We prove Theorem 3 via an iterative algorithm. Our algorithm first determines the release-time and deadline of each database via a pass over the list of constraints **C** in $O(m + n)$-time. It then loops through the shifts starting from the first one until all databases are assigned to a shift, and at each iteration assigns the databases with the earliest deadline among the already released ones while respecting the shift capacity constraints. This can be accomplished in $O(n \cdot \lg n)$ time by using a heap data structure.

We next show by Theorem 4 that all the 4 models of the SADM problem with relative timing constraints are **NP-hard** through a reduction from the classical 3-PARTITION problem [13].

Theorem 4. *The SADM problem is* **NP-hard** *for all the 4 models captured by the notation* $\langle const \mid * \mid rel \mid * \rangle$.

Proof. We first establish **NP-hardness** for the model $\langle const \mid unif \mid rel \mid used \rangle$ via a many-one reduction from the classical 3-PARTITION problem to the decision version of the SADM problem under the model $\langle const \mid unif \mid rel \mid used \rangle$.

In the classical 3-PARTITION problem, we are given a multiset of $3t$ positive integers $S = \{x_1, x_2, \ldots, x_{3t}\}$ with $\sum_{x_i \in S} x_i = tD$ for some integer D, such that each x_i satisfies $\frac{D}{4} < x_i < \frac{D}{2}$. The goal is to decide whether S can be partitioned into t groups of size 3 such that each group sums to exactly D.

Given a 3-PARTITION instance, we construct the corresponding SADM instance under the model $\langle const \mid unif \mid rel \mid used \rangle$ as follows:

- The SADM instance has tD databases with unit size, i.e., $w_i = 1$ for each database B_i. So, for every integer $x_i \in S$ of the 3-PARTITION instance, the SADM instance has x_i databases. The databases $B_1, B_2, \cdots, B_{x_1}$ correspond to x_1, the databases $B_{x_1+1}, \cdots, B_{x_1+x_2}$ correspond to x_2, and so on.
- The shift capacities are uniform and the capacity of each shift is D, i.e., $l_i = D$ for each shift i. Since all databases have unit size, each shift can accommodate D databases.
- For every $x_i \in S$ of the 3-PARTITION instance, the SADM instance has x_i non-strict inequality constraints that ensure all the corresponding databases of x_i are to be scheduled to migrate in the same shift. Precisely, SADM instance has the constraints $s_1 \leq s_2 \leq \cdots \leq s_{x_1} \leq s_1$ for x_1, and the constraints $s_{(\sum_{j=1}^{i-1} x_j)+1} \leq s_{(\sum_{j=1}^{i-1} x_j)+2} \leq \cdots s_{\sum_{j=1}^{i} x_j} \leq s_{(\sum_{j=1}^{i-1} x_j)+1}$ for x_i with $i \geq 1$. The constructed SADM instance has no other temporal constraints or absolute constraints.

All we need to complete the proof is to show that the optimal value of the constructed SADM instance is t if it corresponds to a "yes" instance of the 3-PARTITION problem, and higher otherwise.

Let I be an instance of the 3-PARTITION problem. Assume that I is a "yes" instance. In I, the elements of S can be partitioned into t groups of size 3 such that each group sums to exactly D. For any i with $1 \leq i \leq t$, the corresponding databases of the elements of S in group i can be scheduled to migrate in shift i. Thus the optimal value of the constructed SADM instance is at most t. It cannot be less than t by the generalized pigeonhole principle since there are tD databases with unit size and the capacity of each shift is D.

Let us now assume that I is a "no" instance. For the purpose of contradiction, we also assume the optimal solution to the corresponding SADM instance is at most t. Since the optimal solution to the corresponding SADM instance cannot be less than t by the generalized pigeonhole principle, it is t. Then, we have exactly D databases in each used shift. For any i with $1 \leq i \leq t$, consider the set of databases assigned to the actually used shift with ith smallest index. For any $x_j \in S$, we have either all the databases corresponding to x_j are in this shift, or none due to relative timing constraints. Since for any $x_j \in S$ we have $\frac{D}{4} < x_j < \frac{D}{2}$, the set of databases in this shift are corresponding to the 3 integers in S that adds up to D. We obtain a contradiction since this is true for every used shift.

Notice that since the shift capacities are uniform and the relative timing constraints only constrain some subset of databases to migrate in the same shift, the contents of any two shifts can be exchanged in the constructed SADM instance without affecting the feasibility of the solution. Hence, a solution to the constructed SADM instance that uses t shifts can use the first t shifts for any t. Thus, the reduction holds for the model $\langle const \mid unif \mid rel \mid last\rangle$. Since the models $\langle const \mid unif \mid rel \mid last\rangle$ and $\langle const \mid unif \mid rel \mid used\rangle$ are the most restricted models captured by the notation $\langle const \mid * \mid rel \mid *\rangle$, the reduction holds for all 4 of the models captured by the notation $\langle const \mid * \mid rel \mid *\rangle$.

We should note that the size of the constructed SADM instance is polynomial in the size of the given 3-PARTITION instance in the above reduction, if the 3-PARTITION instance is represented in unary. The proof is sound since the 3-PARTITION problem is strongly **NP-hard**. □

4 Experimental Study

In this section we present our heuristic approaches and experimental results for the models captured by the notation $\langle arb \mid non-unif \mid * \mid *\rangle$. Instances are generated in the following ways: i) assigning random numbers to parameters, ii) assigning random numbers to the missing problem specific values of known instances of related problems in the literature. We developed genetic algorithms for the models under consideration. For each instance, the specific genetic algorithm is executed 10 times and the best solution is fed to CPLEX as the initial solution to the Integer Program (IP) presented in Sect. 4.2. An improved solution and a lower-bound for each instance is obtained from CPLEX with 5 min time limit. In the rest of the section, we present the data generation process, the mathematical formulation, genetic algorithms we developed and the analysis of the experimental results.

4.1 Data Generation Process

For the models with no timing constraints, we generated 360 instances (10 instances per instance type) by assigning random numbers to parameters by a similar approach used in [27]. Additionally, 84 instances are generated by choosing random values for shift capacities from 3 different ranges using the

Hard28 [6] benchmark instances, which is known as challenging for the BIN-PACKING problem [26]. The range of parameters, where the values are chosen uniformly at random, of the 36 instance types are listed below:

- *Number of databases and shifts:* $n \in \{50, 100, 250, 500\}$.
- *Shift capacities:* $l_i \in [0.34L, 1.66L), [0.5L, 1.5L), [0.67L, 1.33L)$, with L being the expected capacity of a shift. L is selected as 100 in randomly generated instances.
- *Database sizes:* $w_i \in [25, 39], [20, 119], [40, 99]$.

For the models with only absolute constraints, the 444 (=360 + 84) instances for the models with no timing constraints are expanded with deadline and release-time values for each database. For each database B_i, the deadline d_i is chosen uniformly at random from the range $[1, n]$, and then the release-time r_i is chosen uniformly at random from the range $[1, d_i]$.

For the models with relative timing constraints, a total of medium and large-sized 600 instances are generated by modifying medium and large-sized 200 instances constructed for the Simple Assembly Line Balancing Problem (SALBP) in [25] as follows:

- The precedence relations of SALBP instances are randomly converted into strict or non-strict inequality constraints.
- The task times of the SALBP instances are used as the size of databases.
- The cycle time in SALBP instances are constant and equal to 1000. In the SADM instances, shift capacities are selected uniformly at random from the following 3 ranges: $[340, 1665], [500, 1499], [670, 1329]$.
- Each database is assigned a deadline or a release-time constraint with probability 0.16, and both a deadline and release-time constraint with probability 0.04.

Notice that three corresponding SADM instances with relative constraints are constructed for each SALBP instance. Half of the instances are medium-sized ($n = 50$), and the other half are large-sized ($n = 100$). If a database has exactly one of deadline or a release-time, it is chosen uniformly at random from the range $[1, n]$. If a database has both release-time and deadline, they are chosen as in the models with only absolute constraints. In our experiments, infeasible instances are replaced with additional feasible instances generated with the same procedure.

4.2 Mathematical Formulations

In order to measure the performance of our heuristic algorithms, we compare the solutions returned by them against the lower-bound obtained from CPLEX by using the following mathematical formulation.

$$
\begin{aligned}
&\text{minimize } z\\
&\text{subject to}\\
&\sum_{j=1}^{n} x_{ij} \quad = 1, \qquad \forall i = 1, ..., n && (1)\\
&\sum_{i=1}^{n} w_i \cdot x_{ij} \quad \leq l_j \cdot y_j, \qquad \forall j = 1, ..., n && (2)\\
&\sum_{j=1}^{n} j \cdot x_{ij} \quad \leq d_i, \qquad \forall i = 1, ..., n && (3)\\
&\sum_{j=1}^{n} j \cdot x_{ij} \quad \geq r_i, \qquad \forall i = 1, ..., n && (4)\\
&\sum_{j=1}^{n} j \cdot x_{kj} \quad \leq \sum_{j=1}^{n} j \cdot x_{ij}, \qquad \forall i = 1, ..., n, \forall k \in NI_i && (5)\\
&\sum_{j=1}^{n} j \cdot x_{kj} \quad < \sum_{j=1}^{n} j \cdot x_{ij}, \qquad \forall i = 1, ..., n, \forall k \in SI_i && (6)\\
&\sum_{j=1}^{n} y_j \quad = z, && (7)\\
&j \cdot y_j \quad \geq z, \qquad \forall j = 1, ..., n && (8)\\
&x_{ij} \in \{0, 1\}, \qquad \forall i, j = 1, ..., n && (9)\\
&y_j \in \{0, 1\}, \qquad \forall j = 1, ..., n && (10)
\end{aligned}
$$

Decision variable x_{ij} equals to 1, if B_i is assigned to shift j, and 0 otherwise. Decision variable y_j equals to 1, if shift j is used, and 0 otherwise.

Constraint 1 ensures that each database is assigned to a shift. Shift capacities are enforced by constraint 2. Constraints 3 and 4 enforce absolute timing constraints, where d_i (r_i) represents the deadline (release-time) of database B_i. Constraints 5 and 6 enforce relative timing constraints, where NI_i (SI_i) represents the set of non-strict (strict) inequalities of the form $s_k \leq s_i$ ($s_k < s_i$). For models with optimization function *used*, constraint 7 forces z to be the number of actually used shifts. For models with optimization function *last*, constraint 8 enforces z to be greater than or equal to the index of the last used shift.

For the models without any timing constraints, our mathematical formulation contains the constraints 1, 2, 9 and 10. For the models with absolute timing constraints, our mathematical formulation contains the constraints 1–4, 9 and 10. For the models with both absolute and relative timing constraints, our mathematical formulation contains the constraints 1–6, 9 and 10. Additionally, constraint 7 is used if the optimization function is *used*, and constraint 8 is used otherwise.

4.3 Genetic Algorithms

A genetic algorithm is typically specified by its following parts: fitness function, encoding scheme, initial population generation, and the production of next generations. In what follows, we explain our design choices for each part.

Fitness Function: Every genetic algorithm uses a fitness function to evaluate the quality of a solution, which is referred to as the fitness of a solution. In order to distinguish solutions with the same objective function value, fitness functions are designed as a function of the objective function value and some problem specific criteria. We used the following three problem specific criteria in our design of the fitness function.

The first criterion used is similar in nature to the squared bin efficiency [9] introduced for the BIN-PACKING problem. It aims to produce solutions with nearly full and nearly empty bins instead of half-full bins, since nearly empty bins can be eliminated more easily. Also nearly empty bins could potentially take more additional items than nearly half-full bins. This can be directly translated into SADM problem as squared shift efficiency (SSE):

$$SSE = \sum_{j=1}^{n} (U_j/L_{max})^2,$$

where U_j denotes the cumulative sizes of the databases assigned to shift j, and L_{max} is the largest shift capacity.

The second criterion makes use of the maximum of the remaining capacities of the used shifts, which we denote by R_{max}. We use R_{max} to determine the potential of a solution to eliminate a shift. If there is a shift j with $U_j \leq R_{max}$, the databases assigned to shift j can be moved to the shift with R_{max} available capacity. The *potential* is defined as follows:

$$potential = \frac{1}{2 + R_{max}}$$

The third criterion penalizes solutions that violate constraints. For the 4 models captured by the notations $\langle arb \mid non-unif \mid \phi \mid *\rangle$ and $\langle arb \mid non-unif \mid abs \mid *\rangle$, it is easy and effective to allow only shift capacity constraint violations. On the other hand, for the remaining 2 models captured by the notation $\langle arb \mid non-unif \mid rel \mid *\rangle$, finding a feasible solution is harder and allowing not only the shift capacity constraint violations, but also the absolute and relative timing constraint violations leads to obtaining better solutions than otherwise. Note that in the final solution returned by the genetic algorithm, there would be no constraint violations. Penalty is defined as the function $(1 + CP) \cdot (1 + AP) \cdot (1 + RP)$, where capacity penalty (CP), absolute penalty (AP), and relative penalty (RP) are defined as follows:

- Capacity Penalty$(CP) = \sum_{j=1}^{n} e(j)$, where e(j) $= \begin{cases} 0, & \text{if } U_j \leq l_j \\ U_j - l_j, & \text{otherwise} \end{cases}$

- Absolute Penalty(AP) = number of violated absolute timing constraints
- Relative Penalty(RP) = number of violated relative timing constraints

The fitness function is then defined as follows:

$$fitness = \frac{SSE}{(z + potential) \cdot penalty}$$

where z represents the optimization function value.

Encoding Scheme: Our genetic algorithms use the group-based encoding scheme since it is known to perform better than the alternatives, i.e., bin-based (shift-based) and object-based encodings, for the BIN-PACKING problem [9]. Additionally, application of the crossover operator is time efficient when the group-based encoding scheme is used. In the group-based encoding scheme, each gene represents the group of databases that are assigned to the same shift. In the example of Fig. 1, the first gene G_1 consists of the database B_1, which is the only database assigned to the first shift. The second gene G_2 consists of the databases B_2, B_3 and B_4, which are assigned to the second shift.

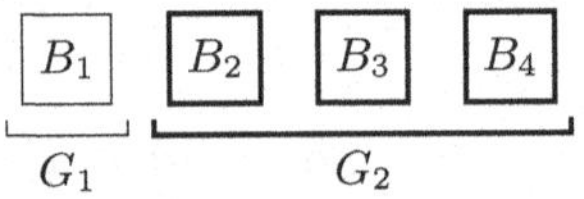

B_1 B_2 B_3 B_4

G_1 G_2

Fig. 1. An example for the group-based encoding scheme.

Initial Population Generation: Initial solutions are generated by a combination of the FirstFit (FF) and the FirstFitDecreasing (FFD) [7] heuristics with random shuffling of databases or limiting the usable shifts. For the models $\langle arb \mid non - unif \mid \phi \mid last\rangle$ and $\langle arb \mid non - unif \mid abs \mid last\rangle$, 99 initial solutions are generated by first randomly shuffling databases and then using the FF heuristic. 1 initial solution is generated using the FFD heuristic. The only difference in the models $\langle arb \mid non - unif \mid \phi \mid used\rangle$ and $\langle arb \mid non - unif \mid abs \mid used\rangle$ is that the shifts are sorted in non-increasing order with respect to their capacities before FF and FFD heuristics are used. For the models with relative timing constraints, i.e., $\langle arb \mid non - unif \mid rel \mid *\rangle$, 250 initial solutions are generated by setting *start index* to $0, 1, \ldots, 249$ and using FF heuristic. The first *start index* shifts are considered only if a database cannot be assigned to the remaining shifts without violating a constraint. Additional 250 initial solutions are generated by setting *start index* to an integer randomly selected from $[0, n]$.

Production of Next Generation: While producing the next generation, elitism rule is used and fittest 10% of the solutions are transferred to the next generation directly. Rest of the 90% of the population is replaced by offsprings created from

2 parents that are selected via a 2-way tournament. To produce offsprings, we use an extended version of the approach in [26] since in our problem shifts have varying capacities. Let U_j denote the cumulative size of the databases assigned to shift j. Procedure first sorts both parents' shifts in non-increasing order with respect to U_j, then similar to the MERGE procedure of the MERGE-SORT algorithm [5], combines shifts by selecting the shift with largest U_j value by comparing the left-most unprocessed shifts of both parents. Selected shift is discarded if one of the followings holds: i) the shift is already passed to the offspring, ii) any database in the shift is already assigned to another shift of the offspring, iii) the capacity constraint of the shift is violated, iv) the optimization function value of the offspring is not better than both of its parents. If the shift is not discarded, it is passed to the offspring. After this process some databases might be left unassigned. These databases are assigned using the FFD and the FF heuristics to create 2 offsprings, fitter one of which is returned. After an offspring is created, a local search procedure inspired by MTP's dominance rule for the BIN-PACKING problem [20] is applied.

In this local search procedure, the 3 shifts with the smallest load are emptied out if the optimization function is *used*. For the optimization function (*last*) the last 3 shifts are emptied out instead. Then procedure tries to replace unassigned databases with either databases with less cumulative size or more databases with same cumulative size from already used shifts. This approach aims to improve the shift efficiency and increase the probability of placing unassigned databases. The procedure tries to replace databases in groups of m since one-to-one replacements are less likely. To illustrate, at most m unassigned databases replace at most m databases all of which assigned to the same shift, in a single replacement. The procedure searches for the best replacement exhaustively. Quality of the replacement and the time spent for finding the best replacement increase exponentially as m increases. Thus m is selected as 2 since it offers the best time-quality trade-off in our case. If no further replacement is possible, remaining unassigned databases are assigned using the FFD heuristic. The local search procedure is reiterated if the previous iteration increased the *fitness* of the solution.

4.4 Experimental Setup

All algorithms are written in Java, compiled and run using JDK version 11.01 with 12 GB heap size. Integer Program is created using CPLEX Java API and run with 12 GB memory limit (after reaching memory limit, CPLEX starts swapping and compressing). All test are executed on the same computer which has 3.7 Ghz (4.3 Ghz Turbo) 64-bit AMD Ryzen 7 2600X 6-core 12-thread CPU and 16 GB DDR4 3200 MHz RAM running Windows 10 Education. CPLEX version 12.62 is used.

4.5 Results and Analysis

Our genetic algorithms terminated under 60 s for all instances. The solutions returned by the genetic algorithms are used to warm start the integer program, which is executed with 5 min time limit. We present a comparison of the quality of the following solutions: i) solution returned by the genetic algorithm, ii) solution returned by CPLEX on the IP presented in Sect. 4.2 with 5 min time limit, where the solution to the genetic algorithm is used as the initial solution, iii) the lower bound for the optimal solution returned by the CPLEX.

Table 1. Comparison of genetic algorithm and lower bound

	$\langle \phi \vert\ used\rangle$	$\langle abs \vert\ used\rangle$	$\langle rel \vert\ used\rangle$	$\langle \phi \vert\ last\rangle$	$\langle abs \vert\ last\rangle$	$\langle rel \vert\ last\rangle$
Max %GAP	9.56	13.95	20.93	6.32	1.42	8.83
Avg %GAP	2.73	4.53	9.04	1.29	0.15	2.04
StdDev	2.03	2.68	4.71	1.43	0.31	1.95

Table 1 provides a comparison of the objective function values of the solutions returned by the genetic algorithms and that of the lower bound provided by CPLEX. For all instances, the genetic algorithm produced solutions that are close to the optimal.

Table 2. Comparison of CPLEX after genetic algorithm and lower bound

	$\langle \phi \vert\ used\rangle$	$\langle abs \vert\ used\rangle$	$\langle rel \vert\ used\rangle$	$\langle \phi \vert\ last\rangle$	$\langle abs \vert\ last\rangle$	$\langle rel \vert\ last\rangle$
Max %GAP	8.25	8.51	11.29	4.45	0.22	0.24
Avg %GAP	1.70	1.36	2.77	0.60	0.15	0.04
StdDev	2.02	1.69	2.48	0.91	0.31	0.06

Table 2 provides a comparison of the objective function values of the solutions returned by the CPLEX (executed 5 min time limit and the solution returned by the genetic algorithm is used as the initial solution) and that of the lower bound provided by CPLEX. We see that CPLEX significantly improved the initial solutions.

5 Conclusion

We introduced a variant of the database migration problem called the Security-Aware Database Migration (SADM) problem. The database migration problem has been studied from the perspective of test cost minimization; [29] documents several results with respect to this objective. Here, we focused on two optimization measures, viz., minimizing the total number of shifts used and minimizing the index of the last shift used. Both these optimization measures arise in the context of minimizing security risks. All the models in our framework except the ones captured by the notation $\langle const \mid * \mid abs \mid used \rangle$ have been classified as being either in **P** or **NP-hard**. For various **NP-hard** models, we developed genetic algorithms that produce solutions that are within at most 9.49% of the optimal in most of the cases. These solutions are further improved by using CPLEX and the improved solutions are within 3.67% of the optimal in more than 85% of the cases. In future work, we will focus on establishing the computational complexity of the models captured by the notation $\langle const \mid * \mid abs \mid used \rangle$.

References

1. Behm, A., Geppert, A., Dittrich, K.R.: On the migration of relational schemas and data to object-oriented database systems. Technical report, University of Zurich (1997)
2. Brodal, G.S., Frigioni, D., Marchetti-Spaccamela, A. (eds.): WAE 2001. LNCS, vol. 2141. Springer, Heidelberg (2001). https://doi.org/10.1007/3-540-44688-5
3. Chatterjee, A., Segev, A.: Data manipulation in heterogeneous databases. SIGMOD Rec. **20**(4), 64–68 (1991)
4. Chon, H.D., Agrawal, D., El Abbadi, A.: Data management for moving objects. IEEE Data Eng. Bull. **25**(2), 41–47 (2002)
5. Cormen, T.H., Leiserson, C.E., Rivest, R.L., Stein, C.: Introduction to Algorithms, 3rd edn. The MIT Press, Cambridge (2009)
6. Delorme, M., Iori, M., Martello, S.: BPPLIB: a library for bin packing and cutting stock problems. Optim. Lett. **12**(2), 235–250 (2017). https://doi.org/10.1007/s11590-017-1192-z
7. Dósa, G., Sgall, J.: First fit bin packing: a tight analysis. In: 30th International Symposium on Theoretical Aspects of Computer Science, STACS 2013, Kiel, Germany, 27 February–2 March 2013, pp. 538–549 (2013)
8. Drumm, C., Schmitt, M., Do, H.H., Rahm, E.: Quickmig: automatic schema matching for data migration projects. In: Proceedings of the Sixteenth ACM Conference on Information and Knowledge Management, CIKM 2007, Lisbon, Portugal, 6–10 November 2007, pp. 107–116 (2007)
9. Falkenauer, E.: A hybrid grouping genetic algorithm for bin packing. J. Heuristics **2**(1), 5–30 (1996)
10. Ferrandina, F., Meyer, T., Zicari, R., Ferran, G., Madec, J.: Schema and database evolution in the O2 object database system. In: VLDB 1995, Proceedings of 21th International Conference on Very Large Data Bases, Zurich, Switzerland, 11–15 September 1995, pp. 170–181 (1995)
11. Gandhi, R., Halldórsson, M.M., Kortsarz, G., Shachnai, H.: Improved results for data migration and open shop scheduling. In: Díaz, J., Karhumäki, J., Lepistö, A., Sannella, D. (eds.) ICALP 2004. LNCS, vol. 3142, pp. 658–669. Springer, Heidelberg (2004). https://doi.org/10.1007/978-3-540-27836-8_56
12. Gandhi, R., Mestre, J.: Combinatorial algorithms for data migration to minimize average completion time. Algorithmica **54**(1), 54–71 (2009)
13. Garey, M.R., Johnson, D.S.: Computers and Intractability: A Guide to the Theory of NP-Completeness. W. H. Freeman, New York (1979)

14. Goldman, R., McHugh, J., Widom, J.: From, semistructured data to XML: migrating the lore data model and query language. In: ACM SIGMOD Workshop on the Web and Databases, WebDB 1999, Philadelphia, Pennsylvania, USA, 3–4 June 1999. Informal Proceedings, pp. 25–30 (1999)
15. Golubchik, L., Khuller, S., Kim, Y.-A., Shargorodskaya, S., Wan, Y.-C.J.: Data migration on parallel disks. In: Albers, S., Radzik, T. (eds.) ESA 2004. LNCS, vol. 3221, pp. 689–701. Springer, Heidelberg (2004). https://doi.org/10.1007/978-3-540-30140-0_61
16. Hall, J., Hartline, J.D., Karlin, A.R., Saia, J., Wilkes, J.: On algorithms for efficient data migration. In: Proceedings of the Twelfth Annual Symposium on Discrete Algorithms, Washington, DC, USA, 7–9 January 2001, pp. 620–629 (2001)
17. Hirofuchi, T., Ogawa, H., Nakada, H., Itoh, S., Sekiguchi, S.: A live storage migration mechanism over WAN for relocatable virtual machine services on clouds. In: 9th IEEE/ACM International Symposium on Cluster Computing and the Grid, CCGrid 2009, Shanghai, China, 18–21 May 2009, pp. 460–465 (2009)
18. Jensen, M., Schwenk, J., Gruschka, N., Iacono, L.L.: On technical security issues in cloud computing. In: IEEE International Conference on Cloud Computing, CLOUD 2009, Bangalore, India, 21–25 September 2009, pp. 109–116 (2009)
19. Khuller, S., Kim, Y.A., Wan, Y.J.: Algorithms for data migration with cloning. In: Proceedings of the Twenty-Second ACM SIGACT-SIGMOD-SIGART Symposium on Principles of Database Systems, San Diego, CA, USA, 9–12 June 2003, pp. 27–36 (2003)
20. Martello, S., Toth, P.: Lower bounds and reduction procedures for the bin packing problem. Discret. Appl. Math. **28**(1), 59–70 (1990)
21. McBrien, P., Poulovassilis, A.: Automatic migration and wrapping of database applications - a schema transformation approach. In: Proceedings of Conceptual Modeling - ER 1999, 18th International Conference on Conceptual Modeling, Paris, France, 15–18 November 1999, pp. 96–113 (1999)
22. Meier, A.: Providing database migration tools - a practicioner's approach. In: VLDB 1995, Proceedings of 21th International Conference on Very Large Data Bases, Zurich, Switzerland, 11–15 September 1995, pp. 635–641 (1995)
23. Myllymaki, J.: Effective web data extraction with standard XML technologies. In: Proceedings of the Tenth International World Wide Web Conference, WWW 10, Hong Kong, China, 1–5 May 2001, pp. 689–696 (2001)
24. Narayanan, D., Thereska, E., Donnelly, A., Elnikety, S., Rowstron, A.I.T.: Migrating server storage to SSDs: analysis of tradeoffs. In: Proceedings of the 2009 EuroSys Conference, Nuremberg, Germany, 1–3 April 2009, pp. 145–158 (2009)
25. Otto, A., Otto, C., Scholl, A.: Systematic data generation and test design for solution algorithms on the example of salbpgen for assembly line balancing. Eur. J. Oper. Res. **228**(1), 33–45 (2013)
26. Quiroz-Castellanos, M., Cruz Reyes, L., Torres-Jiménez, J., Santillán, C.G., Fraire Huacuja, H.J., Alvim, A.C.F.: A grouping genetic algorithm with controlled gene transmission for the bin packing problem. Comput. OR **55**, 52–64 (2015)
27. Scholl, A., Klein, R., Jürgens, C.: Bison: a fast hybrid procedure for exactly solving the one-dimensional bin packing problem. Comput. OR **24**(7), 627–645 (1997)
28. Seo, B., Zimmermann, R.: Efficient disk replacement and data migration algorithms for large disk subsystems. TOS **1**(3), 316–345 (2005)

29. Subramani, K., Caskurlu, B., Velasquez, A.: Minimization of testing costs in capacity-constrained database migration. In: Algorithmic Aspects of Cloud Computing - 4th International Symposium, ALGOCLOUD 2018, Helsinki, Finland, 20–21 August 2018. Revised Selected Papers, pp. 1–12 (2018)
30. Wang, J., Lochovsky, F.H.: Data extraction and label assignment for web databases. In: Proceedings of the Twelfth International World Wide Web Conference, WWW 2003, Budapest, Hungary, 20–24 May 2003, pp. 187–196 (2003)

Scalable and Hierarchical Distributed Data Structures for Efficient Big Data Management

Spyros Sioutas[1], Gerasimos Vonitsanos[1], Nikolaos Zacharatos[1], and Christos Zaroliagis[1,2(✉)]

[1] Department of Computer Engineering and Informatics, University of Patras, 26504 Patras, Greece
{sioutas,mvonitsanos,zacharato,zaro}@ceid.upatras.gr
[2] Computer Technology Institute and Press "Diophantus", Patras University Campus, 26504 Patras, Greece

Abstract. In this work, we survey state of the art hierarchical distributed data structures for the efficient handling of big data, in scenarios where the dominant operation is range queries which have to be answered in real-time. Our main focus is on structures that exhibit stable scalability.

1 Introduction

A great challenge faced by most organizations nowadays concerns their data management. Due to the data endlessly flowing in from sources such as social media activities, Internet of Things (IoT) [6] devices, online streaming services, location based web information, mobile phone usage and consumer preferences expressed on the web, a data-driven revolution is taking place. Analyzing all that information fast can lead to:

- Better decision making based on data-driven insights
- Increased productivity
- Reduced production cost
- Quick fraud detection
- Better customer service

In order to achieve efficient big data management, several infrastructures have been developed. The most popular ones are decentralized systems and MapReduce [5] models.

Decentralized systems, although existed for many years, they have become very popular nowadays and are promoted as the future of Internet networking. They are widely used for sharing resources and store very large data sets, using systems of small computers instead of large costly servers. Typical examples include cloud computing environments, peer-to-peer (P2P) systems and the Internet.

I. Brandic et al. (Eds.): ALGOCLOUD 2019, LNCS 12041, pp. 122–160, 2020.
https://doi.org/10.1007/978-3-030-58628-7_8

In decentralized systems, data are stored at the network nodes and the most crucial operations are data search and data updates. A decentralized network is represented by a graph, a logical *overlay network*, where its nodes correspond to the network nodes, while its arcs may not correspond to existing communication links, but to communication paths. The complexity (cost) of an operation is measured in terms of the number of messages issued during its execution (internal computations at nodes are considered insignificant). A typical assumption is that messages between nodes are of constant size, they are sent through the communication links, and that communication is asynchronous. Moreover, there is an upper bound on the time needed for a node to send a message and receive an acknowledgement. This facilitates the identification of communication problems (e.g., when communication links or nodes are down).

With respect to its *structure*, the overlay supports the operations *Join* (of a new node v; v communicates with an existing node u in order to be inserted into the overlay) and *Departure* (of an existing node u; u leaves the overlay announcing its intent to other nodes of the overlay). Moreover, the overlay implements an *indexing scheme* for the stored data, supporting the operations *Insert* (a new element), *Delete* (an existing element), *Search* (for an element), and *Range Query* (for elements in a specific range). Throughout this paper, we shall denote by N the number of network nodes and by n the size of data ($N \ll n$).

In terms of efficiency, an overlay network should address the following issues:

- Fast queries and updates: updates and queries must be executed in a minimal number of communication rounds, using a minimal number of messages.
- Ordered data: keeping the data in order facilitates the implementation of various enumeration queries when compared to a simple dictionary that can only answer membership queries.
- Size of nodes: the size of a node is the routing information (links and related data) maintained by this node and it is not related to the number of data elements stored in it. Keeping the size of a node small allows for more efficient update operations, but in general reduces the efficiency of access operations while aggravating fault tolerance.
- Fault tolerance: the structure should be able to discover and heal failures at nodes or links.
- Load balancing: it refers to the distribution of data elements on the nodes. The goal of load balancing is to distribute equally the n elements stored in the N nodes of the network (typically $N \ll n$). That is, if there are N nodes and n data elements, ideally each node should carry approximately k elements, where $\lfloor n/N \rfloor \leq k \leq \lfloor n/N \rfloor + 1$.

MapReduce is a programming model and an associated implementation for processing and generating big data sets with a decentralized algorithm on a cluster (collection of compute servers or nodes), with a designated node as master and the other nodes designated as workers. A MapReduce task consists usually of the following five-step computation.

1. Partition: input is being split and assigned to each worker.
2. Map: each worker node applies the map function to its local data, and writes the output to a temporary storage.
3. Shuffle: worker nodes redistribute data based on the output keys (produced by the map function), such that all data belonging to one key is located on the same worker node.
4. Reduce: worker nodes now process each group of output data, per key, in parallel.
5. Join Results: workers combine their local output data to create the final output result.

The reason why both decentralized architecture networks and MapReduce models became so popular is that in order to increase the computing power of the network/cluster, you can simply add more nodes, so that tasks are divided to more nodes and therefore executed faster, compared with the client-server model, where a brand new server machine is required.

Range query processing in decentralized network environments is a notoriously difficult problem to solve both efficiently and scalably. In cloud infrastructures, a most significant and apparent requirement is the monitoring of thousands of computer nodes, which often requires support for range queries: consider range queries issued in order to identify under-utilized nodes so as to assign them more tasks, or to identify overloaded nodes so as to avoid bottlenecks in the cloud.

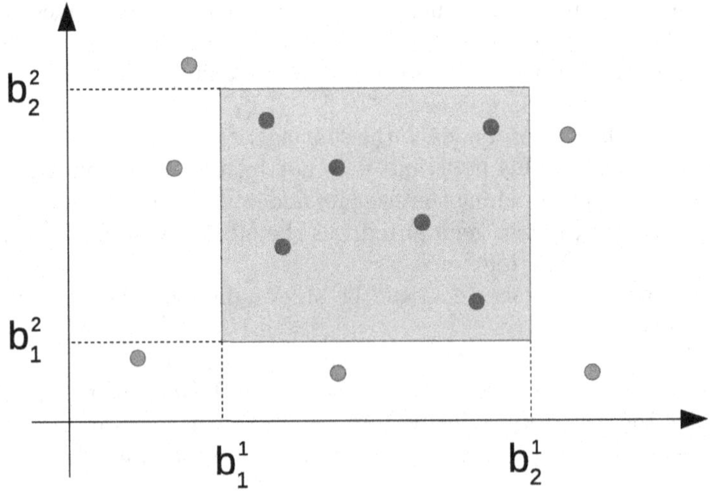

Fig. 1. Two dimensional range query (Color figure online)

The most fundamental, one-dimensional query (also known as the *interval query*) involves retrieving all records x where their value is between an upper bound b_1 and a lower bound b_2, that is, $b_1 \leq value(x) \leq b_2$. Evidently, generalizations to higher dimensions are derived easily. A multi-dimensional query involves retrieving all records $x = (x_1, \ldots, x_d)$ for which $b_1^i \leq value(x_i) \leq b_2^i$, $\forall$ $1 \leq i \leq d$, where d denotes the number of dimensions, b_1^i and b_2^i denote the lower and upper bounds on each dimension of the query respectively, and $value(x_i)$ denotes the value of the elements in the i-th dimension. Each query forms a hyper-rectangle of d dimensions which contains all the elements that satisfy it. For instance (cf. Fig. 1), the two-dimensional range query forms a rectangle on the plane. Red points represent those elements that satisfy the query.

The two dimensional query is very popular because it can answer geographical as well as trajectory queries. Multi-dimensional queries are typically used when browsing online for products, where every filter that you apply is one more dimension on the range query. Many applications require the management and the analysis of massive multi-dimensional datasets.

Overlay structures for decentralized systems can be divided in two big categories: hash-based structures and hierarchical-based structures. Both have their pros and cons, therefore choosing one highly depends on the needs of the users and the applications considered. Hash-based structures (e.g., CAN [15], Chord [19]) use probabilistic methods to distribute the workload among nodes equally, have good exact match query times, but slow range query times [22] since hashing destroys the ordering. On the other hand, hierarchical-based structures support range queries more naturally and efficiently as well as a wider range of operations, since they maintain the ordering of data, but lack the simplicity of hash-based systems.

Due to the importance of the range query problem, we focus in this work on hierarchical overlay structures that support directly range and more complex queries. The main goal of this work is to *present and review* state-of-the-art structures for efficient big data management that exhibit stable scalability.

Over the last years, many data structures have been implemented to address the range query problem on decentralized systems as well as to address the aforementioned efficiency issues of overlay structures. In this framework, we review four important hierarchical structures with their variations, and a ring based one. In particular, we review the following structures.

1. Hierarchical Structures
   (a) BATON [9] and BATON* [8]
   (b) D^2-Tree [3] and D^3-Tree [16]
   (c) ART [18] and ART^+ [17]
   (d) SPIS (SPark-based Interpolation Search Tree) [14]
2. Ring-based structures
   (a) P-Ring [4]

The rest of the paper is organized as follows. In Sect. 2 we survey the most popular hierarchical data structures, while in Sect. 3 we survey the ring-based structures. In Sect. 4 we provide a comparison of all structures. We conclude in Sect. 5.

2 Hierarchical Tree-Based Structures

In this section, we present the hierarchical tree-based structures BATON [9], BATON* [8], D^2-Tree [3], D^3-Tree [16], ART [18], ART^+ [17], and SPIS [14].

2.1 BATON

2.1.1 Structure

The Balance Tree Structure for P2P Networks (BATON) [9] is the first overlay network based on a balanced tree structure that can support both exact match and range queries. It is based on a binary balanced tree structure in which each node of the tree is maintained by a node. Each node in the network (cf. Fig. 2) stores a link to its parent, a link to its left child, a link to its right child, a link to its left adjacent node, a link to its right adjacent node, a left routing table to selected nodes on its left hand side at the same level, and a right routing table to selected nodes on its right hand side at the same level. While the tree structure is binary, it has scalability and robustness similar to that of the B-tree.

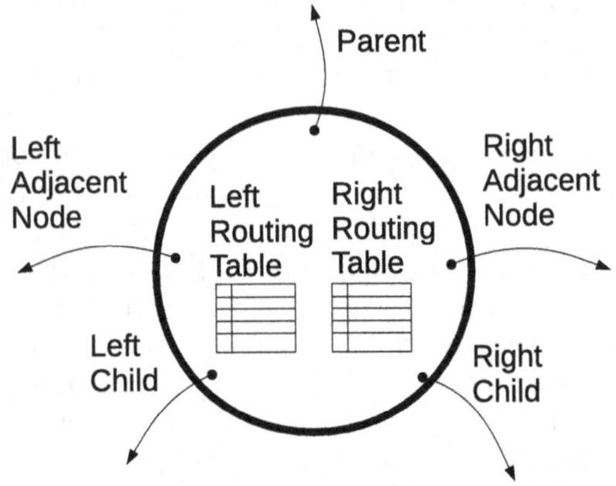

Fig. 2. A node of the BATON structure

Each node of the BATON structure is associated with a *level* and a *number*. The level of the root node is 0, its immediate children are at level 1 and so on. The level of any node is one greater than the level of its parent. Hence the maximum level number in the tree is one less than the height of the tree (which can not be greater than $1.44 \log N$ [11]).

At level L there are at most 2^L nodes in a binary tree. The nodes are numbered from 1 to 2^L (from left to right) within each level, regardless of whether there is a node currently instantiated at that position. The pair of level and number precisely determine the location of a node in the binary tree.

Every physical compute node has an IP address or some other network ID, which can be used to locate the node and communicate with it. Thus every node has a logical ID, which consists of number and level, and a physical ID which consists of its IP address.

The links that each node maintains are the physical IDs of each node. Links to selected neighbors are maintained by means of two special sideway routing tables: a *left routing table* and a *right routing table*. Each of these routing tables contains links to nodes at the same level with numbers that are less (respectively greater) than the number of the source node by a power of 2. The j-th element in the left (right) routing table at node numbered m contains a link to the node at number $m - 2^{j-1}$ (respectively $m + 2^{j-1}$) at the same level in the tree. If there is no such node, an entry is still made in the routing table, but marked as null. A routing table is considered full if all valid links are not null.

Adjacency links are based on an in-order traversal of the tree. Given a node x, the node immediately prior to it in the traversal is *left adjacent* to it, and the node immediately after x is *right adjacent* to it. Note that adjacent nodes may be at different levels of the tree.

2.1.2 Node Join/Departure

A new node that wants to join the network, must know at least one node inside the network. The former sends to the latter a JOIN request which is being carried out in two phases. The first phase is to determine where the new node should join. The second phase is to insert the new node at a specific place and update all the necessary links of the network. The complexity of this action is $\log N$ steps for finding a place for the joining node and $\mathcal{O}(\log N)$ cost for updating the routing tables (which is more efficient than other P2P systems, which usually require $\mathcal{O}(\log^2 N)$ for updating the routing tables).

Only leaf nodes can voluntarily leave the network, and only if their departure will not affect the tree balance. In any other case, any node that wishes to leave the network must find a replacement for itself, which can only be a leaf whose absence does not affect the tree balance. If the leaf node can leave without disrupting the tree balance, it sends a *LEAVE* message to is neighbor nodes, so they can update their routing tables. If a leaf node (that can not leave because it will disrupt the tree balance) or a inner node wishes to leave, then it sends a *FIND REPLACEMENT* message to the network starting from the same level and moving down in order to find a leaf node that will take their place. This process takes at most as many steps as the height of the tree which is $\mathcal{O}(\log N)$. The BATON needs $\log N$ steps to find a replacement node and $\mathcal{O}(\log N)$ cost for updating the routing tables.

2.1.3 Fault Tolerance

In case of a node failure, the node's IP will become unreachable. The first node to discover an unreachable IP must report it to its father which takes care to manage the node failure and update the routing tables.

It has already been described how a node failure is handled. Fault tolerance denotes the ability of the BATON structure to continue its operation, by routing the messages around the missing node. There are two axes in which messages can travel in BATON, vertical and horizontal. The horizontal axis uses the left and right routing tables links of the nodes, while the vertical axis uses the parent/children and adjacency links. The horizontal axis is naturally fault tolerant, since there is a logarithmic expansion of links and therefore a larger number of paths. The vertical axis is rendered fault tolerant because it can create paths that include different levels of the tree. These additional links that BATON stores suffice to provide efficient recovery even with a large number of node failures.

2.1.4 Load Balancing

The BATON is also equipped with a load balancing mechanism. Its goal is to adjust the range of values in the nodes in order to achieve an equal computational load across the network. This is accomplished through data migrations between adjacent nodes (for internal and leaf nodes), and node re-position in the tree (only for leaf nodes).

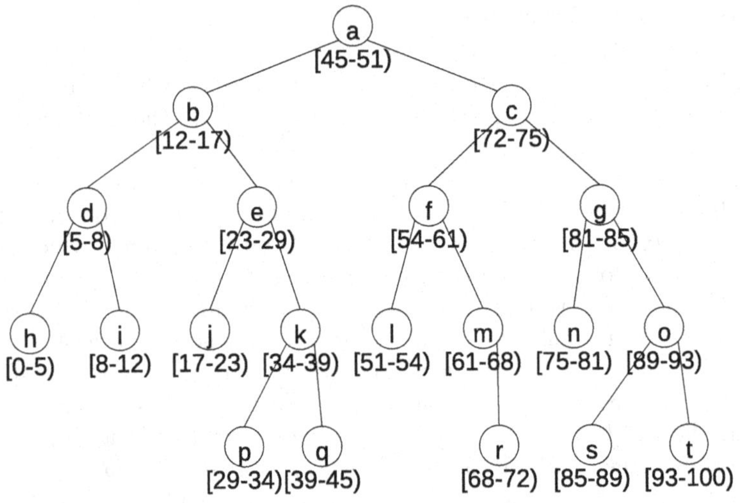

Fig. 3. Range of values for each node of BATON

2.1.5 Queries

In order to answer exact and range queries, a range (or interval) of values is assigned to each node (both leaf and internal). The range of values managed by a node is required to be to the right of the range managed by its left subtree and less than the range managed by its right subtree. Figure 3 shows an instance of BATON for range values $0 - 100$. It is similar to the B^{+}-tree indexing, but internal nodes also manage a range of data values directly. The queries do not start from the root, but from a random node of the structure.

The search operation in BATON first checks the horizontal axis (using right and left routing tables' links) then the vertical axis (using parent/children & adjacency links) to locate the correct node. A search operation for key k issued at node x works as follows. First, node x checks its own range. If k is within its range, the local index is searched and the search is stopped. Otherwise, it checks its right (left) routing table, if k is greater (less) than its own range to find the rightmost (leftmost) node y that its lower (upper) bound is less (greater) than k. Node x forwards the request to y. This step is performed until no node in the routing tables satisfies the condition. The last node that completed the process now forwards the request to its right (left) child if it exists or its right (left) adjacent node until the correct node is found. The complexity of this process is $\mathcal{O}(\log N)$.

Range query works in the same manner. It follows the same steps, until it finds an intersection of the node range value (interval) with the searched range. Once the intersection is found, partial answers for the range query have always been answered. It then continues to the left and/or to the right, following the adjacency links to cover the remainder search range. Its complexity is $\mathcal{O}(\log N)$ to find the intersection and $\mathcal{O}(1)$ to cover each of the remainder nodes. An answer to a range query that its range is spread across M nodes, requires $\mathcal{O}(\log N + M)$ steps.

2.1.6 Experimental Evaluation

In [9], an experimental evaluation was carried out in a network containing 1000 to 10000 nodes. For a network of size N, $1000 \cdot N$ values were inserted in batches in the domain of $[1, 100000000)$. For each test, 1000 exact queries and 1000 range queries are executed and the average cost is taken. For comparison purposes, CHORD [19] and a Multiway-tree proposed in [12] (which is a simplified version of BATON) were used.

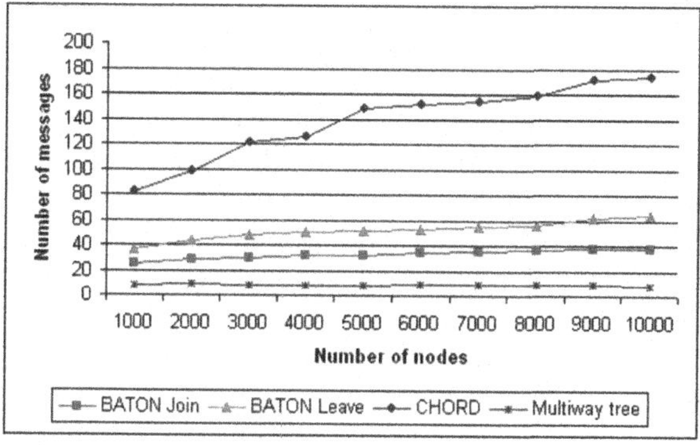

Fig. 4. Updating routing tables in BATON, CHORD and Multiway trees

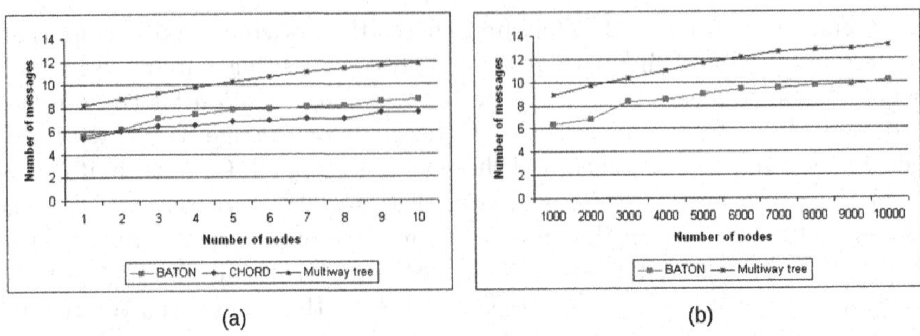

Fig. 5. BATON, CHORD and multiway trees: (a) exact match query; (b) range query

Figures 4 and 5 compare the number of nodes (x-axis) with the number of messages exchanged (y-axis) for routing table updating, exact match and range queries on BATON, CHORD and Multiway-tree structures. We observe that the exchange of messages in BATON remain almost stable, regardless of the number of the network size.

2.2 BATON*

2.2.1 Structure

BATON* [8] is very similar to the BATON structure, but with some core differences.

Each node in BATON* can have up to m children (also called *fanout*) instead of two as in the original structure. In addition to maintaining links to children, the parent node also has to keep track of the ranges of values managed by their children.

Neighbor routing tables at a node maintain links to selected neighbor nodes at the same level which have a distance equal to $d \cdot m^i$, where $d = 1, .., m - 1$ and $i \geq 0$, from the node itself. For example, in Fig. 6, the left routing table of node o maintains links to n, m, l, k, g (shown as purple), which have a distance equal to $1 \cdot 4^0, 2 \cdot 4^0, 3 \cdot 4^0, 1 \cdot 4^1$ and $2 \cdot 4^1$, respectively. Similarly, the right routing table of o maintains links to nodes p, q, r, s. The maximum number of links in routing tables of a node at level L is bounded by $(m - 1) \cdot L$.

For a BATON* structure of fanout m, a range of values managed by a node is greater than the ranges of values managed by the first $\lfloor m/2 \rfloor$ children nodes while less than ranges of values managed by the last $\lceil m/2 \rceil$ children nodes. For instance, in Fig. 6, the range of values managed by o is greater than those of y, x, n, but smaller than those of z, d, p, q.

The cost of search in BATON* becomes $\mathcal{O}(\log_m N)$, as expected. Moreover, the cost of updating routing tables becomes $\mathcal{O}(m \cdot \log_m N)$. It is clear that by increasing the fanout of a node to reduce the cost of the search, the size of the routing tables is increased, and hence the cost of table updating.

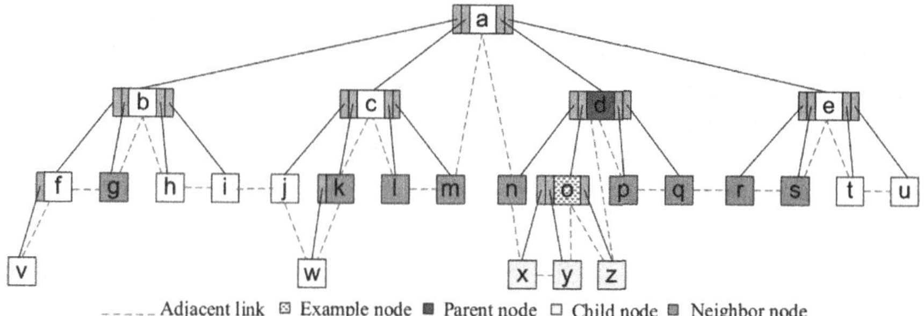

Fig. 6. BATON* structure

2.2.2 Node Join/Departure

A node of the BATON* can only accept a new joining node as a child if it has full neighbor routing tables but does not have m children. Otherwise, it has to forward the join request to either its parent, its lower level adjacent node, or a neighbor node that does not have enough children. In a similar manner, a node can only leave its current position if it does not cause the tree to become unbalanced. Otherwise, it has to find a replacement node by sending a leave request to its lower level adjacent node.

The cost of finding a place for a new joining node or finding a replacement node is $\mathcal{O}(\log_m N)$ since the height of the tree is $\mathcal{O}(\log_m N)$. The cost of updating the routing table is $\mathcal{O}(m \cdot \log_m N)$ for their neighbor routing tables since the maximum number of neighbor nodes a node can have is $\mathcal{O}(m \cdot \log_m N)$, and each of these has to add or remove an entry. Also a newly inserted node has to construct its own routing tables, with up to $\mathcal{O}(m \cdot \log_m N)$ entries, each of which can be obtained in constant time through its parent. In addition, there is a parent link and two adjacency links to create/delete. There can be no children links for a node being joined or departed. Summing these up, the total cost of node join or departure is $\mathcal{O}(m \cdot \log_m N)$.

2.2.3 Fault Tolerance

Fault tolerance in BATON* is very similar to that of its predecessor (BATON). Having even more links on the vertical axis, routing around missing nodes becomes much easier and cheaper, thus making BATON* highly fault tolerant.

2.2.4 Load Balancing

Load balancing in BATON* has two forms. Exchanging data with adjacent nodes, or remove underloaded nodes and place them in overloaded regions of the tree. The former is the easiest and cheapest form of load balancing, however it will not suffice when there are global imbalances. In occasions like these, the latter form of load balancing is used.

Since BATON* employs the tree structure, internal nodes cannot be easily removed, and hence the latter form of load balancing is only possible for leaf nodes. In general, if a node is overloaded, it first tries to do load balancing with its adjacent nodes. If there is no lightly loaded adjacent nodes, it then tries to find a lightly loaded leaf node to do load balancing. Once such a node is found, that node has to perform a forced leave from its current position and a forced join to the new position to share the workload of the overloaded node.

2.2.5 Queries

Searching in BATON* is very similar to BATON. The sole difference is that when the search request has to be forwarded to a suitable child node, there are $m/2$ options instead of two.

A node u receiving a search request checks to see if there is a neighbor node it knows about which is more appropriate to handle the search. If the searched value is greater than u's upper bound, while there is no right hand side neighbor node of u whose lower bound is less than the searched value, then u checks to find the most suitable child to forward the request. That is the rightmost child whose lower bound is less than the searched value. Similarly, if the searched value is less than the node's lower bound while there is no left hand side neighbor node whose upper bound is greater than the searched value, then the node has to try to find the leftmost child whose upper bound is greater than the searched value, to forward the search request.

The range query algorithm is modified in an analogous way.

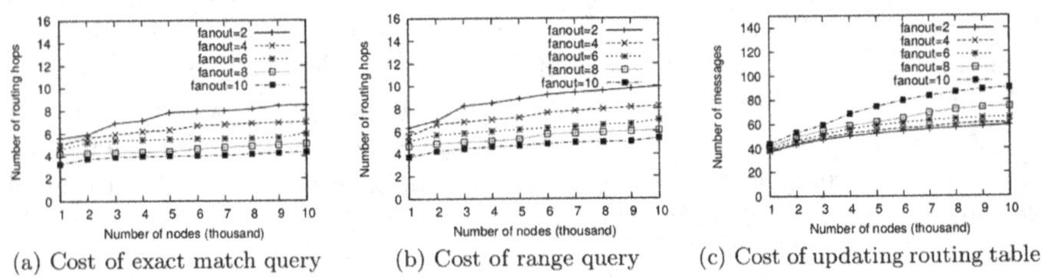

(a) Cost of exact match query (b) Cost of range query (c) Cost of updating routing table

Fig. 7. Effect of varying fanout values in BATON*

2.2.6 Experimental Evaluation

In [8], an experimental evaluation was carried out in networks consisted of 1000 to 10000 nodes and the fanout m used was from 2 to 10. For a network of size N, $1000 \cdot N$ values were inserted in batches in the domain of $[1, 1000000000)$. For each test, 1000 exact queries and 1000 range queries are executed and the average cost is taken.

Figure 7 shows the effect of the different fanouts on an exact match query, on a range query and on the cost of updating routing tables. It is clear that by increasing the fanout, exact match queries and range queries become faster at the expense of slower routing table updating. In order for BATON* to become really efficient, one has to tune the fanout to his own needs to get the best results.

Figure 8 shows how much node failure BATON and BATON* can withstand before they are unable to complete a lookup operation. It is obvious that the larger the fanout, the more fault tolerant the structure is.

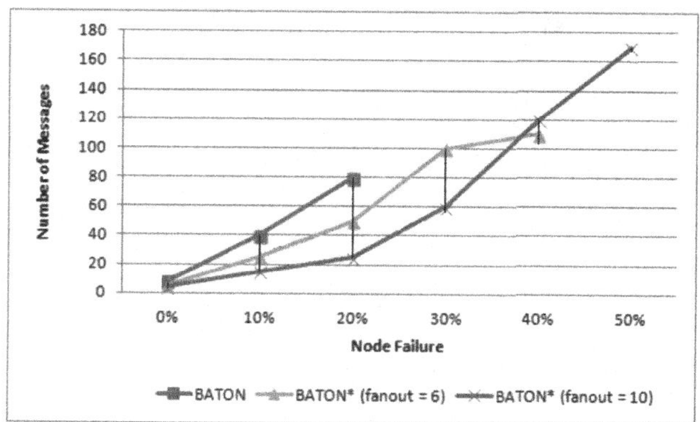

Fig. 8. Lookup operations with node failures in BATON and BATON*

2.3 D^2-Tree

2.3.1 Structure

The Deterministic Decentralized tree (D^2-Tree) [3] is a hierarchical overlay consisting of two levels as shown in Fig. 9. The upper level of the overlay is a perfect binary tree (PBT). The leaves of the tree are representatives of the buckets that constitute the lower level of the overlay. Each bucket is a set of $\mathcal{O}(\log N)$ nodes and it is structured as a doubly linked list. Each node of the bucket points to the node which is a leaf of the PBT and is called the *representative* of the bucket. Additionally it maintains its routing table w.r.t the nodes of all buckets.

Each node in the upper binary tree, maintains an additional set of links to other nodes apart from the standard links which form the tree. More specifically each node v in the tree maintains the following links (cf. Fig. 10):

- Links to its father (if there is one) and its children.
- Links to its adjacent nodes based on an in-order traversal of the tree.
- Links to its leftmost and rightmost leaves of its subtree.
- Links to nodes at the same level as v. These links facilitate an exponential search on the nodes of the same level. Assume that node v lies at level l. In a binary tree, the maximum number of nodes at level l is equal to 2^l. Node v maintains at most $2l$ links: l links to nodes to the right and l links to nodes to the left. The links are distributed in exponential steps, that is the first link

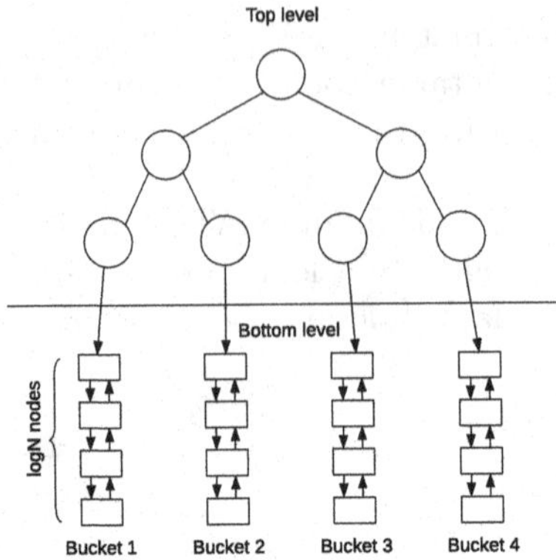

Fig. 9. The D^2-Tree structure

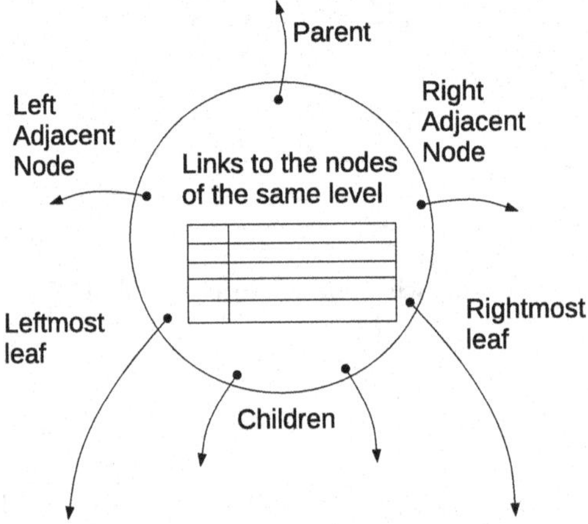

Fig. 10. A D^2-Tree node

points to a node (if there is one) 2^0 positions to the left (right), the second 2^1 positions to the left (right), and the i-th link 2^{i-1} positions to the left (right). These links constitute the routing table of v.

Regarding the complexity bounds, the D^2-Tree:

- uses $\mathcal{O}(\log N)$ space per node;
- achieves a deterministic $\mathcal{O}(\log N)$ query bound;
- achieves a deterministic (amortized) $\mathcal{O}(\log N)$ update bound for elements as well as for node joins and departures;
- exhibits a deterministic (amortized) $\mathcal{O}(\log N)$ bound for load-balancing;
- supports ordered data queries optimally, and tolerates node failures.

2.3.2 Node Join/Departure

When a node z makes a join request to v, then this node is forwarded to its left adjacent leaf u. Then, node z is added to the doubly linked list representing the bucket of u by manipulating a constant number of links. The routing table of z is updated.

When a node v leaves (departs from) the network, then it is replaced by its left adjacent node u (if there is no left adjacent node, then the right one is chosen), which in turn is replaced by its first node z in its bucket as shown in Fig. 11. Link and data information are copied from v to u and from u to z.

When a node v is discovered to be unreachable, its left adjacent node u is first located. This is accomplished by traversing the path to the rightmost leaf starting from the left child of v. Node u fills the gap of v and the first child z in the bucket of u fills the gap left by u. The data contents of u are not moved to another node, but the navigation data (routing tables and other links) are moved to node z that takes its place. Node u has its routing tables recomputed, its links to adjacent nodes set, and the links to the rightmost and leftmost leaves of its subtree are copied from its left and right child respectively.

The join and departure of nodes may cause the size of the buckets to be uneven, which in the long run renders the structure unbalanced. To control the size of the buckets, a weight-based approach is used.

2.3.3 Fault Tolerance

If a node v discovers that node u is unreachable, then it contacts a sibling of u through the routing tables of the siblings of v. This sibling of u is able to reconstruct all links of node u and a node departure of u is initiated, which resolves this failure.

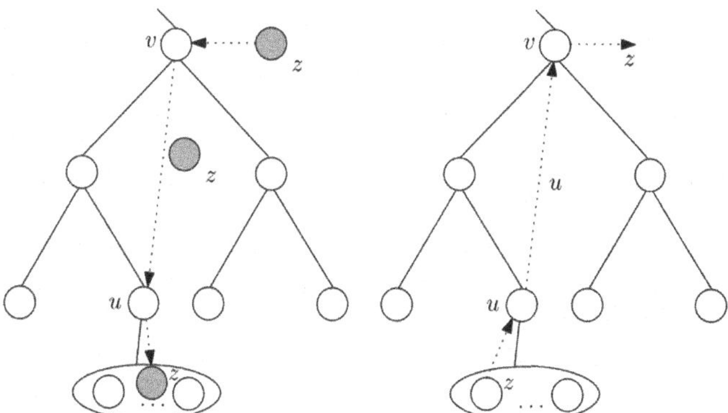

Fig. 11. D^2-tree: To the left (right), the join of z (departure of u) is depicted. The *dotted* labeled *arrows* represent the movement of the nodes denoted by the label.

Due to the way the search operation is implemented, near to root nodes are not crucial, and their failure will not cause more problems that the failure of any other node.

2.3.4 Load Balancing

In the D^2-Tree, the index from the overlay structure is separated using the load balancing mechanism. The number of elements per node is dynamic w.r.t. node joins and departures and it is controlled by the load-balancing mechanism. Moreover, the number of nodes of the perfect binary tree is not connected by any means to the number of elements stored in the structure. The overlay structure supports the operations of node join and node departure, while at the same time it tackles failures of nodes whenever these are discovered.

The load balancing technique of D^2-Tree distributes almost equally the elements among nodes by making use of weights. Weights are used to define a metric of load balance, which shows how uneven the load is between nodes. When the load is uneven, then a data migration process is initiated to equally distribute elements.

The load balancing technique can be described in two steps. The first step is a mechanism that allows efficient local updates of weight information when elements are added or removed at the leaves, which is necessary to avoid hotspots, and the next step is the load-balancing scheme in the tree overlay.

Assume that the overlay structure is denoted by T. When an element is added/removed to/from a leaf u in T, the weights on the path from u to the root must be updated. Assume that node v lies at height h and its children $v_1, v_2, ..., v_s$ are at height $h-1$. The variable *virtual weight* $b(v)$ of v is defined as the weight stored in node v. In particular, for a node v the algorithm maintains the *virtual weight invariant* that $b(v)$ is approximately equal to $e(v)+\sum_{i=1}^{s} b(v_i)$, where $e(v)$ denotes the number of elements residing in a node v.

Assume that an update takes place at leaf u. The path from u to the root is traversed until a node z is found, for the virtual weight invariant holds. Let v be the child of z, for which the virtual weight invariant does not hold. The weights are then recomputed in the path from u to v. Node's z weight information is updated by taking the sum of the weights written in its children plus the number of elements residing at z.

The load balancing mechanism redistributes the elements among nodes when the load between nodes is not distributed equally enough, but it does not tamper with the structure of T. For ease of exposition, assume that T is binary (the algorithm generalizes easily for trees whose nodes have a O(1) number of children).

Let node v at height h have two children p and q at height $h-1$. The density $d(v)$ of v denotes the mean number of elements per node in the subtree of v. Let $c(p,q) = \frac{d(p)}{d(q)}$ denotes the *criticality* of the two brother nodes p and q, representing their difference in densities. The algorithm maintains also the *criticality invariant*, namely that $\frac{1}{c} \leq c(p,q) \leq c$, for some $1 < c \leq 2$. That is, there are no large differences between densities. For instance, choosing $c = 2$ implies that the density of any node can be at most half of that of its brother.

Combining the two steps, each time an update takes place at leaf u, weights in the path from u to the root are updated until a node z is found for which the virtual weight invariant holds. Weights from u to z's child are recomputed. Then, the highest ancestor w of u is located where the criticality invariant is violated, and a node redistribution between w and his brother takes place.

2.3.5 Queries

The search for an element a in the overlay may be initiated from any node v at level l that has range of values $[x_v, x'_v]$. Let z be the node with range of values containing a. Assume without loss of generality that $x'_v < a$. Then, by using the routing tables of v, level ℓ is searched for a node u with right sibling w (if there is such a sibling) such that $x'_u < a$ and $x_w > a$ unless a is in the range of u and the search terminates. This step has $\mathcal{O}(\ell)$ cost, since it simulates a binary search.

If the search continues, then node z will either be an ancestor of u or w or in the subtree rooted at the right child $r(u)$ of u or in the subtree rooted at the left child $l(w)$ of w. First, the rightmost leaf r of u and the leftmost leaf l of w are located. If $x'_r \geq a$ then a is in the subtree of $r(u)$ and symmetrically if $x_l \leq a$ then a is in the subtree of $l(w)$. Note that at most one of these cases may hold for a. For instance, if $x'_r \geq a$ then an ordinary top down search from node $r(u)$ suffices to find z in $\mathcal{O}(\log N)$ steps (or in its bucket). Symmetrically, this is true also for $l(u)$. However, if both cases do not hold, then z is an ancestor of u or w. In this case a bottom-up search is initiated from u towards the root. This step can be carried out in $\mathcal{O}(\log N)$ steps as well.

A range query $[a, b]$ initiated at a node v, invokes a search operation for element a. Node u that contains a returns to v all elements in this range. If all elements of u are reported, then the range query is forwarded to the right adjacent node (based on the in-order traversal) and continues until an element larger than b is reached for the first time.

2.4 D^3-Tree

The Dynamic Deterministic Decentralized Tree (D^3-Tree) [16] is an extension of D^2-Tree that adopts all of its strengths and extends it in two respects: it introduces an enhanced fault tolerant mechanism and it is able to answer efficiently search queries when massive node failures occur. D^3-Tree achieves the same deterministic (worst-case or amortized) bounds as D^2-Tree for search, update and load-balancing operations, and answers search queries in $\mathcal{O}(\log N)$ amortized cost under massive node failures.

The D^3-Tree has a significantly small redistribution rate (structure redistributions after node joins or departures), while element load-balancing is rarely necessary. It also achieves a significant success rate in element queries, even under massive node failures.

2.4.1 Structure

Similar to the D^2-Tree, the D^3-Tree consists of two levels. The upper level is a Perfect Binary Tree (PBT) of height $\mathcal{O}(\log N)$. The leaves of this tree are representatives of the buckets that constitute the lower level of the D^3-Tree. Each bucket is a set of $\mathcal{O}(\log N)$ nodes which are structured as a doubly linked list as shown in Fig. 9. Each node v of the D^3-Tree maintains an additional set of links (described below) to other nodes apart from the standard links which form the tree. The first four sets are inherited from the D^2-Tree, while the fifth set is a new one that contributes in establishing a better fault-tolerance mechanism.

- Links to its father and its children.
- Links to its adjacent nodes based on an in-order traversal of the tree.
- Links to nodes at the same level as v. The links are distributed in exponential steps; the first link points to a node (if there is one) 2^0 positions to the left (right), the second 2^1 positions to the left (right), and the i-th link 2^{i-1} positions to the left (right). These links constitute the routing table of v and require $\mathcal{O}(\log N)$ space per node.
- Links to leftmost and rightmost leaf of its subtree. These links accelerate the search process and contribute to the structure's fault tolerance when a considerable number of nodes fail.
- For leaf nodes only, links to the buckets of the nodes in their routing tables. The first link points to a bucket 2^0 positions left (right), the second 2^1 positions to the left (right) and the i-th link 2^{i-1} positions to the left (right). These links require $\mathcal{O}(\log N)$ space per node and keep the structure fault tolerant, since each bucket has multiple links to the PBT.

2.4.2 Node Joins/Departures

When a node z makes a join request to v, v forwards the request to an adjacent leaf u. If u is a PBT node, the request is forwarded to the left adjacent node, w.r.t. the in-order traversal, which is definitely a leaf (unless v is a leaf itself). In case v is a bucket node, the request is forwarded to the bucket representative, which is a leaf. Then, node z is added to the doubly linked list of the bucket represented by u. In node joins, a simplification is made, that the new node is clear of elements and it is placed after the most loaded node of the bucket. Thus the load is shared and the new node stores half of the elements of the most loaded one.

When a node v leaves the network, it is replaced by an existing node, so as to preserve the in-order adjacency. All navigation data are copied from the departing node v to the replacement node, along with the elements of v. If v is an internal PBT node, then it is replaced by the first node z in its bucket. If v is a leaf, then it is directly replaced by z. Then v is free to depart.

2.4.3 Node Redistribution

Node redistribution guarantees that if there are z nodes in total in the y buckets of the subtree of v, then after the redistribution each bucket maintains either $\lfloor z/y \rfloor$ or $\lfloor z/y \rfloor + 1$ nodes. The redistribution in the subtree v works as follows.

Assume that the subtree v at height h has K buckets. A traversal of all the buckets is carried out to determine the exact value $|v|$, which denotes the number of nodes in the buckets of the subtree of v. The redistribution starts from the rightmost bucket b and it is performed in an in-order fashion so that elements in the nodes remain unaffected. Assume that b has q extra nodes that must be transferred to other buckets. Since bucket b maintains a link to the next bucket on the left, b', the extra nodes q are transferred there, while the internal nodes of PBT are also updated (because the in-order traversal must remain untouched). Finally, bucket b informs b' to take over, and the same procedure applies again with b' as the source bucket. The case where q nodes must be transferred to bucket b from b' is symmetric. In the case that b' does not have the q nodes that b needs, b' has to find them on the remaining buckets on the left, so it travels towards the leftmost bucket of the subtree until $q \leq \sum_{i=1}^{s} |b_i|$, where $|b_i|$ is the size of the i-th bucket on the left. Then, nodes of b_s move towards b' one bucket at a time, until it goes to b' and finally into b.

2.4.4 Load Balancing

The load balancing technique in a subtree v (with $|v|$ nodes in the subtree) is carried out as follows. A bottom-up calculation of the weights in all nodes of v is performed, to find $w(v)$ of v. The algorithm starts from the right most node w of the rightmost bucket b and it is performed in an in-order fashion. Assume that w has m extra elements which must be transferred to node w'.

- If w is a bucket node, w' is its left node, unless w is the first node of the bucket and then w' is the bucket representative.
- If w is a leaf node, then w' is the left in-order adjacent of w.
- If w is an internal binary node, then its left in-order adjacent is a leaf and w' is the last node of its bucket.

The first m elements removed from w and are added to end of the element queue of w', in order to preserve the indexing structure of the tree. The ranges of both w and w' nodes are updated respectively. The case where m elements must be transferred from w' to w is symmetric. When w' contains less elements than the m elements that w needs, it travels towards the leftmost node of the subtree following the in-order traversal, until $m \leq \sum_{i=1}^{s} e(u_i)$, where $e(u_i)$ is the number of elements of the i-th node on the left. Then the elements of u_s are transferred to u_{s-1}, from u_{s-1} to u_{s-2} and so on, until the m elements are moved from w' to w.

2.4.5 Fault Tolerance

When a node w discovers that v is unreachable, the network initiates a *node withdrawal* procedure by reconstructing the routing tables of v, in order for v to be removed smoothly, as if v was departing. If v belongs to a bucket, it is removed from the structure and the links of its adjacent nodes are updated. In case v is an internal binary node, its right adjacent node u is first located, in order to replace v.

If v is a leaf, then it should be replaced by the first node u in its bucket. In the D^2-Tree, if a leaf was found unreachable, contacting its bucket would be infeasible, since the only link between v and its bucket would have been lost. This weakness was eliminated in the D^3-Tree, by maintaining multiple links towards each bucket, distributed in exponential steps (in the same way as the horizontal adjacency links). This way, when w is unable to contact v, it contacts directly the first node of its bucket u and u replaces v. Regardless of node's v position in the structure, the elements stored in v are lost.

2.4.6 Queries

The search for an element a may be initiated from any node v at level l. If v is a bucket node, then if its range contains a the search terminates, otherwise the search is forwarded to the bucket representative, which is a binary node. If v is a PBT node, then let z be the node with range of values containing a, $a \in [x_z, x'_z]$ and assume without loss of generality that $x'_v < a$. The opposite case is completely symmetric. A horizontal binary search is performed at level l using the routing tables of v. More specifically, the rightmost links of the routing tables are followed until a node q is found, such that $x_q > a$, or until the rightmost node q_r of level l is reached. If the first case holds, a is between q and the last visited node in the left of q. The search continues to the left, decreasing the travelling step by one. The algorithm continues travelling left and right while gradually decreasing the travelling step until it finds a node u with sibling w (if there is such sibling) such that $x'_u < a$ and $x_w > a$. If the second case holds, then $x'_{q_r} < a$ and according to the in-order traversal, the search continues to the right subtree of q_r. If a is in the range of any of the visited nodes of level l, the search terminates.

Having located nodes u and w, the horizontal search is terminated and a vertical search is initiated. Node z will either be the common ancestor of u and w, or it will be in the right subtree rooted at u, or in the left subtree rooted at w. Node u contacts the rightmost leaf y of its subtree. If $x_y > a$ then an ordinary top down search from node u will suffice to find z. Otherwise node z is in the bucket of y, or in its right in-order adjacent node (this is also the common ancestor of u and w), or in the subtree of w.

Overall, the search for an element a is carried out in $\mathcal{O}(\log N)$ steps.

A range query $[a, b]$ initiated at a node v, invokes a search operation for element a. Node z that contains a returns to v all elements in its range. If all elements of u are reported, then the range query is forwarded to the right adjacent node (based on the in-order traversal) and continues until an element larger than b is reached for the first time.

2.4.7 Queries with Node Failures

In a network with node failures, an unsuccessful search for element a refers to the cases where either z (the node with range of values containing a, i.e., $a \in [x_z, x'_z]$) is unreachable, or there is a path to z but the search algorithm can not follow it to locate z due to failures of intermediate nodes. D^2-Tree provides a preliminary fault-tolerant mechanism that succeeds only in the case of a few node failures. That mechanism cannot deal with massive node failures (also known as churn) i.e., its search algorithm may fail to locate a. The difference in D^3-Tree is that during the horizontal search, if the most distant right adjacent of v located in position 2^j is unreachable, v keeps contacting its right adjacent nodes by checking positions $2^{j-1}, 2^{j-2}, \ldots$ (i.e., by decreasing repeatedly the exponent by 1), until it finds a node q which is reachable.

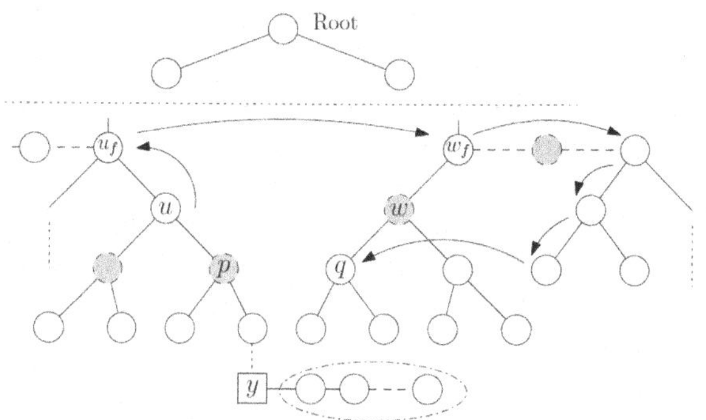

Fig. 12. Example of vertical search between u and unreachable w

In case $x'_q < a$ the search continues to the right using the most distant right adjacent of q. Otherwise, the search continues to the left and q contacts its most distant left adjacent p which is in the right of v. If p is unreachable, q does not decrease the exponent by 1, but contacts directly its nearest left adjacent (at position 2^0) and asks it to search to the left. This improvement reduces the number of messages that are meant to fail, because of the exponential positions of nodes in routing tables and the nature of binary horizontal search.

A vertical search to locate z is always initiated between two siblings u and w, which are either both active, or one of them is unreachable, as shown in Fig. 12 where the left sibling u is active and w, the right one, is unreachable. In both cases, the subtree of the active sibling is searched first, then the common ancestor is contacted and then, if the other sibling is unreachable, the active sibling tries to contact its corresponding child (right child for left sibling and left child for right sibling). When the child is found the search is forwarded to its subtree.

In general, when node u wants to contact the left (right) child of unreachable node w, the contact is accomplished through the routing table of its own left (right) child. If its child is unreachable (Fig. 12), then u contacts its father u_f and u_f contacts the father of w, w_f. Then w_f contacts its grandchild through its left and right adjacents and their grandchildren.

In the case where the initial node v is a bucket node, then if its range contains a the search terminates, otherwise the search is forwarded to the bucket representative. If the bucket representative has failed, the bucket contacts its other representatives right or left, until it finds a representative that is reachable. Then the procedure continues as described above for the case of a binary node.

2.4.8 Experimental Evaluation

In [16], an experimental evaluation was carried out in networks consisting from 1000 to 10000 nodes. For a size of network N, $1000 \times N$ elements were inserted. The number of passing messages between the nodes was used to measure the performance of the system.

For Node Join/Departures. $2 \times N$ nodes were updated. Figure 13 shows that the D^3-Tree update and redistribution mechanism achieves a better amortized redistribution cost, compared to those of BATON, BATON* and P-Ring.

Cost of Queries with/without Node Failures. To measure the network performance for the operation of single queries, experiments were conducted for each N (1000 to 10000), performing $2M$ (M is the number of binary nodes) searches. The search cost is shown in Fig. 14.

To measure the network performance for the operation of element search with node failures, experiments were conducted for different percentages of node failures: 10%, 20%, 30%, 40%, 50%, 75%. For each value of N considered (in the range from 1000 to 10000) and node failure percentage, $2M$ searches were performed. In order to get a better estimation of the search cost, a different set of nodes was forced to fail each time. Figure 15 depicts the increase in search cost when massive node failures take place in D^3-Tree, BATON, different fanouts of BATON* and P-Ring. The graph is irrelevant to N.

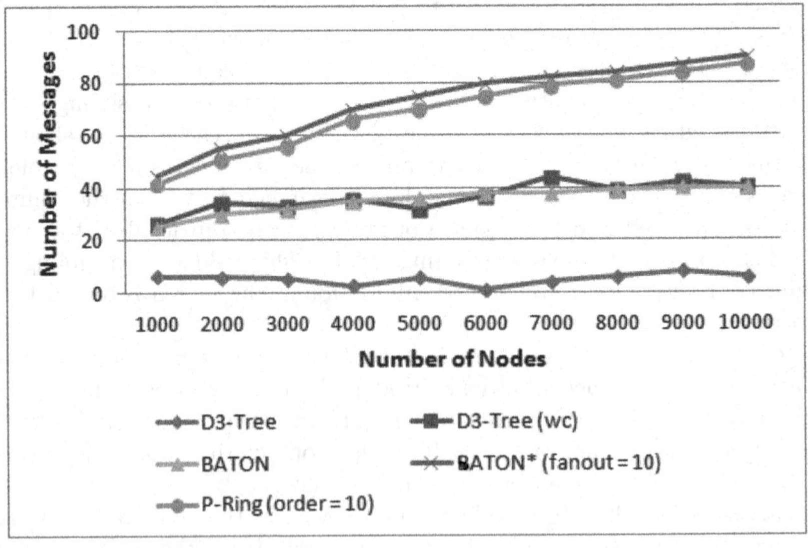

Fig. 13. Average messages for node updates

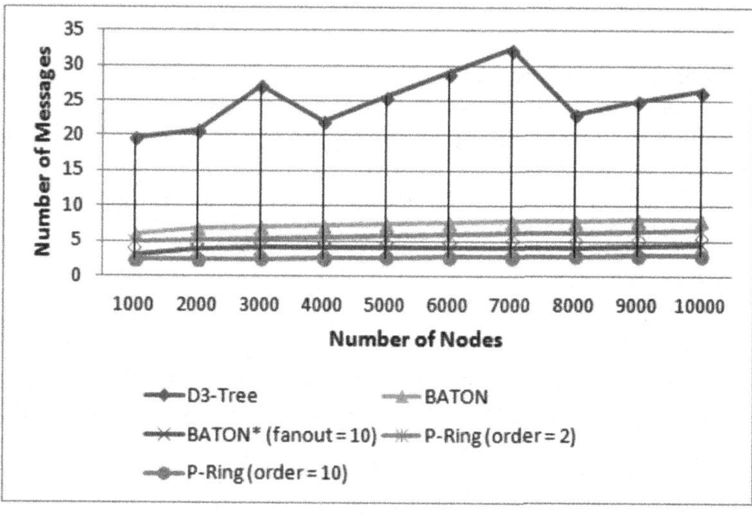

Fig. 14. Cost of queries without node failures

We observe that D^3-Tree can withstand up to 50% node failure while keeping the search cost low. P-Ring and BATON* (both of fanout/order 10) can withstand the same percentage of node failure, but the cost of search operation rises above that of the D^3-Tree after 30%. BATON can not handle the search operations after 20% of node failure, while BATON* (with fanout 6) can withstand up to 40%.

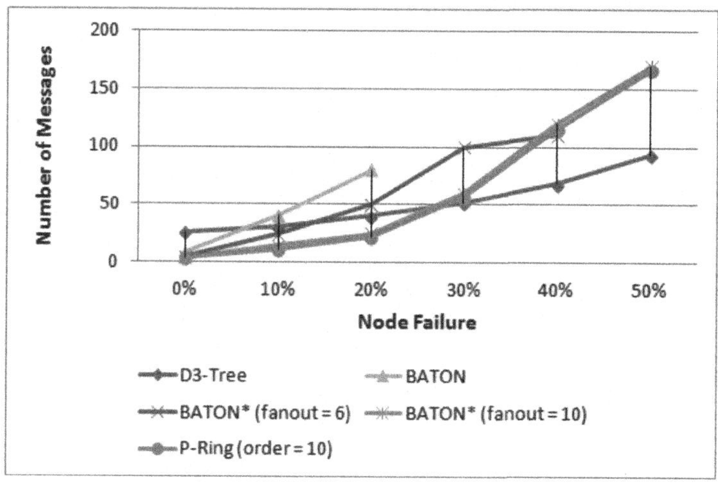

Fig. 15. Cost of queries under node failure

2.5 ART

The Autonomous Range Tree (ART) [18] is an exponential tree structure, which remains unchanged with high probability (w.h.p.), and organizes a number of fully dynamic buckets of nodes. The communication cost of query and update operations is $\mathcal{O}(\log_2 b \log N)$ hops, where $b = 2^{2^i}$, $i = 1, 2, 3...$ Moreover, ART is a fully dynamic and fault-tolerant structure, which supports the join/leave node operations in $\mathcal{O}(\log \log N)$ expected number of hops w.h.p.

2.5.1 Structure

One of the basic components of the ART structure is the Level Range Tree (LRT). LRT will be called upon to organize collections of nodes at each level of ART. LRT is built by grouping nodes having the same ancestor and organizing them in a tree structure recursively. The innermost level of nesting (recursion) will be characterized by having a tree in which no more than b nodes share the same direct ancestor, where b is a double-exponentially power of two. Thus, multiple independent trees are imposed on the collection of nodes. Figure 16 shows the LRT structure for $b = 2$.

The degree of the nodes at level $i > 0$ is $d(i) = t(i)$, where $t(i)$ indicates the number of nodes at level i. It holds that $d(0) = b$ and $t(0) = 1$. Let n be w-bit keys. Each node with label i (where $1 \leq i \leq N$) stores ordered keys that belong in the range $[(i-1)\ln n, i\ln n - 1]$, where $N = n/lnn$ is the number of nodes. Each node is also equipped with a table named Left Spine Index (LSI), which stores pointers to the nodes of the left-most spine. Furthermore, each node of the left-most spine is equipped with a table named Collection Index (CI), which stores pointers to the collections of nodes presented at the same level (see pointers directed to collections of last level). Nodes having the same father belong to the same collection.

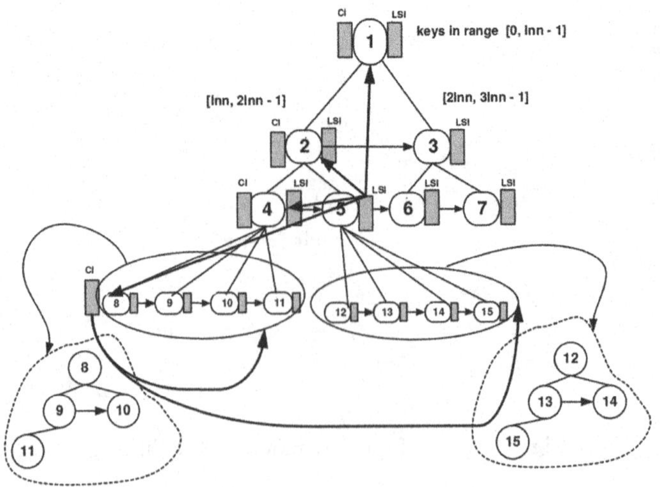

Fig. 16. The LRT structure for $b = 2$

ART stores cluster of nodes only, each of which is structured as an independent decentralized architecture (it can be BATON*, Chord, Skip-Graphs, etc). The backbone-structure of ART is exactly the same with LRT. Moreover instead of LSI, which reduces the robustness of the whole system, a Random Spine Index routing table is introduced, which stores pointers to randomly chosen cluster nodes.

2.5.2 Node Joins/Departures

The operation of join/leave of nodes inside a cluster-node is modelled as the combinatorial game of balls in bins presented in [10]. In this way, for a random sequence of join/leave node operations drawn from a distribution of density $\mu(\cdot)$, the expected load w.h.p. of each cluster-node never exceeds $\Theta(\log N)$ in size and never becomes zero. In skew sequences, though, the load of each cluster-node may become $\Theta(N)$ in the worst case.

When a node wants to join the network, it is assumed that this node is accompanied by a key, and that key designates the exact position in which the new node must be inserted. If an empty node u makes a join request at a particular node v (which is called *entrance node*) then there is no need to get to a different cluster node than the one in which u belongs. Similarly, the algorithm for the departure of a node u assumes that the departure can be made from any node in the ART structure. This may not be desirable, and in many applications it is assumed that the choice for departure of node u can be made only from this node.

2.5.3 Fault Tolerance

In the ART structure, the overlay of cluster nodes remains unchanged in the expected case w.h.p., so in each cluster_node the algorithms for node failure and restructuring are those inherited by the decentralized architecture used.

2.5.4 Queries

The search algorithm gets as input a node in which the query is initiated, and a key to search. The first step of the algorithm is to locate the levels of the ART where the desired cluster nodes are located. This is achieved by using the RSI index. The next step is to locate the correct cluster node in the right level. The first position of RSI (notated as RSI[1]) always points to the next cluster node at the same level. Following RSI[1], the correct cluster node can be found at the right level. The final step is to search inside the decentralized structure that each cluster node holds to locate the key.

The Range search algorithm gets as input a node in which the query is initiated and a range of keys $[k_l, k_r]$. It then calls the search algorithm on the same node with key k_l and by exploiting the order of the keys on each node it performs a right linear scan until it finds a key $K > k_r$.

2.5.5 Experimental Evaluation

In [18] an experimental evaluation was carried out, including a detailed performance comparison with BATON*. In particular, each cluster-node is implemented as a BATON*. The network was tested with different number of nodes ranging up to 500000. The data inserted was 2000 times the size of the network, with numbers in the universe [1, ..., 1000000000] inserted in batches, following beta, uniform and power law distributions. For each test, 1000 exact match queries and 1000 range queries were executed, and the average costs of operations are calculated.

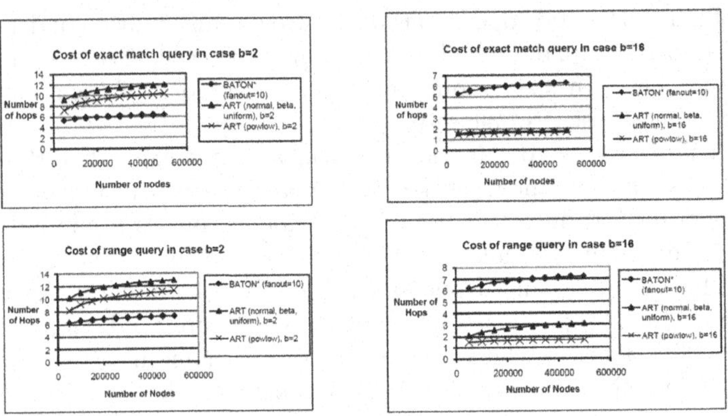

Fig. 17. Exact and range query times of BATON* and ART with $b = 2, 16$ for normal, beta, uniform and power-law input distributions

We observe in Fig. 17 that except for the case where $b = 2$ (right part of Fig. 17), the ART structure outperforms BATON* structure in both exact and range queries by a wide margin.

2.6 ART$^+$

ART$^+$ [17] is similar to its predecessor ART, regarding the structure's outer level. Their difference, which introduces performance enhancements, lies in the fact that each cluster-node of ART$^+$ is structured as a D^3-Tree.

2.6.1 Structure

The backbone structure of ART$^+$ (cf. Fig. 18) is similar to the Level Range Tree (LRT), in which some interventions have been made to improve its performance and increase the robustness of the whole system. ART$^+$ is built by grouping cluster-nodes having the same ancestor and organizing them in a tree structure recursively. A cluster-node is defined as a bucket of ordered nodes. The innermost level of nesting (recursion) will be characterized by having a tree in which

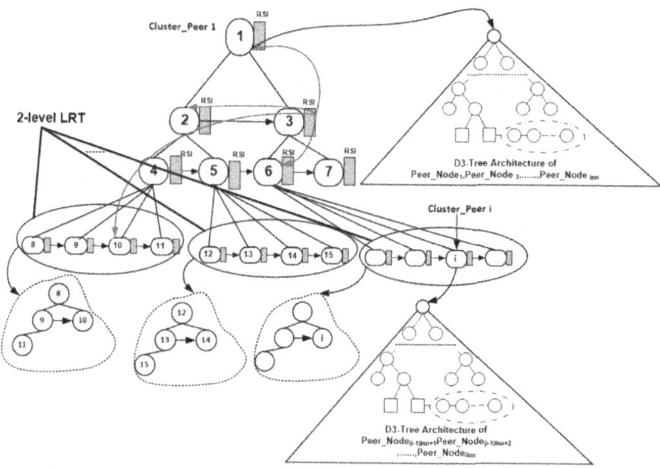

Fig. 18. ART$^+$ structure

no more than b cluster-nodes share the same direct ancestor (where $b = 2^{2^i}$, $i = 1, 2, 3..$). Thus, multiple independent trees are imposed on the collection of cluster-nodes. The height of ART$^+$ is $\mathcal{O}(\log \log_b N)$ in the worst case. The ART$^+$ structure remains unchanged w.h.p.

Similarly to ART, the degree of the cluster-nodes at level $i > 0$ is $d(i) = t(i)$, where $t(i)$ indicates the number of cluster-nodes at level i. It holds that $d(0) = b$ and $t(0) = 1$. At initialization step, the first node, the $(\ln n + 1)$-th node, the $(2 \cdot \ln n + 1)$-th node and so on are chosen as bucket representatives.

Let n be w-bit keys, N be the total number of nodes and N' be the total number of cluster-nodes. Each node with label i (where $1 \leq i' \leq N$) of a random cluster stores ordered keys that belong in the range $[(i' - 1) \ln^2 n, i' \ln^2 n - 1]$, where $N' = n/\ln n$. Each cluster-node with label i' (where $1 \leq i' \leq N'$) stores ordered nodes with sorted keys belonging in the range $[(i' - 1) \ln^2 n, i' \ln^2 n - 1]$, where $N' = n/\ln^2 n$ or $N' = N/\ln n$ is the number of cluster-nodes.

ART$^+$ stores cluster-nodes only, each of which is structured as an independent decentralized architecture, which changes dynamically after node join/leave and element insert/delete operations inside it.

In contrast to its predecessor, ART, whose inner level was structured as a BATON*, each cluster-node of ART$^+$ is structured as a D^3-Tree. Each cluster-node is equipped with a routing table named Random Spine Index (RSI), which stores pointers to cluster-nodes belonging to a random spine of the tree (instead of the LSI of LRT which stores pointers to the nodes of the left-most spine, decreasing this way the robustness of the structure). Moreover, instead of using fat Collection Index (CI) tables, which store pointers to the collections of nodes presented at the same level, the appropriate collection of cluster-nodes is accessed by using a 2-level LRT structure.

2.6.2 Node Joins/Departures

In ART$^+$, the overlay of cluster-nodes remains unaffected in the expected case w.h.p., when nodes join or leave the network.

A node u can make a join/leave request to a node v, which is located at cluster node W. Since the expected size of W is w.h.p. $O(\log^k N)$, for some $k = O(1)$, the node join/leave can be carried out in $\mathcal{O}(\log \log N)$ hops. The outer structure of ART$^+$ remains unchanged w.h.p. as mentioned before, but each D^3-Tree structure changes dynamically after node join/leave operations. According to D^3-Tree performance evaluation, the node join/leave can be carried out in $\mathcal{O}(\log \log N)$ hops.

Similarly to ART, the operation of join/leave of nodes inside a cluster-node is modelled as the combinatorial game of balls in bins presented in [10]. In this way, for a random sequence of join/leave node operations drawn from a distribution of density $\mu(\cdot)$, the expected load w.h.p. of each cluster-node never exceeds $\Theta(\log N)$ in size and never becomes zero. In skew sequences, though, the load of each cluster-node may become $\Theta(N)$ in worst case.

2.6.3 Fault Tolerance

In the ART$^+$ structure, similarly to ART, the overlay of cluster-nodes remains unchanged in the expected case w.h.p., so in each cluster-node the algorithms for node failure and restructuring are those of the decentralized architecture used. D^3-Tree is a highly fault-tolerant structure, since it supports procedures for node withdrawal and handles massive node failures efficiently.

2.6.4 Queries

Since the structure's maximum number of nesting levels is $\mathcal{O}(\log_b \log N)$ and at each nesting level i the standard LRT structure has to be applied in $N^{1/2^i}$ collections, the whole searching process requires $\mathcal{O}(\log_b^2 \log N)$ hops. Then, the target node has to be located by searching the respective decentralized structure. Since there is a polylogarithmic load in each cluster node, the total query complexity of $\mathcal{O}(\log_b^2 \log N)$ follows.

By exploiting the order of the keys on each node, it turns out that a range query requires $\mathcal{O}(\log_b^2 \log N + |A|)$ hops, where $|A|$ is the answer size.

2.6.5 Experimental Evaluation

In [17], the performance of ART$^+$ was evaluated by experiments that ran on different number of nodes N from 50000 to 500000. Each cluster node stores no more than $0.75 \log^2 N$ nodes in smooth distributions (as proved in [18]) and no more than $2.5 \log^2 N$ nodes in non-smooth distributions. Moreover, the elements inserted were $2000 \cdot N$ which are numbers from the universe [1, .., 1.000.000.000]. The number of passing messages was used to measure the performance.

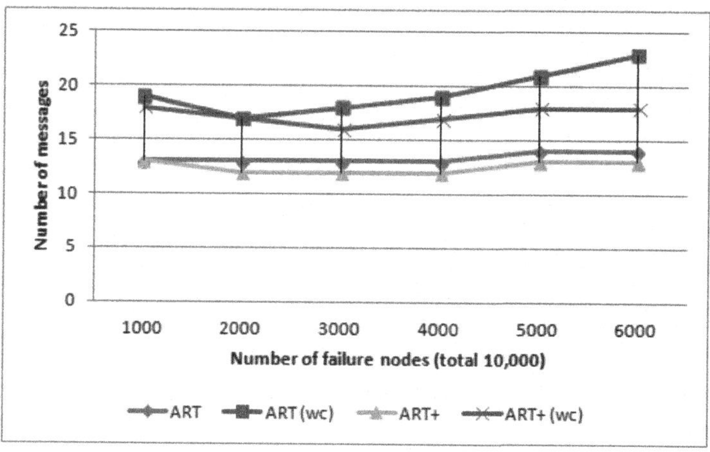

Fig. 19. Lookup Operations with Node Failures in ART and ART$^+$

Cost of Queries under massive node failures. In case of massive node failures, the search algorithm has to find alternative paths to overcome the unreachable nodes. Thus, an increase in node failures results in an increase in search costs. To evaluate the system in case of massive failures, the system was initiated with 10000 nodes and they were let to randomly fail without recovering. Since the backbone of ART$^+$ remains unaffected w.h.p., the search cost is restricted inside a cluster-node (D^3-Tree), meaning that parameter b does not affect the overall expected cost. Figure 19 illustrates the effect of massive failures of ART and ART$^+$.

Cost of Load-Balancing Operations. To evaluate the cost of load-balancing, the network was tested with a variety of distributions. For a network of N total nodes, $2N$ node updates were performed. Both ART and ART$^+$ remain unaffected w.h.p., when nodes join or leave the network, thus the load-balancing performance is restricted inside a cluster-node (BATON* for ART, and D^3-Tree for ART$^+$), meaning that parameter b does not affect the overall cost. The load-balancing cost is depicted in Fig. 20a. Both expected and worst case values are depicted in the same graph.

Experiments confirm that ART$^+$ has an $\mathcal{O}(\log\log N)$ load-balancing performance, instead of the ART performance of $\mathcal{O}(m \cdot \log_m \log N)$. Thus, even in the worst case scenario, the ART$^+$ outperforms ART, since D^3-Tree has a more efficient load-balancing mechanism than BATON*; cf. Fig. 20b.

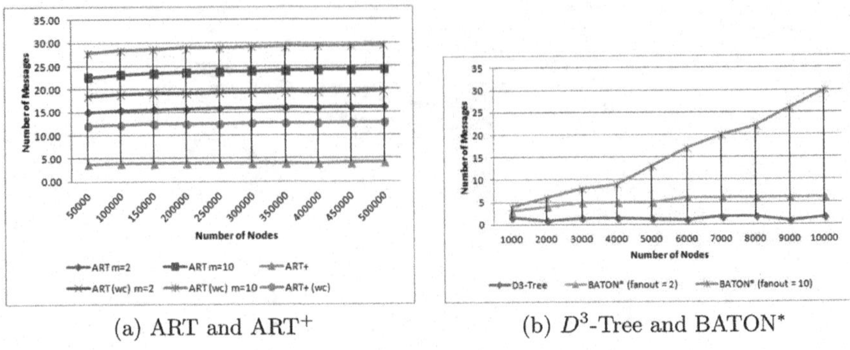

(a) ART and ART$^+$

(b) D^3-Tree and BATON*

Fig. 20. Cost of load-balancing operation.

2.7 SPark-based Interpolation Search Tree (SPIS)

Spark [21] is the successor of Hadoop [20], which is the open source implementation of the MapReduce model. In [14], the classic Interpolation Search Tree [13] was integrated into Spark's [21] distributed environment. Spark uses *Resilient Distributed Datasets* (RDDs) as its fundamental data organization scheme. An RDD is an immutable (i.e., read-only) distributed collection of objects. The datasets are divided into partitions, which are further computed on different nodes of the cluster. However, *Data Frames* (DFs) are also supported that provide more rich semantics and also provide additional optimizations for running SQL queries over distributed data.

The classic Interpolation Search Tree (IST) has the following properties:

- It requires space $\mathcal{O}(n)$ for a data set of cardinality n.
- The amortized insertion and deletion cost is $\mathcal{O}(\log\log n)$
- The expected search time on data sets with smooth probability density is $\mathcal{O}(\log\log n)$
- The worst case search time is $\mathcal{O}((\log n)^2)$.
- The data structure supports sequential access in linear time and operations Predecessor, Successor, and Min in time $\mathcal{O}(1)$. In particular, it can be used as a priority queue.

In [14], the Spark's RDD API was used since the focus was in providing faster search capabilities at the partition level. Since RDDs are immutable, inserting (deleting) elements in (from) the tree (even though the tree supports such actions) were not a concern, and the focus was on search and range queries. Range search queries turned out to be faster than Spark's built-in functions. Figure 21 shows how the sorting and partitioning is done in Spark's distributed environment.

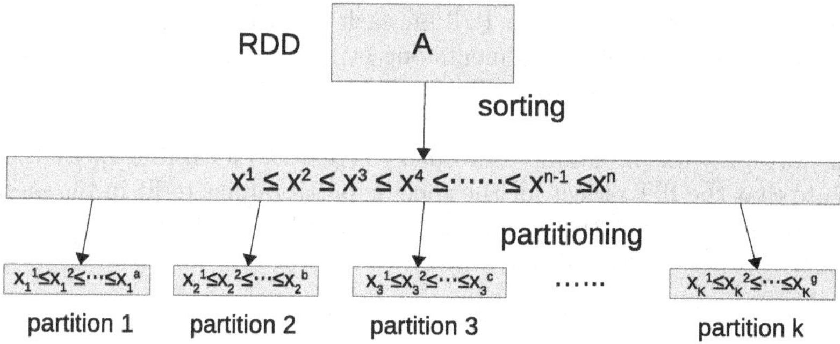

Fig. 21. Spark's sorting procedure

2.7.1 Structure

The Interpolation Search Tree (IST) is a multi-way tree, where the degree of a node depends on the cardinality of the set stored below it. It requires $\mathcal{O}(n)$ space for an element set of cardinality n. More precisely, the degree of the root is $\Theta(n^a)$, for some constant $0 < a < 1$. The root splits the set into $\Theta(n^{1-a})$ subsets. The children of the root have degree equal to $\Theta(n^{(1-a)a})$. An illustration of an IST can be found in Fig. 22.

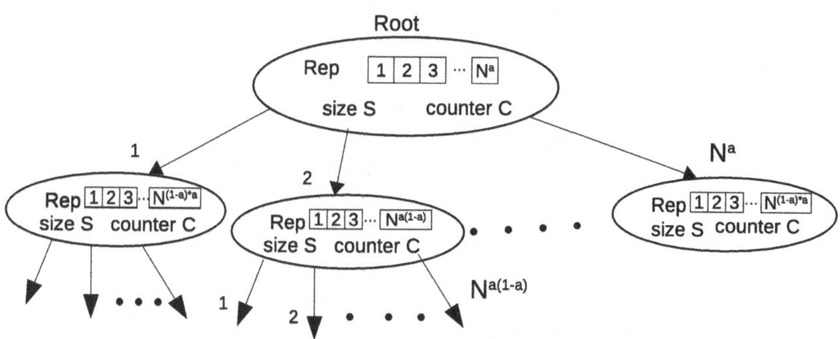

Fig. 22. Interpolation Search Tree

Each node u in the IST is associated with (i) a REP_u array, which contains a sample of the subset of elements that is stored below u; (ii) a variable S_u, which denotes the size of the subset; and (iii) a variable C_u, which counts how many insertions/deletions have been performed since the last rebuilding (of the IST) that involved u; cf. Fig. 22.

The idea is that on every partition of the RDD an IST is created that manages the elements of that same partition. The Spark's sorting function was used to sort and partition the elements to the worker nodes. After sorting is completed, each partition holds roughly the same number of sorted elements.

The next step is to create an IST on each partition. Instead of using the insertion algorithm to add the elements one by one in the tree, a bulk-insertion is used to insert all sorted elements in the tree, and globally rebuild it from the root.

This way, only one rebuilding is needed to create an ideal IST for each partition. Note that the IST object for the specific partition has to fit in the memory of each worker. However, this issue can be resolved since the input dataset can be split in a larger number of partitions if necessary.

2.7.2 Fault Tolerance

Spark operates on top of fault tolerant systems, like Hadoop Distributed File System (HDFS), making all the RDDs fault tolerant. Since RDDs are immutable, Spark keeps the lineage of the deterministic operations that were used on the input dataset to create it. If due to a worker node failure any partition is lost, then that partition can be recomputed to another worker node from the original dataset using the lineage of operations.

2.7.3 Queries

The classic search algorithm performs interpolation search in the REP array of every node of the tree, starting from the root, in order to locate the subset in which the search should be continued. The expected search time is $\mathcal{O}(\log\log(n))$.

In Spark, the search algorithm works as follows. Each partition is queried with they key that has to be searched. If the key is inside the partition's interval, the search algorithm is performed on the IST of the same partition returning true or false depending on whether the key exists in the structure or not. If the key is not inside the partition's interval, nothing is returned. Thus only one partition executes the search algorithm for each key that is queried.

The algorithm for a range query in the interval $[min, max]$ works in a similar manner. Each partition is queried with min and max, and all elements with keys between those values have to be returned.

Let x_i^F denote the first item of the i-th partition and let x_i^L denote the last item of the i-th partition. The following algorithm is concurrently executed in each partition i.

- If min is inside the i-th partition's interval $[x_i^F, x_i^L]$, then the search algorithm is performed and the corresponding element B is found.
    - If max is inside the partition's interval, then the search algorithm is performed again and the corresponding element E is found. All elements in-between B and E are returned.
    - Else if max isn't inside the partition's interval, then E is assigned to the last element of the partition (x_i^L). All elements in-between B and E are returned.
- Else if max is inside the i-th partition's interval, then the search algorithm is performed and the corresponding element E is found. B is assigned to the first element of the partition (x_i^F). All elements in-between B and E are returned.

- Else if $min < x_i^F$ and $max > x_i^L$, the whole partition is returned.
- Else if none of the above happens, zero is returned.

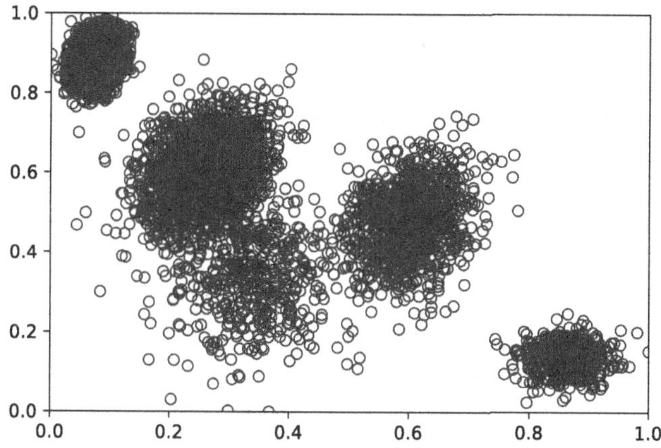

Fig. 23. Dataset distribution for SPIS

2.7.4 Experimental Evaluation

In [14], an experimental evaluation was conducted on a cluster with 32 physical computing machines running Hadoop 2.7 and Spark 2.1.0. Synthetic datasets were used for the experimentation with different cardinalities. The dataset contained one-dimensional values that were produced by a mixture of Gaussian distributions. The selection of this dataset was based in the fact that many real-world datasets contain clusters and are frequently modeled as Gaussian mixtures. Figure 23 presents such a distribution in the two-dimensional space. In the experiments, the projection in the x and y axis were used, in order to construct the one-dimensional dataset for the performance evaluation.

Two kinds of experiments were performed. First a runtime performance test, comparing three different algorithmic techniques, one using IST (A), and two using Spark's built-in features (F and M).

Technique A consists of the following steps.

- Create an RDD by referencing the dataset file. Map its contents to Float numbers. Sort and partition the RDD to the workers.
- Generate an array of 5000 random float pairs in the interval $[0, 1]$ to perform range search queries. The array is created at the Driver node and broadcasted to all workers in the cluster.
- Create an IST on each partition.
- Execute 5000 Range Queries on the IST of each partition using the pairs of the array as input parameters, and monitor the total runtime.

Technique M consists of the following steps.

- Create an RDD by referencing the dataset file. Map its contents to Float numbers. Sort and partition the RDD to the Workers.
- Generate an array of 5000 random float pairs in the interval [0, 1] (to perform range search queries).
- Using *mapPartition* and *find* functions, perform 5000 range queries on the elements of each partition.

Technique F consists of the following steps.

- Create an RDD by referencing the dataset file. Map its content to Float numbers.
- Generate an array of 100 random float pairs in the interval [0, 1] (to perform range search queries).
- Filter the input RDD using the elements of the array as bounds.

Since the number of queries is different, it is only logical to compare the elapsed time per query for all algorithmic techniques. The corresponding results are given in Table 1. The runtime results correspond to 32 Spark Workers.

Table 1. Runtime performance comparison.

Input size $\times 10^6$	Number of partitions	A (ms)	M (ms)	F (s)
10	64	7.88	13.46	2.58
20	64	8.74	19.58	5.22
100	128	12.2	83.12	2.46
200	128	14.5	125.04	4.28
1000	512	56.54	507.14	15.10

We observe that algorithmic technique A is significantly faster than Spark's built-in techniques F and M. The difference is more evident for bigger datasets.

The second set of experiments was carried out in order to test the scalability of the proposed organization scheme. Using an input dataset of ten million float numbers, 5000 range queries were performed on the IST while gradually adding more Workers to the cluster.

The total runtime also includes sorting time. Sorting is performed by three Workers (note that the file is stored in three partitions in the HDFS) before being split across the cluster. This is the reason behind the significant improvement in the first three tests. After that, the runtime is steadily decreases which shows the good scalability of the proposed approach; see Fig. 24.

3 Decentralized Ring-Based Structures

3.1 P-Ring

P-Ring [4] is implemented in the context of a modular framework that identifies and separates the different functional components of an overlay index structure.

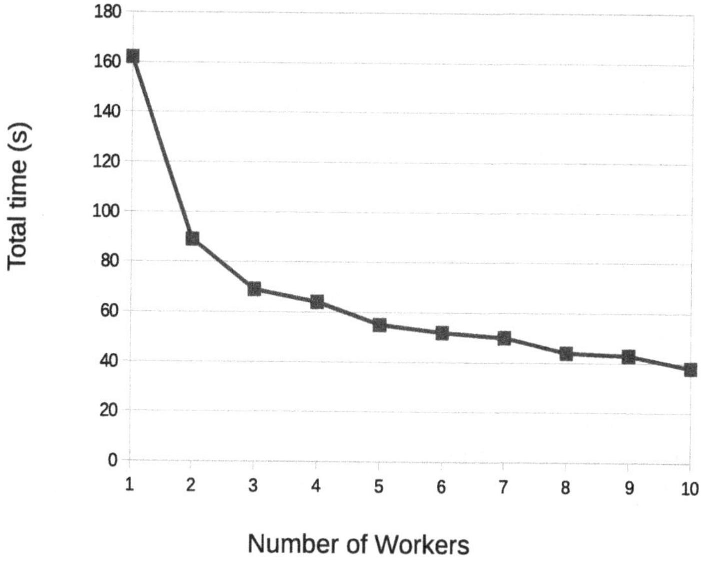

Fig. 24. Scalability performance

3.1.1 Structure

The P-Ring consists of the following four levels.

Fault Tolerant Ring: The Fault Tolerant Ring connects the nodes in the system along a ring, and provides reliable connectivity among these nodes even in the case of failures. For a node p, $succ(p)$ (respectively, $pred(p)$) denotes the node adjacent to p in a clockwise (resp., counter-clockwise) traversal of the ring. The Ring provides methods to get the address of the successor or predecessor, insert a new successor, join the ring or leave the ring (of course, a node can just fail). The Ring also generates events such as *newSuccessor*, and *newPredecessor-Value* that can be caught by higher layers and processed either synchronously or asynchronously.

Data Store: The Data Store, built on top of the Fault Tolerant Ring, is responsible for distributing the items to nodes. Ideally, the distribution should be uniform so that each node stores about the same number of items. The Data Store provides API methods to insert and delete items into and from the system.

Content Router: The Content Router, built on top of the Data Store, is responsible for efficiently routing messages to nodes that have items satisfying a given predicate.

Replication Manager: The Replication Manager, built on top of the Data Store, ensures that items assigned to a node are not lost if that node fails. The Replication Manager algorithms were used, where the items stored at a node are replicated by its successors in the ring.

P-Ring nodes are divided in owner nodes and helper nodes. Helper nodes are not assigned any items. The rest are called owner nodes. The helpers change over time and help with node joins/departures.

3.1.2 Load Balancing

The search key space is ordered on a ring, wrapping around the highest value. The Data Store partitions this ring space into ranges and assigns each of these ranges to a different node. The system is initiated with one owner node that owns the entire indexing domain. All other nodes join the system as helper nodes, and become owner nodes during load balancing.

Whenever the number of items in a node's p Data Store becomes larger than a bound u, an overflow occurs. Then, node p tries to *split* its assigned range and its items with a helper node.

Whenever the number of items in p's Data Store becomes smaller than a bound l, an underflow occurs. Then, p tries to acquire a larger range and more items from its successor in the ring. In this case, the successor either *redistributes* its items with p, or gives up its entire range to p and becomes a helper node.

Let now discuss in detail the basic operations when an overflow or an underflow occurs.

A node p that overflows executes a *split* operation. During a split, node p tries to find a helper p' and transfer half of its items, and the corresponding range to p', After p' is found, half of the items are removed from p and its range is split accordingly. Then, p invites p' to join the ring as its successor. Using the information received from p, p' initializes its index components and joins the ring.

If there is an underflow at node p, then a *merge and redistribution* is executed. Node p invokes the merge function on its successor in the ring. The successor sends back the action decided, *merge* or *redistribute*, a new range, and the list of items that are to be re-assigned to p. Then, p appends the new range and the new items to its own. The invoked node $p' = succ(p)$, checks whether a redistribution of items is possible between the two "siblings". If indeed, then it sends some of its items and the corresponding range to p. If a redistribution is not possible, then p' gives up all its items and its range to p, and becomes a helper node.

3.1.3 Fault Tolerance

Node failures and insertions as well as splits and merges at the Data Store level, disrupt the consistency of the Content Router. A simple *Stabilization Process* is executed on each node periodically that repairs the inconsistencies of Content Router. This process guarantees that the Content Router structure eventually becomes fully consistent as long as the nodes remain connected at the ring level.

3.1.4 Experimental Evaluation

To evaluate the load balancing of the system and show that the P-Ring achieves good load balance at low cost, a simulated environment and a real implementation were tested in [4].

Initially, 256 nodes were inserted, and no items. Then, items were randomly inserted/deleted in three phases: insert only, insert and delete, and delete only. In each phase 50000 operations are executed at the rate of 1 operation/second. Three different distributions for the items inserted were tested: uniform, Zipf 0.5, and Zipf 1. The domain is [1, 65536]. The items to be deleted are chosen uniformly at random from the existing items.

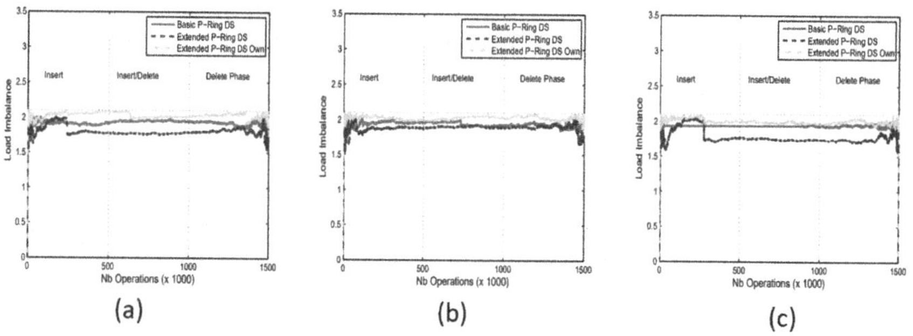

Fig. 25. P-Ring Imbalance (a) uniform, (b) Zipf 0.5, (c) Zipf 1

Figure 25 shows the imbalance measured every 60 simulated operations. The three subfigures are very similar, showing that regardless of the data skew, the system maintains its load balance. Next, the performance of the P-Ring Content Router is investigated, where the search cost (number of messages required to evaluate a range query, averaged over 100 random searches) is measured. The main variable component in the cost of range queries is finding the item with the smallest qualifying value, so only that cost is reported. P-Ring is compared to BATON*, Chord and Skip Graphs [1].

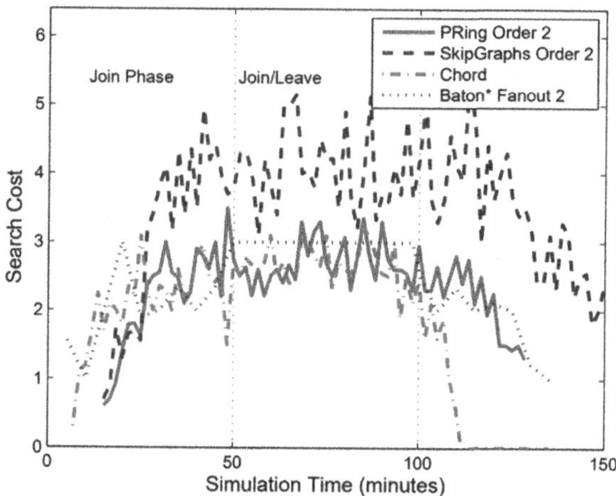

Fig. 26. Search performance

Figure 26 illustrates the search cost of P-Ring's Content Router, Skip Graphs, BATON* and Chord. It is clear that P-Ring's cost is lower than the cost of Skip Graphs and approximately equal to the cost of BATON* and Chord.

4 Comparison of Hierarchical Structures

In this Section we provide a comparison of the overlay structures presented in the previous sections. Table 2 demonstrates the complexities of the overlay structures for the operations of: Range Search, Insert/Delete Key, Maximum size of routing tables, and Join/Depart Node.

Table 2. Time complexities of structures' actions.

Structures	Range search	Insert/Delete key	Max size of routing table	Join/Depart node
BATON [9]	$\mathcal{O}(\log N)$	$\mathcal{O}(\log N)$	$\mathcal{O}(\log N)$	$\overline{\mathcal{O}}(\log N)$
BATON* [8]	$\mathcal{O}(\log_m N)$	$\overline{\mathcal{O}}(m \cdot \log_m N)$	$\mathcal{O}(m \cdot \log_m N)$	$\overline{\mathcal{O}}(m \cdot \log_m N)$
D^2-Tree [3]	$\mathcal{O}(\log N)$	$\tilde{\mathcal{O}}(\log N)$	$\mathcal{O}(\log N)$	$\tilde{\mathcal{O}}(\log N)$
D^3-Tree [16]	$\mathcal{O}(\log N)$	$\tilde{\mathcal{O}}(\log N)$	$\mathcal{O}(\log_m N)$	$\tilde{\mathcal{O}}(\log N)$
ART [18]	$\hat{\mathcal{O}}(\log_b^2 \log N)$	$\overline{\mathcal{O}}(m \cdot \log_m \log N)$	$\mathcal{O}(N^{1/4}/\log^c N)$	$\overline{\mathcal{O}}(m \cdot \log_m \log N)$
ART$^+$ [17]	$\hat{\mathcal{O}}(\log_b^2 \log N)$	$\tilde{\mathcal{O}}(\log \log N)$	$\mathcal{O}(N^{1/4}/\log^c N)$	$\tilde{\mathcal{O}}(\log \log N)$
P-Ring [4]	$\mathcal{O}(\log_d N)$	$\tilde{\mathcal{O}}(d \cdot \log_d N)$	$\mathcal{O}(\log N)$	$\tilde{\mathcal{O}}(d \cdot \log_d N)$
SPIS [14]	$\mathcal{O}(\log \log(n/N))$	$\tilde{\mathcal{O}}(1)$	$\mathcal{O}((n/N)^a)$	$\tilde{\mathcal{O}}(1)$

N: number of nodes; n: number of elements with $(N << n)$; m: fanout;
d: order of the ring; a: constant $0 < a < 1$; $\tilde{O}$: amortized bound; $\overline{O}$: expected amortized bound.

In the case of node failure in the SPIS structure, a replica of the respective partition is ready to be assigned to another worker, while in case of node join, a simple repartition of the data is performed.

We notice that the SPIS solution is the fastest when it comes to Insert/Delete Key and Join/Depart Node, since the actions on the RDDs (or Dataframes) partitions of Spark Cluster, occur mostly in memory and in bulk processing fashion. For this reason (bulk processing), the complexities of insert/delete key and join/departure node operations are amortized.

As Table 2 shows, all the structures have different complexities on every operation. This means that there is no clear answer on which structure is the best to use. It highly depends on the nature of the problem, the type of network, and the application at hand that determines which operations uses more than others.

5 Conclusions

In this work we focused on range query processing for big data. We presented and reviewed state-of-the-art hierarchical (and not DHT-based) distributed overlay structures for efficient big data management that exhibit stable scalability.

References

1. Aspnes, J., Shah, G.: Skip graphs. In: Proceedings 14th Annual ACM-SIAM Symposium on Discrete Algorithms (SODA), Baltimore, MD, pp. 384–393 (2003)
2. Barkai, D.: Technologies for sharing and collaborating on the net. In: 1st International Conference on Peer-to-Peer Computing (P2P 2001), 27–29 August 2001, Linköping, Sweden, pp. 13–28 (2001)
3. Brodal, G.S., Sioutas, S., Tsichlas, K., Zaroliagis, C.: D^2-tree: a new overlay with deterministic bounds. In: Cheong, O., Chwa, K.-Y., Park, K. (eds.) ISAAC 2010. LNCS, vol. 6507, pp. 1–12. Springer, Heidelberg (2010). https://doi.org/10.1007/978-3-642-17514-5_1
4. Crainiceanu, A., Linga, P., Machanavajjhala, A., Gehrke, J., Shanmugasundaram, J.: Load balancing and range queries in P2P systems using P-Ring. ACM Trans. Internet Technol. **10**(4), 1–30 (2011)
5. Dean, J., Ghemawat, S.: Mapreduce: simplified data processing on large clusters. Commun. ACM **51**(1), 107–113 (2008)
6. Ding, G., Wang, L., Wu, Q.: Big data analytics in future internet of things. CoRR, abs/1311.4112 (2013)
7. Ganesan, P., Bawa, M., Garcia-Molina, H.: Online balancing of range-partitioned data with applications to peer-to-peer systems. In: (e)Proceedings of the Thirtieth International Conference on Very Large Data Bases, VLDB 2004, Toronto, Canada, 31 August–3 September 2004, pp. 444–455 (2004)
8. Jagadish, H.V., Ooi, B.C., Tan, K.-L., Vu, Q.H., Zhang, R.: Speeding up search in peer-to-peer networks with a multi-way tree structure. In: Proceedings of the ACM SIGMOD International Conference on Management of Data, Chicago, Illinois, USA, 27–29 June 2006, pp. 1–12 (2006)
9. Jagadish, H.V., Ooi, B.C., Vu, Q.H.: BATON: a balanced tree structure for peer-to-peer networks. In: Proceedings of the 31st Conference on Very Large Databases (VLDB 2005), Trondheim, Norway, pp. 661–672 (2005)
10. Kaporis, A.C., Makris, C., Sioutas, S., Tsakalidis, A.K., Tsichlas, K., Zaroliagis, C.D.: Improved bounds for finger search on a RAM. Algorithmica **66**(2), 249–286 (2013)
11. Knuth, D.E.: The Art of Computer Programming, vol. III, 2nd edn. Addison-Wesley, Redwood City (1998)
12. Liau, C.Y., Ng, W.S., Shu, Y., Tan, K.-L., Bressan, S.: Efficient range queries and fast lookup services for scalable P2P networks. In: Ng, W.S., Ooi, B.-C., Ouksel, A.M., Sartori, C. (eds.) DBISP2P 2004. LNCS, vol. 3367, pp. 93–106. Springer, Heidelberg (2005). https://doi.org/10.1007/978-3-540-31838-5_7
13. Mehlhorn, K., Tsakalidis, A.K.: Dynamic interpolation search. In: Automata, Languages and Programming, 12th Colloquium, Nafplion, Greece, 15–19 July 1985, Proceedings, pp. 424–434 (1985)
14. Papadopoulos, A.N., Sioutas, S., Zacharatos, S., Zaroliagis, C.: Efficient distributed range query processing in apache spark. In: Proceedings of 19th IEEE/ACM International Symposium on Cluster, Cloud and Grid Computing - CCGRID 2019, pp. 569–575. IEEE Computer Society (2019)
15. Ratnasamy, S., Francis, P., Handley, M., Karp, R.M., Shenker, S.: A scalable content-addressable network. In: SIGCOMM, pp. 161–172 (2001)
16. Sioutas, S., Sourla, E., Tsichlas, K., Zaroliagis, C.: D^3-tree: a dynamic deterministic decentralized structure. In: Bansal, N., Finocchi, I. (eds.) ESA 2015. LNCS, vol. 9294, pp. 989–1000. Springer, Heidelberg (2015). https://doi.org/10.1007/978-3-662-48350-3_82

17. Sioutas, S., Sourla, E., Tsichlas, K., Zaroliagis, C.: ART$^+$: a fault-tolerant decentralized tree structure with ultimate sub-logarithmic efficiency. In: Karydis, I., Sioutas, S., Triantafillou, P., Tsoumakos, D. (eds.) ALGOCLOUD 2015. LNCS, vol. 9511, pp. 126–137. Springer, Cham (2016). https://doi.org/10.1007/978-3-319-29919-8_10
18. Sioutas, S., Triantafillou, P., Papaloukopoulos, G., Sakkopoulos, E., Tsichlas, K.: Art: Sub-logarithmic decentralized range query processing with probabilistic guarantees. J. Distrib. Parallel Databases (DAPD) **31**(1), 71–109 (2012)
19. Stoica, I., Morris, R., Karger, D., Kaashoek, M.F., Balakrishnan, H.: Chord: a scalable peer-to-peer lookup service for internet applications. SIGCOMM Comput. Commun. Rev. **31**(4), 149–160 (2001)
20. White, T.: Hadoop: The Definitive Guide. O'Reilly (2015)
21. Zaharia, M., et al.: Apache spark: a unified engine for big data processing. Commun. ACM **59**(11), 56–65 (2016)
22. Zhang, Y., Liu, L., Li, D., Liu, F., Lu, X.: DHT-based range query processing for web service discovery. In: Proceedings of the IEEE International Conference on Web Services (ICWS 2009), Los Angeles, CA, pp. 477–484, IEEE, July 2009

Author Index

Printed in the United States
By Bookmasters